THE INTERNATIONAL SCIENTIFIC SERIES

THE LIFE AND GROWTH OF LANGUAGE

THE INTERNATIONAL SCIENTIFIC SERIES

THE LIFE AND GROWTH OF LANGUAGE

AN OUTLINE OF LINGUISTIC SCIENCE

WILLIAM DWIGHT WHITNEY

GYAN

Published by

GYAN

Gyan Publishing House
5, Ansari Road
Daryaganj, New Delhi-110002
Phone: 011-47034999, 9811692060
E-mail: books@gyanbooks.com

Distribution Network
gyanbooks.com
India, USA, Canada, UK, Australia, France

ISBN : 978-81-212-6182-1 (PB)
First Published, 1888

2nd Impression 2021

Printed at: Gyan Press, Delhi.

The
Life and Growth of Language
Author: William Dwight Whitney

THE INTERNATIONAL SCIENTIFIC SERIES.

VOLUME XVI.

THE

INTERNATIONAL SCIENTIFIC SERIES.

Each book complete in One Volume, 12mo, and bound in Cloth.

1. FORMS OF WATER: A Familiar Exposition of the Origin and Phenomena of Glaciers. By J. TYNDALL, LL. D., F. R. S. With 25 Illustrations. $1.50.

2. PHYSICS AND POLITICS; Or, Thoughts on the Application of the Principles of "Natural Selection" and "Inheritance" to Political Society. By WALTER BAGEHOT. $1.50.

3. FOODS. By EDWARD SMITH, M. D., LL. B., F. R. S. With numerous Illustrations. $1.75.

4. MIND AND BODY: The Theories of their Relation. By ALEXANDER BAIN, LL. D. With 4 Illustrations. $1.50.

5. THE STUDY OF SOCIOLOGY. By HERBERT SPENCER. $1.50.

6. THE NEW CHEMISTRY. By Professor J. P. COOKE, of Harvard University. With 31 Illustrations. $2.00.

7. ON THE CONSERVATION OF ENERGY. By BALFOUR STEWART, M. A., LL. D., F. R. S. With 14 Illustrations. $1.50.

8. ANIMAL LOCOMOTION; or, Walking, Swimming, and Flying. By J. B. PETTIGREW, M. D., F. R. S., etc. With 130 Illustrations. $1.75.

9. RESPONSIBILITY IN MENTAL DISEASE. By HENRY MAUDSLEY, M. D. $1.50.

10. THE SCIENCE OF LAW. By Professor SHELDON AMOS. $1.75.

11. ANIMAL MECHANISM: A Treatise on Terrestrial and Aërial Locomotion. By Professor E. J. MAREY. With 117 Illustrations. $1.75.

12. THE HISTORY OF THE CONFLICT BETWEEN RELIGION AND SCIENCE. By J. W. DRAPER, M. D., LL. D. $1.75.

13. THE DOCTRINE OF DESCENT AND DARWINISM. By Professor OSCAR SCHMIDT (Strasburg University). With 26 Illustrations. $1.50.

14. THE CHEMICAL EFFECTS OF LIGHT AND PHOTOGRAPHY. By Dr. HERMANN VOGEL (Polytechnic Academy of Berlin). Translation thoroughly revised. With 100 Illustrations. $2.00.

15. FUNGI: Their Nature, Influences, Uses, etc. By M. C. COOKE, M. A., LL. D. Edited by the Rev. M. J. Berkeley, M. A., F. L. S. With 109 Illustrations. $1.50.

16. THE LIFE AND GROWTH OF LANGUAGE. By Professor WILLIAM DWIGHT WHITNEY, of Yale College. $1.50.

17. MONEY AND THE MECHANISM OF EXCHANGE. By W. STANLEY JEVONS, M. A., F. R. S. $1.75.

18. THE NATURE OF LIGHT, with a General Account of Physical Optics. By Dr. EUGENE LOMMEL. With 188 Illustrations and a Table of Spectra in Chromo-lithography. $2.00.

19. ANIMAL PARASITES AND MESSMATES. By Monsieur VAN BENEDEN. With 83 Illustrations. $1.50.

20. FERMENTATION. By Professor SCHÜTZENBERGER. With 28 Illustrations. $1.50.

21. THE FIVE SENSES OF MAN. By Professor BERNSTEIN. With 91 Illustrations. $1.75.

22. THE THEORY OF SOUND IN ITS RELATION TO MUSIC. By Professor PIETRO BLASERNA. With numerous Illustrations. $1.50.

23. STUDIES IN SPECTRUM ANALYSIS. By J. NORMAN LOCKYER, F. R. S. With 6 Photographic Illustrations of Spectra, and numerous Engravings on Wood. $2.50.

24. A HISTORY OF THE GROWTH OF THE STEAM-ENGINE. By Professor R. H. THURSTON. With 163 Illustrations. $2.50.

25. EDUCATION AS A SCIENCE. By ALEXANDER BAIN, LL. D. $1.75.

26. STUDENTS' TEXT-BOOK OF COLOR; Or, Modern Chromatics. With Applications to Art and Industry. By Professor OGDEN N. ROOD, Columbia College. New edition. With 130 Illustrations. $2.00.

27. THE HUMAN SPECIES. By Professor A. DE QUATREFAGES, Membre de l'Institut. $2.00.

28. THE CRAYFISH: An Introduction to the Study of Zoölogy. By T. H. HUXLEY, F. R. S. With 82 Illustrations. $1.75.

29. THE ATOMIC THEORY. By Professor A. WURTZ. Translated by E. Cleminshaw, F. C. S. $1.50.

30. ANIMAL LIFE AS AFFECTED BY THE NATURAL CONDITIONS OF EXISTENCE. By KARL SEMPER. With 2 Maps and 106 Woodcuts. $2.00.

31. SIGHT: An Exposition of the Principles of Monocular and Binocular Vision. By JOSEPH LE CONTE, LL. D. With 132 Illustrations. $1.50.

32. GENERAL PHYSIOLOGY OF MUSCLES AND NERVES. By Professor J. ROSENTHAL. With 75 Illustrations. $1.50.

33. ILLUSIONS: A Psychological Study. By JAMES SULLY. $1.50.

34. THE SUN. By C. A. YOUNG, Professor of Astronomy in the College of New Jersey. With numerous Illustrations. $2.00.

New York: D. APPLETON & CO., 1, 3, & 5 Bond Street.

35. VOLCANOES: What they Are and what they Teach. By JOHN W. JUDD, F.R.S., Professor of Geology in the Royal School of Mines. With 96 Illustrations. $2.00.

36. SUICIDE: An Essay in Comparative Moral Statistics. By HENRY MORSELLI, M.D., Professor of Psychological Medicine, Royal University, Turin. $1.75.

37. THE FORMATION OF VEGETABLE MOULD, THROUGH THE ACTION OF WORMS. With Observations on their Habits. By CHARLES DARWIN, LL. D., F. R. S. With Illustrations. $1.50.

38. THE CONCEPTS AND THEORIES OF MODERN PHYSICS. By J. B. STALLO. $1.75.

39. THE BRAIN AND ITS FUNCTIONS. By J. LUYS. $1.50.

40. MYTH AND SCIENCE. By TITO VIGNOLI. $1.50.

41. DISEASES OF MEMORY: An Essay in the Positive Psychology. By TH. RIBOT, author of "Heredity." $1.50.

42. ANTS, BEES, AND WASPS. A Record of Observations of the Habits of the Social Hymenoptera. By Sir JOHN LUBBOCK, Bart., F. R. S., D. C. L., LL. D., etc. $2.00.

43. SCIENCE OF POLITICS. By SHELDON AMOS. $1.75.

44. ANIMAL INTELLIGENCE. By GEORGE J. ROMANES. $1.75.

45. MAN BEFORE METALS. By N. JOLY, Correspondent of the Institute. With 148 Illustrations. $1.75.

46. THE ORGANS OF SPEECH AND THEIR APPLICATION IN THE FORMATION OF ARTICULATE SOUNDS. By G. H. VON MEYER, Professor in Ordinary of Anatomy at the University of Zürich. With 47 Woodcuts. $1.75.

47. FALLACIES: A View of Logic from the Practical Side. By ALFRED SIDGWICK, B. A., Oxon. $1.75.

48. ORIGIN OF CULTIVATED PLANTS. By ALPHONSE DE CANDOLLE. $2.00.

49. JELLY-FISH, STAR-FISH, AND SEA-URCHINS. Being a Research on Primitive Nervous Systems. By GEORGE J. ROMANES. $1.75.

50. THE COMMON SENSE OF THE EXACT SCIENCES. By the late WILLIAM KINGDON CLIFFORD. $1.50.

51. PHYSICAL EXPRESSION: Its Modes and Principles. By FRANCIS WARNER, M. D., Assistant Physician, and Lecturer on Botany to the London Hospital, etc. With 51 Illustrations. $1.75.

52. ANTHROPOID APES. By ROBERT HARTMANN, Professor in the University of Berlin. With 63 Illustrations. $1.75.

---

53. THE MAMMALIA IN THEIR RELATION TO PRIMEVAL TIMES. By OSCAR SCHMIDT. $1.50.

54. COMPARATIVE LITERATURE. By HUTCHESON MACAULAY POSNETT, M. A., LL. D., F. L. S., Barrister-at-Law; Professor of Classics and English Literature. University College, Aukland, New Zealand; author of "The Historical Method," etc. $1.75.

55. EARTHQUAKES AND OTHER EARTH MOVEMENTS. By JOHN MILNE, Professor of Mining and Geology in the Imperial College of Engineering, Tokio, Japan. With 38 Figures. $1.75.

56. MICROBES, FERMENTS, AND MOULDS. By E. L. TROUESSART. With 107 Illustrations. $1.50.

57. THE GEOGRAPHICAL AND GEOLOGICAL DISTRIBUTION OF ANIMALS. By ANGELO HEILPRIN. $2.00.

58. WEATHER. A Popular Exposition of the Nature of Weather Changes from Day to Day. With Diagrams. By Hon. RALPH ABERCROMBY. $1.75.

59. ANIMAL MAGNETISM. By ALFRED BINET and CHARLES FÉRÉ, Assistant Physician at the Salpêtrière. $1.50.

60. INTERNATIONAL LAW, with Materials for a Code of International Law. By LEONE LEVI, Professor of Common Law, King's College. $1.50.

61. THE GEOLOGICAL HISTORY OF PLANTS. With Illustrations. By Sir J. WILLIAM DAWSON, LL. D., F. R. S. $1.75.

62. ANTHROPOLOGY. An Introduction to the Study of Man and Civilization. By EDWARD B. TYLOR, D. C. L., F. R. S. Illustrated. $2.00.

63. THE ORIGIN OF FLORAL STRUCTURES, THROUGH INSECT AND OTHER AGENCIES. By the Rev. GEORGE HENSLOW, M. A., F. L. S., F. G. S. With 88 Illustrations.

THE INTERNATIONAL SCIENTIFIC SERIES.

THE

LIFE AND GROWTH

OF

LANGUAGE:

AN OUTLINE OF LINGUISTIC SCIENCE.

BY

WILLIAM DWIGHT WHITNEY,

PROFESSOR OF SANSKRIT AND COMPARATIVE PHILOLOGY IN YALE COLLEGE.

PREFACE.

The present work needs only a few words by way of introduction. That its subject calls for treatment in the series of which it forms a part, especially at this time, when men's crude and inconsistent views of language are tending to crystallize into shape, no labored argument is required to prove. Very discordant opinions as to the basis and superstructure of linguistic philosophy are vying for the favor, not of the public only, but even of scholars, already deeply versed in the facts of language-history, but uncertain and comparatively careless of how these shall be coördinated and explained. Physical science on the one side, and psychology on the other, are striving to take possession of linguistic science, which in truth belongs to neither. The doctrines taught in this volume are of the class of those which have long been widely prevalent among students of man and his institutions; and they only need to be exhibited as amended and supported, not crowded out or overthrown, by the abundant new knowledge which the century has yielded, in order to win an acceptance well-nigh universal. They who hold them have been too much overborne hitherto by the ill-founded claims of men who arrogate a special scientific or philosophic profundity.

After one has once gone over such a subject upon a carefully matured and systematic plan, as I did in my "Language and the Study of Language" (New York and London, 1867), it is not possible, when treating it again for the same public, to avoid following in the main the same course; and readers of the former work will not fail to observe many parallelisms between the two. Even a part of the illustrations formerly used have been turned again to account; for, if it be made a principle to draw the chief exemplifications of the life and growth of language from our own tongue, there are certain matters—especially our most important recent formative endings and auxiliaries—which must be taken, because they are most available for the needed purpose. Nor has the basis of linguistic facts and their classification undergone during the past eight years such change or extension as should show conspicuously in so compendious a discussion as this. Accordingly, I present here an outline of linguistic science agreeing in many of its principal features with the former one; the old story told in a new way, under changed aspects and with changed proportions, and with considerably less fullness of exposition and illustration.

The limits imposed on the volume by the plan of

the series have compelled me to abbreviate certain parts to which some will perhaps agree with me in wishing that more extension could have been given. Thus, it had been my intention to include in the last chapter a fuller sketch of the history of knowledge and opinion in this department of study. And I have had to leave the text almost wholly without references: although I may here again allege the compendious cast of the work, which renders them little called for; I trust that no injustice will be found to have been done to any. The foundation of my discussion is the now generally accessible facts of language, which are no one man's property more than another's. As for views opposed to my own, while often having them distinctly in mind in their shape as presented by particular scholars, I have hardly ever thought it necessary to report them formally; and I have on principle avoided anything bearing the aspect of personal controversy.

NEW HAVEN, *April*, 1875.

CONTENTS.

CHAPTER I.

INTRODUCTORY: THE PROBLEMS OF THE SCIENCE OF LANGUAGE.

Definition of language. Man its universal and sole possessor. Variety of languages. The study of language; aim of this volume.

LANGUAGE may be briefly and comprehensively defined as the means of expression of human thought.

In a wider and freer sense, everything that bodies forth thought and makes it apprehensible, in whatever way, is called language; and we say, properly enough, that the men of the Middle Ages, for example, speak to us by the great architectural works which they have left behind them, and which tell us very plainly of their genius, their piety, and their valor. But for scientific purposes the term needs restriction, since it would apply else to nearly all human action and product, which discloses the thought that gives it birth. Language, then, signifies rather certain instrumentalities whereby men consciously and with intention represent their thought, to the end, chiefly, of making it known to other men: it is expression for the sake of communication.

The instrumentalities capable of being used for this purpose, and actually more or less used, are various: gesture and grimace, pictorial or written signs, and uttered or spoken signs: the first two addressed to the eye, the last to the ear. The first is chiefly employed by mutes—though not in its purity, inasmuch as these unfortunates are wont to be trained and taught by those who speak, and their visible signs are more or less governed by habits born of utterance; going even so far as slavishly to represent the sounds of speech. The second, though in its inception a free and independent means of expression, yet in its historical development becomes linked as a subordinate to speech, and even finds in that subordination its highest perfection and greatest usefulness.[1] The third is, as things actually are in the world, infinitely the most important; insomuch that, in ordinary use, "language" means utterance, and utterance only. And so we shall understand it here: language, for the purposes of this discussion, is the body of uttered and audible signs by which in human society thought is principally expressed, gesture and writing being its subordinates and auxiliaries.[2]

Of such spoken and audible means of expression no human community is found destitute. From the highest races to the lowest, all men speak; all are able to interchange such thoughts as they have. Language, then, appears clearly "natural" to man; such are his endowments, such his circumstances, such his history—one or all of these—that it is his invariable possession.

Moreover, man is the sole possessor of language. It is true that a certain degree of power of communication, sufficient for the infinitely restricted needs of their gregarious intercourse, is exhibited also by some

[1] See the author's "Language and the Study of Language," p. 448 *seq.*; and his "Oriental and Linguistic Studies," ii. 193–196.

[2] Their natural and historical relations will be further treated of in chapter xiv.

of the lower animals. Thus, the dog's bark and howl signify by their difference, and each by its various style and tone, very different things; the domestic fowl has a song of quiet enjoyment of life, a clutter of excitement and alarm, a cluck of maternal anticipation or care, a cry of warning—and so on. But these are not only greatly inferior in their degree to human language; they are also so radically diverse in kind from it, that the same name cannot justly be applied to both. Language is one of the most marked and conspicuous, as well as fundamentally characteristic, of the faculties of man.

Nevertheless, while human language is thus one as contrasted with brute expression, it is in itself of a variety which is fairly to be termed discordance. It is a congeries of individual languages, separate bodies of audible signs for thought, which, reckoning even those alone of which the speakers are absolutely unintelligible to one another, are very numerous. These languages differ among themselves in every degree. Some are so much alike that their users can with sufficient trouble and care come to understand one another; of others, even a superficial examination shows abundant correspondences; of yet others, similar points of accordance are rarer, and only discoverable by practised study and research; and a great number are to all appearance wholly diverse—and often, not only diverse in respect to the actual signs which they use for their various conceptions, but also as to their whole structure, the relations which they signify, the parts of speech they recognize. And this diversity does not accord with differences of intellectual capacity among the speakers: individuals of every degree of gift are found using, each according to his power, the same identical dialect; and souls of kindred calibre in different societies can hold no communion together. Nor does it accord with geographical divisions; nor yet, in its limits and degrees, with the apparent limits of races. Not seldom, far greater race-differences are met with among the speakers of one language, or of one body of resembling languages, than between those who use dialects wholly unlike one another.

These, and their like, are the problems which occupy the attention of those who pursue the science of language, or linguistic science. That science strives to comprehend language, both in its unity, as a means of human expression and as distinguished from brute communication, and in its internal variety, of material and structure. It seeks to discover the cause of the resemblances and differences of languages, and to effect a classification of them, by tracing out the lines of resemblance, and drawing the limits of difference. It seeks to determine what language is in relation to thought, and how it came to sustain this relation; what keeps up its life and what has kept it in existence in past time, and even, if possible, how it came into existence at all. It seeks to know what language is worth to the mind, and what has been its part in the development of our race. And, less directly, it seeks to learn and set forth what it may of the history of human development, and of the history of races, their movements and connections, so far as these are to be read in the facts of language.

No reflecting and philosophizing people has ever been blind to the exceeding interest of problems like these, or has failed to offer some contribution toward their solution. Yet the body of truth discovered in earlier times has been so small, that the science of language is to be regarded as a modern one, as much so as geology and chemistry; it belongs, like them, to the nineteenth century. To review its history is no part of our present task; no justice could be done the subject within the space that could be spared it in this volume; and the few words that we can bestow upon it will be better said in the last chapter than here. Although of so recent growth, the science of language is already one of the leading branches of modern inquiry. It is not less comprehensive in its material, definite in its aims, strict in its methods, and rich and fruitful in its results, than its sister sciences. Its foundations have been laid deep and strong in the thorough analysis of many of the most important human tongues, and the careful examination and classification of nearly all the rest. It has yielded to the history of mankind as a whole, and to that of the different races of men, definite truths and far-reaching glimpses of truth which could be won in no other way. It is bringing about a re-cast of the old methods of teaching even familiar and long-studied languages, like the Latin and Greek; it is drawing forward to conspicuous notice others of which, only a few years ago, hardly the names were known. It has, in short, leavened all the connected branches of knowledge, and worked itself into the very structure of modern thought, so that no one who hears or reads can help taking some cognizance of it. No educated person can afford to lack a clear conception of at least a brief connected outline of a science possessing such claims to attention.

The design of this volume, accordingly, is to draw out and illustrate the principles of linguistic science, and to set forth its results, with as much fullness as the limited space at command shall allow. The study is not yet so developed and established as not to include subjects respecting which opinions still differ widely and deeply. But direct controversy will be avoided; and the attempt will be made to construct an argument which shall commend itself to acceptance by the coherence of its parts and the reasonableness of its conclusions. In accordance with the plan of the series of treatises into which this enters as a member, simplicity and popular apprehensibility will be everywhere aimed at. To start from obvious or familiar truths, to exemplify by well-known facts, will be found, it is believed, the best way to arrive with assurance at the ultimate results sought after. The prime facts of language lie, as it were, within the easy grasp of every man who speaks—yet more, of every man who has studied other languages than his own—and to direct intelligent attention toward that which is essential, to point out the general in the midst of the particular and the fundamental underneath the superficial, in matters of common knowledge, is a method of instruction which cannot but bear good fruit.

CHAPTER II.

HOW EACH INDIVIDUAL ACQUIRES HIS LANGUAGE: LIFE OF LANGUAGE.

Language learned, not inherited or made, by the individual; process of children's learning to speak; what this involves, outside the province of the linguistic student. Origin of particular words. Character of a word as sign for a conception. Mental training in learning language; determination of the inner form of language from without; constraint and advantage in the process. Acquisition of a second language, or of more than one; learning even of native speech a never-ending process. Imperfection of the word as sign; language only the apparatus of thought.

THERE can be asked respecting language no other question of a more elementary and at the same time of a more fundamentally important character than this: how is language obtained by us? how does each speaking individual become possessed of his speech? Its true answer involves and determines well-nigh the whole of linguistic philosophy.

There are probably few who would not at once reply that we learn our language; it is taught us by those among whom our lot is cast in childhood. And this obvious and common-sense answer is also, as we shall find on a more careful and considerate inquiry, the correct one. We have to look to see what is implied in it.

In the first place, it sets aside and denies two other conceivable answers: that language is a race-characteristic, and, as such, inherited from one's ancestry, along with color, physical constitution, traits of character, and the like; and that it is independently produced by each individual, in the natural course of his bodily and mental growth.

Against both these excluded views of the acquisition of language may be brought such an array of facts so familiar and undeniable that they cannot be seriously upheld. Against the theory of a language as a race-characteristic may be simply set, as sufficient rebutting evidence, the existence of a community like the American, where there are in abundance descendants of African, of Irish, of German, of southern European, of Asiatic, as well as of English ancestors, all using the same dialect, without other variety than comes of differences of locality and education, none showing a trace of any other "mother-tongue" or "native speech." But the world is full of such cases, on the small scale and on the large. Any child of parents living in a foreign country grows up to speak the foreign speech, unless carefully guarded from doing so; or, it speaks both this and the tongue of its parents, with equal readiness. The children of missionary families furnish the most striking examples of this class: no matter where they may be in the world, among what remotely kindred or wholly unrelated dialects, they acquire the local speech as "naturally" as do the children of the natives. And it is only necessary that the child of English or German or Russian parents, born in their native country, should (as is often done) be put with a French nurse, and hear French alone spoken about it, and it will grow up to speak French first and

French only, just as if it were a French child. And what is French, and who are its speakers? The mass of the people of France are Celts by descent, with characteristic Celtic traits which no mixture or education has been able to obliterate; but there is hardly an appreciable element of Celtic in the French language; this is almost purely a Romanic dialect, a modern representative of the ancient Latin. There are few unmixed languages in the world, as there are few unmixed races; but the one mixture does not at all determine the other, or measure it. The English is a very striking proof of this; the preponderating French-Latin element in our vocabulary gets its most familiar and indispensable part from the Normans, a Germanic race, who got it from the French, a Celtic race, who got it from the Italians, among whom the Latin-speaking community were at first a very insignificant element, numerically. It is useless to bring up further examples; the force of those here given will be sufficiently supported by our later inquiry into the actual processes of acquisition of language.

So far as the other theory, that of independent production by each person of his own speech, implies that each inherits from his ancestors a physical constitution which makes him develop unconsciously the same speech as theirs, it is virtually coincident with the first theory, and the same facts tell with crushing weight against it; so far as it is meant to imply that there is a general likeness in intellectual constitution between members of the same community which leads them to frame accordant systems of expression, it is equally without support from facts; for the distribution of human dialects is as irreconcilable with that of natural capacity and bent as with that of physical form among human beings. Every variety of gift is found among those who employ, each with his own degree of skill and capacity, the same speech; and souls of commensurate calibre in different communities are unable to have intercourse together.

We come, then, to consider directly the process by which the child becomes able to speak a certain language—a process sufficiently under every one's observation to allow of general and competent criticism of any attempted description of it. We cannot, it is true, follow with entire comprehension all the steps of evolution of the infantile and childish powers; but we can understand them well enough for our purpose.

The first thing which the child has to learn, before speech is possible, is to observe and distinguish; to recognize the persons and things about him, in their concrete individuality, and to notice as belonging to them some of their characteristic qualities and acts. This is a very brief description of a very intricate psychological process—which, however, it does not belong to the student of language to draw out in greater detail. There is involved in it, we may further remark in passing, nothing which some of the lower animals may not achieve. At the same time, the child is exercising his organs of utterance, and gaining conscious command of them, partly by a mere native impulse to the exertion of all his native powers, partly by imitation of the sound-making persons about him: the child brought up in solitude would be comparatively silent. This physical process is quite analogous with the training of the hands: for some six months the child tosses them about, he knows not how or why; then he begins to notice them and work them under command, till at length he can do by conscious volition whatever is within their power. Control and management of the organs of utterance comes much more slowly; but the time arrives when the child can imitate at least some of the audible as well as the visible acts of others; can reproduce a given sound, as a given gesture. But before this, he has learned to associate with some of the objects familiar to him the names by which they are called; a result of much putting of the two together on the part of his instructors. Here is seen more markedly, at least in degree, the superiority of human endowment. The association in question is doubtless at the outset no easy thing, even for the child; he does not readily catch the idea that a set of sounds belongs to and represents a thing—any more than, when older, the idea that a series of written characters represents a word; but their connection is set so often and so distinctly before him as to be learned at last, just as the connection is learned between sugar and pleasure to the taste, between a rod and retribution for misbehavior. And every child begins to know things by their names long before he begins to call them. The next step is to imitate and reproduce the familiar name, usually at first in the most imperfect way, by a mere hint of the true sound, intelligible only to the child's constant attendants; and when that step is taken, then for the first time is made a real beginning of the acquisition of language.

Though not all children start with the acquisition cf precisely the same words, yet their limit of variety is but a narrow one. We may take as fair examples of at least the very early ones the childish names for 'father' and 'mother,' namely *papa* and *mamma*, and the words *water*, *milk*, *good*. And we have to notice especially both how wholly external is the process which makes the child connect these particular names with their respective ideas, and how empirical and imperfect are the ideas themselves. What is really implied in *papa* and *mamma*, the child does not in the least know; to him they are only signs for certain loving and caring individuals, distinguished most conspicuously by differences of dress; and the chance is (and it not seldom chances) that he will give the same names to other individuals showing like differences; the real relation of male and female parent to child he comes to comprehend only much later—not to speak of the physiological mysteries involved in it, which no man yet comprehends. As little does he understand the real nature of water and milk; he knows no more than that, among the liquids (that name, to be sure, comes much later, but not till long after the child has realized the distinction of liquid and solid) constantly brought before him there are two which he readily distinguishes, by look and by taste, and to which other people give these names; and he follows their example. The names are provisional, convenient nuclei for the gathering of more knowledge about; where the liquids come from will be learned by and by, and their chemical constitution, perhaps, in due time. As for *good*, the first association of the term is probably with what has a pleasant taste; then what is otherwise agreeable comes to be comprehended under the same name; it gets applied to behavior which is agreeable to the parents, as judged by a standard which the child himself is far from understanding—and this transfer to a moral sphere is by no means an easy one; as he grows up, the child is (perhaps) all the time learning to distinguish more accurately between *good* and *bad;* but he is likely to be at the last baffled by finding that the wisest heads in the world have been and are irreconcilably at variance as to what *good* really means—whether it implies only utility, or an independent and absolute principle.

These are only typical examples, fairly illustrating the whole process of speech-getting. The child begins as a learner, and he continues such. There is continually in presence of his intellect more and better than he can grasp. By words he is made to form dim conceptions, and draw rude distinctions, which after experience shall make truer and more distinct, shall deepen, explain, correct. He has no time to be original; far more rapidly than his crude and confused impressions can crystallize independently into shape, they are, under the example and instruction of others, centred and shaped about certain definite points. So it goes on indefinitely. The young mind is always learning words, and things through words; in all other cases as really, if not so obviously, as when, by description and picture or by map and plan, it is led to form some inaccurate half-conception of the animal *lion* or the city *Peking*. The formal distinctions made by the inflectional system of even so simple a language as English, and by words of relation, are at first out of the child's reach. He can grasp and wield only the grosser elements of speech. He does not apprehend the relation of one and more than one clearly enough to use the two numbers of nouns; the singular has to do duty for both; and so also the root-form of the verb, to the neglect of persons, tenses, and moods. It is an era in his education when he first begins to employ preterits and plurals and their like. So with the pronouns. He is slow to catch the trick of those shifting names, applied to persons according as they are speaking, spoken to, or spoken of; he does not see why each should not have an own name, given alike in all situations: and he speaks of himself and others by such a name and such only, or blunders sorely in trying to do otherwise—till time and practice set him right.[1] Thus, in every respect, language is the expression of matured and practised thought, and the young learner enters into the use of it as fast as natural capacity and favoring circumstances enable him to do so. Others have observed, and classified, and abstracted; he only reaps the fruit of their labors. It is precisely as when the child studies mathematics; he goes over and appropriates, step by step, what others have wrought out, by means of word and sign and symbol; and he thus masters in a few years what it has taken generations and ages to produce, what his unaided intellect could never have produced; what, perhaps, he could never independently have produced a single item of, having just mental force enough to follow and acquire it: though also, perhaps, he has capacity to increase it by and by, adding something new for those to learn who come after him—even as the once educated speaker may come to add, in one way and another (as will be pointed out later), new stores of expression to language.

In all this, now, is involved infinitely more than linguistic science has any call to deal with and explain. Let us consider, for example, the word *green*. Its presence in our vocabulary implies first the physical cause of the color, wherein is involved the whole theory of optics: and this concerns the physicist; it is for him to talk of the ether and its vibrations, and of the fre-

[1] The amount of sapient philosophy which has been aimlessly expended on this simple fact—as if it involved the metaphysical distinction of the *ego* and the *non-ego*—is something truly surprising.

quency and length of the waves which produce the sensation of greenness. Then there is the structure of the eye: its wondrous and mysterious sensitiveness to just this kind of vibration, the apparatus of nerves which conveys the impression to the brain, the cerebral structure which receives the impression: to treat of all this is the duty of the physiologist. His domain borders and overlaps that of the psychologist, who has to tell us what he can of the intuition and resulting conception, considered as mode and product of mental action, of the power of apprehension and distinction and abstraction, and of the sway of consciousness over the whole. Then, in the hearing of the word *green* is involved the wonderful power of audition, closely akin with that of vision: another sensitive apparatus, which notes and reports another set of vibratory waves, in another vibrating medium: it falls, like vision, into the hands of the physicist and physiologist. They, too, have to do with the organs of utterance, which produce the audible vibration; with their obedience to the directions of the will: directions given but not executed under the review of consciousness, and implying that control of the mind over the muscular apparatus of the body which is by no means the least of mysteries. We might go on indefinitely thus, noticing what is included in the simplest linguistic act; and behind all would lie as a background the great mystery of existence and its cause, which no philosophy has yet been able to do more than recognize. Every part of this is of interest and importance to the linguistic scholar, but each in its own way and degree: and his specific and central business is with none of it, but rather with something else. This, namely: there exists an uttered and audible sign, *green*, by which, in a certain community, are designated a certain class of kindred shades among the infinitely varied hues of nature and of art; and every person who, by birth or by immigration or as a visitor (a bodily visitor, or only a mental one, as student of its literature), comes into the community in question, learns to associate that sign with the given group of shades, and to understand and employ it as designating them; and he learns to classify the infinity of hues under that and certain other signs, of like nature and use. About this pivotal fact all the other matters involved fall into position as more or less nearly auxiliary; from it as point of view they are judged and have their value estimated. Language, both in its single items and as a whole, is primarily the sign of the idea, the sign with its accompanying idea; and to take any other department of the questions involved as the central one is to throw the whole into a false position, distorting the proportions and relations of every part. And, as the science of language seeks after causes, endeavors to explain the facts of language, the primary inquiry respecting this fact is: how came this sign to be thus used? what is the history of its production and application? and even, what is its ultimate origin and the reason of it? provided we can reach so far.

For there is, recognizably and traceably, a time when and a reason why many of our words came into use as signs for the ideas they represent. For example, a certain other shade of color, a peculiar red, was produced (with more, of its kind) not many years ago, as result of the chemical manipulation of coal tar, and was, reflectively and artificially, called by its inventor *magenta*, after the name of a place which a great battle had recently made famous. The word *magenta* is just as real and legitimate a part of the English language as *green*, though vastly younger and less important; and those who acquire and use the latter do so in precisely the same manner as the former, and generally with equal ignorance and unconcern as to its origin. The word *gas* is of much longer standing and wider use with us, and has its respectable family of derivatives and compounds—as *gaseous*, *gasify*, *gas-pipe*—and even its colloquial figurative uses—as when we call an empty and sophistical but ready talker *gassy;* but it was the wholly arbitrary invention of a Dutch chemist (Van Helmont), about A. D. 1600. Science was at that time getting so far along as to begin to form the distinct conception of an aëriform or *gaseous* condition of existence of matter; and this name chanced to be introduced and supported in a way that commended it to general acceptance; and so it became the name, and for all Europe. The young now for the most part know it first as the title of a certain kind of *gas*, made practically useful in giving light; but by and by, if fairly educated, they are led in connection with the word to form for themselves the scientific idea of which this is the sign. To trace the history of these two vocables is to inform ourselves as to the time and the circumstances of production of the aniline colors, and as to the taking of a certain important step forward in scientific thinking. We cannot follow so clearly toward or to its source the word *green*, because it is vastly older, reaching back far beyond the period of literary record; but we do seem to arrive by inference at a connection of it with our word *grow*, and at seeing that a *green* thing was named from its being a *growing* thing; and this is a matter of no small interest as bearing on the history of the word.

It is not the place here to follow up this line of in

quiries, and see what is meant by etymologizing, or tracing the history of words toward their origin; the subject is one which will occupy us more properly later. We touch it in passing merely in order to note that the reason of first attribution of a sign to its specific use is one thing, and that the reason of its after employment in that use is another and a very different thing. To the child learning to speak, all signs are in themselves equally good for all things; he could acquire and reproduce one as well as another for a given purpose. In fact, children in different communities do learn every possible variety of names for the same thing: instead of *green*, the German child learns *grün*, the Dutch *groen*, the Swedish *grön*—all related to our *green*, yet not identical with it; and the French child learns *vert*, the Spanish *verde*, the Italian *viride*—a similar group of related yet diverse names; while the Russian says *zelenüi*, the Hungarian *zöld*, the Turk *ishil*, the Arab *akhsar*, and so on. Each of these, and of hundreds of others, is obtained in the same way: the child hears it uttered by those about him under such circumstances as make plain to him what it signifies; by its aid he in part learns to abstract the quality of color from the colored object and conceive it separately; and he learns to combine in one comprehensive conception the different shades of green, distinguishing them together from the other colors, as blue and yellow, into which they pass by insensible gradations. The learner grasps the conception, at least in a measure, and then associates his own word with it by a purely external tie, having been able, if so guided, to form the same association with any other existing or possible word, and not less easily and surely. An internal and necessary tie between word and idea is absolutely non-existent for him; and whatever historical reason there may be is also non-existent to his sense. He may sometimes ask "what for?" about a word, as he does, in his childish curiosity, about everything else; but it makes no difference with the young etymólogist (any more than with the older one) what answer he gets, or whether he gets an answer; to him, the sole and sufficient reason why he should use this particular sign is that it is used by those about him. In the true and proper meaning of the terms, then, every word handed down in every human language is an arbitrary and conventional sign: arbitrary, because any one of the thousand other words current among men, or of the tens of thousands which might be fabricated, could have been equally well learned and applied to this particular purpose; conventional, because the reason for the use of this rather than another lies solely in the fact that it is already used in the community to which the speaker belongs. The word exists *θέσει*, 'by attribution,' and not *φύσει*, 'by nature,' in the sense that there is, either in the nature of things in general, or in the nature of the individual speaker who uses it, any reason that prescribes and determines it.

There is obviously mental training and shaping, as well as mental equipment, in the process of learning to speak. The mental action of the individual is schooled into certain habits, consonant with those of his community; he acquires the current classifications and abstractions and ways of looking at things. To take an example: the quality of color is so conspicuous, and our apprehension of it so urged by the infinity of its manifested differences which are ever before our eyes, that the conception of color is only quickened and rendered more distinct by acquisition of the words which denote it. But in the classification of the shades of hue the phraseology of the language acquired bears a determining part; they fall into order under and about the leading names, as *white*, *black*, *red*, *blue*, *green;* and each hue is tested in the mind by aid of these, and referred to the one or the other class. And different languages make different classifications: some of them so unlike ours, so much less elaborate and complete, that their acquisition gives the eye and mind a very inferior training in distinguishing colors. This is still more strikingly the case as regards number. There are dialects which are in a state of infantile bewilderment before the problem of numeration; they have words for 'one,' 'two,' and 'three;' but all beyond is an undivided 'many.' None of us, it is tolerably certain, would ever have gone farther than that by his own absolutely unassisted efforts; but by words—and only by words; for such is the abstractness of the relations of number that they, more than any others, are dependent for their realization and manageableness on expression—more and more intricate numerical relations have been mastered by us, until finally we are provided with a system which is extensible to every thing short of infinity—the decimal system, namely, or that which proceeds by constant additions of ten individuals of any given denomination to form the next higher. And what is the foundation of this system? Why, as every one knows, the simple fact that we have ten fingers ("digits") on our two hands; and that fingers are the handiest substitutes for figures, the most ready and natural of aids to an unready reckoner. A fact as external and physical as this, and seemingly so trivial, has shaped the whole science of mathematics, and, altogether without his being aware of it, gives form to all the numerical conceptions of each new learner. It is a suggestion of general human experience in the past, transmuted through language into a law for the government of thought in the future.

The same, in varying way and measure, is true of every part of language. All through the world of matter and of mind, our predecessors, with such wisdom as they had at command, have gone observing, deducing, and classifying; and we inherit in and through language the results of their wisdom. So with the distinctions of *living* and *lifeless;* of *animal* and *vegetable* and *mineral;* of *fish* and *reptile* and *bird* and *insect;* of *tree* and *bush* and *herb;* of *rock* and *pebble* and *sand* and *dust.* So with those of *body, life, mind, spirit, soul,* and their kindred. So with the qualities of objects, both physical and moral, and with their relations, through the whole round of the categories: position and succession, form and size, manner and degree: all, in their indefinite multitude, are divided and grouped, like the shades of color, and each group has its own sign, to guide the apprehension and help the discrimination of him who uses it. So, once more, with the apparatus of logical statement: the ability to put a subject and predicate closely together, and to test their correspondence by repeated comparison, comes only by language; and it is the fruitful means whereby old cognitions are corrected and new ones attained. So, in fine, with the auxiliary apparatus of inflections and form-words, wherein various tongues are most of all discordant, each making its own selection of what it will express and what it will leave for the mind to understand without expression.

Every single language has thus its own peculiar framework of established distinctions, its shapes and forms of thought, into which, for the human being who learns that language as his "mother-tongue," is cast the content and product of his mind, his store of impressions, however acquired, his experience and knowledge of the world. This is what is sometimes called the "inner form" of language—the shape and cast of thought, as fitted to a certain body of expression. But it comes as the result of external influence; it is an accompaniment of the process by which the individual acquires the body of expression itself; it is not a product of his internal forces, in their free and undirected workings; it is something imposed from without. It amounts simply to this: that the mind which was capable of doing otherwise has been led to view things in this particular way, to group them in a certain manner, to contemplate them consciously in these and those relations.

There is thus an element of constraint in language-learning. But it is an element of which the learner is wholly unconscious. Whatever language he first acquires, this is to him the natural and necessary way of thinking and speaking; he conceives of no other as even possible. The case could not be otherwise. For even the poorest language in existence is so much better than any one's powers could have produced unaided, that its acquisition would imply a greatly accelerated drawing out and training of the powers of even the most gifted being; the advantage is so great that the disadvantage entirely disappears before it. We, to be sure, looking on from without, can sometimes find reason for regret, saying: "Here is a man of capacities far beyond the average of the degraded community of which he is a member; in justice to those capacities, he should have had his birth where a higher language would have developed them into what they were able to become; only," we should have to add, "this barbarian tongue raises him far above what he could have become had he never learned to speak at all." Moreover, it is far oftener the case that the individual's linguistic lot is beyond his deserts; that he acquires a language above his level, and would have been better fitted by a lower dialect.

It is not easy to over-estimate the advantage won by the mind in the obtaining of a language. Its confused impressions are thus reduced to order, brought under the distinct review of consciousness and within reach of reflection; an apparatus is provided with which it can work, like the artisan with his tools. There is no other parallel so close, as regards both the kind and the degree of assistance afforded, as this between words, the instruments of thought, and those other instruments, the creation and the aids of man's manual dexterity. By as much as, supplied with these, man can traverse space, handle and shape materials, frame textures, penetrate distance, observe the minute, beyond what he could compass with his unequipped physical powers, by so much is the reach and grasp, the penetration and accuracy, of his thought increased by speech. This part of the value of speech is by no means easy to bring to full realization, because our minds are so used to working by and through words that they cannot even conceive of the plight they would be in if deprived of such helps. But we may think, for example, of what the mathematician would be without figures and symbols.

In respect to this general training and equipment of the mind for work, the first acquisition of a language does for the individual what can never be repeated later. When we first take hold of an additional language, we cannot help translating its signs into those we already know; the peculiarities of its "inner form," the non-identity and incommensurability of its shaped and grouped ideas with those of our native speech, escape our notice. As we gain familiarity with it, as our conceptions adapt themselves to its framework and operate directly through it, we come to see that our thoughts are cast by it into new shapes, that its phraseology is its own and inconvertible. Perhaps it is here that we get our most distinct hint of the element of constraint in language-learning. Certainly, the exceptionally-gifted Polynesian or African who should learn a European language—as English, French, German—would find himself prepared for labor in departments of mental action which had before been inaccessible to him, and would realize how his powers had been balked of their best action by the possession of only the inferior instrument. The scholars of the Middle Ages, who employed the Latin for the expression of their higher thought, did so partly because the popular dialects had not yet become enriched to a capacity for aiding the production of such thought and for expressing it.

But in all other respects, the learning of a second language is precisely the same process as the learning of a first, of one's own "mother-tongue." It is the memorizing of a certain body of signs for conceptions and their relations, used in a certain community, existing or extinct—signs which have no more natural and necessary connection with the conceptions they indicate than our own have, but are equally arbitrary and conventional with the latter; and of which we may make ourselves masters to a degree dependent only on our opportunities, our capacity, our industry, and the length of time devoted to the work; even coming to substitute, if circumstances favor, the second language in our constant and ready use, and to become unfamiliar with and forget its predecessor.

We realize better in the case of a second or "foreign," than in that of a first or "native" language, that the process of acquisition is a never-ending one; but it is not more true of the one than of the other. We say, to be sure, of a child who has reached a certain grade that he "has learned to speak;" but we mean by this only that he has acquired a limited number of signs, sufficient for the ordinary purposes of the childish life, together with the power, by much practice, of wielding them with adroitness and general correctness. There are, probably, only a few hundred such signs, all told; and outside their circle, the English is as much an unknown language to the child as is German, or Chinese, or Choctaw. Even ideas which he is fully able to grasp when put into his acquired phraseology are unintelligible if expressed as grown-up men would naturally write them; they must be translated into childish phrase. What he has is especially the central core of language, as we may call it: signs for the most commonly recurring conceptions, words which every speaker uses every day. As he grows older, as his powers develop and his knowledge increases, he acquires more and more; and in different departments, according to circumstances. He who has to turn at once to the hard work of life may add to the first childish store little besides the technical expressions belonging to his own narrow vocation; he, on the other hand, who devotes years to the sole work of getting himself educated, and continues to draw in knowledge through the rest of his life, appropriates constantly larger stores, and rises to higher styles of expression. The ordinary vocabulary of the educated, including a great variety of the technical terms of special branches of knowledge with which the educated man must have at least a degree of acquaintance, he may come to understand and to use with intelligence; but there will be whole bodies of English expression which he cannot wield, as well as styles to which he does not attain. The vocabulary of a rich and long-cultivated language like the English may be roughly estimated at about 100,000 words (although this excludes a great deal which, if "English" were understood in its widest sense, would have to be counted in); but thirty thousand is a very large estimate for the number ever used, in writing or speaking, by a well-educated man; three to five thousand, it has been carefully estimated, cover the ordinary needs of cultivated intercourse; and the number acquired by persons of lowest training and narrowest information is considerably less than this. Nowhere more clearly than here does it appear that one gets his language by a process of learning, and only thus; for all this gradual increase of one's linguistic resources goes on in the most openly external fashion, by dint of hearing and reading and study; and it is obviously only a continuation, under somewhat changed circumstances, of the process of acquisition of the first nucleus; while the whole is parallel to the beginning and growth of one's command of a "foreign" tongue.

The same thing, however, appears clearly enough, if we consider more narrowly the somewhat shifting relations between our linguistic signs and the conceptions for which they stand. The relation is established at first by a tentative process, liable to error and subject to amendment. The child finds out very soon that names do not in general belong to single objects alone, but rather to classes of related objects; and his power of noting resemblances and differences, the most fundamental activity of intellect, is from the first called into lively action and trained by the constant necessity of applying names rightly. But the classes are of every variety of extent, and in part determined by obscure and perplexing criteria. We have noted already the natural and frequent childish error of using *papa* and *mamma* in the sense of 'man' and 'woman;' the child is puzzled, by and by, by finding that there are other *papas* and *mammas*, though he must not call them so. An older child he learns to call, for example, *George;* but he finds that he must not say *George* of other kindred beings; there is another word, *boy*, for that use. But then, again, he makes acquaintance with still other *Georges;* and to find the tie that binds them into a class together is a problem quite beyond his powers. A variety of creatures of very diverse appearance he learns to call *dog;* but he may not take the same liberty with *horse;* though mules and donkeys are much more like horses than greyhounds and lapdogs are like terriers, they must be carefully distinguished in appellation. A sun in a picture is still a *sun;* and in a cultivated community the child soon gets his imagination trained to recognize the pictured representations of things, and to call them by the same names, while still distinctly aware of the relation between thing and picture; while a grown-up untutored savage is completely baffled by such a counterfeit, seeing in it only a confusion of lines and scratches. A toy house or tree is to have the title *house* or *tree;* but a kind of toy human being has the specific name of *doll*. The words of degree have their peculiarities of application: *near* is sometimes at an inch of distance, sometimes at a rod; a *big* apple is not nearly so big as a *little* house; a *long* time means a few minutes or a few years The inconsistencies of expression are numberless; and till added experience explains them, there is room for misapprehensions and blunders. Moreover, there are cases in which the difficulty is much more persistent, or is never wholly removed. *Fish* even adult apprehension makes to include whales and dolphins, till scientific knowledge points out a fundamental difference as underlying the superficial resemblance.

But it is especially in regard to matters of which the knowledge is won in a more artificial way, that the beginner's ideas are vague and insufficient. For example, children are apt to be taught the names and definitions of geographical objects and relations without gaining any real comprehension of what it all means; a map, a more unintelligible kind of picture, is little better than a puzzle; and even older children, or grown men, have defective conceptions which are only rectified by exceptional experience in after-life. Localities, of course, are most incorrectly imagined by those who have not seen them. Of Sedan, Peking, Hawaii, Chimborazo, every well-instructed person knows enough to be able to talk about them; but how imperfectly do we conceive them, as compared with one who has lived at or near them! We have to be extremely careful, in teaching the young, not to push them on too rapidly, lest we prove to have been building up a mere artificial and empty structure of names, without real enlightenment. And yet, something of this is unavoidable, a necessary incident of instruction. A host of grand conceptions are put before the youthful mind, and kept there by a paltry association or two, while it is left for after-development to fill them out to more nearly their true value. The child is ludicrously unable at first to know what is meant by *God*, or *good*, or *duty*, or *conscience*, or the *world*, even as *sun* and *moon*, *weight* and *color*, involve infinitely more than he has an inkling of; but the word, in each case, gives him a definite nucleus, about which more and ever more knowledge may be grouped; he makes a constant approach toward the right conception, even if it be one to which no human wisdom has yet attained. For the condition of the child, after all, differs only in degree from that of the man, and in no very great degree. Our words are too often signs for crude and hasty, for indefinite and indefinable, generalizations. We use them accurately enough for the ordinary practical purposes of life; and most of mankind go through life content with that, letting instruction and experience bring what improvement they may; few have the independence, even if they had the time and ability, to test every name to the bottom, drawing precise limits about each. For the most part, we are loose thinkers and loose talkers, misled into error in an infinity of cases by our ignorance of the terms we glibly use. But even the wisest and most thorough of us is met by the impossibility of giving to speech a preciseness of definition which should exclude misunderstanding and unsound reasoning—especially as to matters of subjective import, where it is hard to bring conceptions to a sharp test. And so the differences of view, even of philosophers, take on the form of verbal questions, controversies hinge on the interpretation of a term, and every writer who aims at exactness has to begin with definitions—to which, then, he finds it impossible to be faithful; some antagonist or successor, perhaps, shows him to have failed of exactness at a critical point, and tumbles into ruins the whole magnificent structure of fancied truth which he had erected.

We see from all this, it may be observed, how far language is from being identical with thought. It is so just as much as the mathematician's figures and symbols are identical with his conceptions of mathematical quantities and relations; and not one whit more. It is, as we noticed at the outset, the means of expression of thought, an instrumentality auxiliary to the processes of thought. An acquired language is something imposed from without upon the methods and results of mental action. It does, indeed, as a frame-work imposed upon a growing and developing body, give shape to that which underlies it, determining the "inner form;" and yet it is everywhere loose and adjustable. While working by it, the mind also works under it, shifting and adapting, changing and improving its classifications, working in new knowledge and better insight. Thus far we have emphasized the passive receptive work of the mind in dealing with language, because that is, especially at the outset, the bulk of its work; in the following chapters we have to take account of its more independent and creative activity.

But nothing that has been said is to be misconstrued into meaning that the mind is not, in all its work, essentially an active and creative force, or that it gets by instruction a faculty which it did not before possess. All that is implied in the power to speak belongs indefeasibly to man, as a part of his natural endowment; but this power is guided in its development, and determined in the result it attains, by the example and in struction of other minds, already developed. It does nothing which it might not have done alone, under favoring circumstances, and with sufficient time—the life-time, namely, of a few score or hundred generations; but for what it actually does, both as regards the how much and the how, it has to thank those about it. Its acquisition of language is a part of its education, in just the same manner and degree as the other parts of education.

CHAPTER III.

THE CONSERVATIVE AND ALTERATIVE FORCES IN LANGUAGE.

Other side of life of language; growth and change; question of its mode and cause. Illustrative passage from oldest English, or Anglo-Saxon; exposition of its differences from modern English: differences of pronunciation; abbreviations and extensions; changes of meaning; of phraseology and construction. Classification of linguistic changes.

We have seen in the foregoing chapter that the individual learns his language, obtaining the spoken signs of which it is made up by imitation from the lips of others, and shaping his conceptions in accordance with them. It is thus that every existing language is maintained in life; if this process of tradition, by teaching and learning, were to cease in any tongue upon earth, that tongue would at once become extinct.

But this is only one side of the life of language. If it were all, then each spoken dialect would remain the same from age to age. In virtue of it, each does, in fact, remain nearly the same; this is what maintains the prevailing identity of speech so long as the identity of the speaking community is maintained—aside from those great revolutions in their circumstances which now and then lead whole communities to adopt the speech of another people. This, then, is the grand conservative force in the history of language; if there were no disturbing and counteracting forces to interfere with its workings, every generation to the end of time would speak as its predecessors had done.

Such, however, as every one knows, is very far from being the case. All living language is in a condition of constant growth and change. It matters not to what part of the world we may go: if we can find for any existing speech a record of its predecessor at some time distant from it in the past, we shall perceive that the two are different—and more or less different, mainly in proportion to the distance of time that separates them. It is so with the Romanic tongues of southern Europe, as compared with their common progenitor the Latin; so with the modern dialects of India, as compared with the recorded forms of speech intermediate between them and the Sanskrit, or with the Sanskrit itself; and not less with the English of our day, as compared with that of other days. An English speaker even of only a century ago would find not a little in our every-day speech which he would understand with difficulty, or not at all; if we were to hear Shakespeare read aloud a scene from one of his own works, it would be in no small part unintelligible (by reason, especially, of the great difference between his pronunciation and ours); Chaucer's English (500 years ago) we master by dint of good solid application, and with considerable help from a glossary; and King Alfred's English (1000 years ago), which we call Anglo-Saxon, is not easier to us than German. All this, in spite of the fact that no one has gone about of set purpose to alter English speech, in any generation among the thirty or forty that have lived between us and Alfred, any more than in our own. Here, then, is another side of the life of language for us to deal with, and to explain, if we can. Life, here as elsewhere, appears to involve growth and change as an essential element; and the remarkable analogies which exist between the birth and growth and decay and extinction of a language and those of an organized being, or of a species, have been often enough noticed and dwelt upon: some have even inferred from them that language is an organism, and leads an organic life, governed by laws with which men cannot interfere.

Plainly, however, we should be overhasty in resorting to such an explanation until after mature inquiry and deliberation. There is no *primâ facie* impossibility that language, if an institution of human device, and propagated by tradition, should change. Human institutions in general go down from generation to generation by a process of transmission like that of language, and they are all modified as they go. On the one hand, tradition is by its very nature imperfect and inaccurate. No one has ever yet been able to prevent what passes from mouth to ear from getting altered on the way. The child always commits blunders, of every kind, in his earlier attempts at speaking: if careful and well trained, he learns later to correct them; but he is often careless and untrained. And all through the life-long process of learning one's "mother-tongue," one is liable to apprehend wrongly and to reproduce inexactly. On the other hand, although the child in his first stage of learning is more than satisfied to take what is set before him and use it as he best can, because his mental development is far short of that which it represents, and its acquisition is urging him on at his best rate of progress, the case does not always continue thus with him: by and by his mind has grown up, perhaps, to the full measure of that which his speech represents, and begins to exhibit its native and surplus force; it chafes against the imposed framework of current expression; it modifies a little its inherited instrument, in order to adapt this better to its own purposes. So, to have recourse to an obvious analogy, one may, by diligent study under instructors, have reached in some single department—as of natural science, mathematics, philosophy—the furthest limits of his predecessors' knowledge, and found them too strait for him; he adds new facts, draws new distinctions, establishes new relations, which the subsisting technical language of the department is incompetent to express; and there arises thus an absolute need of new expression, which must in some way or other be met; and it is met. Every language must prove itself able to signify what is in the minds of its speakers to express; if unequal to that, it would have to abdicate its office; it would no longer answer the purposes of a language. The sum of what all the individual speakers contribute to the common store of thought and knowledge by original work has to be worked into the "inner form" of their language along with and by means of some alteration in its outer form.

Here, then, at any rate, are two obvious forces, having their roots in human action, and constantly operating toward the change of language; and it remains to be seen whether there are any others, of a different character. Let us, then, proceed to examine the changes which actually go on in language, and which by their sum and combined effect constitute its growth, and see what they will say as to the force that brings them about.

And it will be well to begin with a concrete example, a specimen of altered speech, which shall serve as a source of illustration, and as groundwork for a classification of the kinds of linguistic change. The Frenchman would find his best example in a parallel between a phrase of ancient Latin and its correspondent in modern French, with intermediate forms from the older French; the German could trace a passage backward through the Middle to the Old High-German, with hints of a yet remoter antiquity derived from the Gothic; to the English speaker, nothing else is so available as a specimen of the oldest English, or Anglo-Saxon, of a thousand years ago. Let us look, then, at a verse from the Anglo-Saxon gospels, and compare it with its modern counterpart :—

Se Hælend fôr on reste-dæg ofer æceras ; sôthlîce his leorning-cnihtas hyngrede, and hî ongunnon pluccian thâ ear and etan.

No ordinary English reader, certainly, would understand this, or discover that it is the equivalent of the following sentence of our modern version :—

"Jesus went on the sabbath day through the corn ; and his disciples were a hungered, and began to pluck the ears of corn and to eat." (Matthew xii. 1.)

And yet, by translating it as literally as we can, we shall find that almost every element in it is still good English, only disguised by changes of form and of meaning. Thus :—

'The Healing [one] fared on rest-day over [the] acres ; soothly, his learning-knights [it] hungered, and they began [to] pluck the ears and eat.'

Thus although, from one point of view, *and* and *his* are the only words in the Anglo-Saxon passage which are the same also in the English—and not even those really, since their former pronunciation was somewhat different from their present—from another point of view everything is English excepting *se*, 'the,' and *hi*, 'they'—and even those, virtually; since they are cases of inflection of the definite article and third personal pronoun, of which other cases (as *the*, *that*, *they*, and *he*, *his*, *him*) are still in good use with us. Both the discordance and the accordance are complete, according to the way in which we look at them. We will proceed to examine the passage a little in detail, in order to understand better the relations between the older and the newer form.

In the first place, their pronunciation is even more different than is indicated by the written text. There are at least two sounds in the Anglo-Saxon which are unknown in our present speech: namely, the *h* of *cnihtas*, which was nearly or quite the same with the *ch* of the corresponding German word *knecht*, and the *y* of *hyngrede*, which was the German *ü* and French *u*, an *u*(*oo*)-sound with an *i*(*ee*)-sound intimately combined with it. On the other hand, there are sounds in the English which were unknown to the Anglo-Saxon. Our so-called "short *o*," of *on*, was no ancient sound; nor was the "short *u*" of *begun*, *pluck*, which had then the vowel-sound of *book* and *full*; nor was the "short *i*" of *his*, which was more like the French and German short *i*, not markedly different in quality from the true long *i*, our so-called "long *e*," or *ee*-sound. All these are examples of the manifold changes of English pronunciation during the thousand years since Alfred—changes which have altered the whole aspect of our orthoëpy and orthography. And others of them are illustrated in the passage: for instance, our *knight* and *eat* show protractions of the short vowels of *cniht* and *etan*, each typical of a whole class of cases; and the lengthened *i* has been changed into a diphthong, which we call "long *i*" simply because it has taken the place of our former long *i* (*ee*); while we call the real long *i* of *eat* by the false name of "long *e*" for the same reason.

Again, we may observe in the forms of many words the effects of a tendency toward abbreviation. *Reste* and *hyngrede* have lost with us their final *e*, which in Anglo-Saxon, as now in German and Italian, made an additional syllable. *Ongunnon*, *pluccian*, and *etan* have lost both vowel and consonant of a final syllable; and these syllables were the distinctive endings, in the first word of the plural verbal inflection (*ongan*, 'I or he began,' but *ongunnon*, 'we or they began'), in the other two of the infinitive. In *æceras*, 'acres,' and *cnihtas*, 'knights,' though we have saved the final *s* of the plural ending, it no longer makes an additional syllable. And in *sôthlîce*, 'soothly' (i. e. 'truly, verily'), there is a yet more marked abbreviation, to which we shall presently return.

On the other hand, *ear*, 'ears,' and *fôr*, 'fared,' have been extended in modern time by the addition of other pronounced elements. It was the rule in Anglo-Saxon that a neuter noun of one syllable, if of long quantity, had no (nom. or accus.) plural ending. With us, every noun, of whatever gender or quantity (save a few exceptions, of which we need take no account here), takes *s* as its plural sign. As for *fôr*, the Anglo-Saxons conjugated *faran*, 'fare,' as they did *dragan*, 'draw,' and said *fôr*, 'fared,' like *drôh*, 'drew' (compare the corresponding German *fahren fuhr* and *tragen trug*)—that is to say, *faran* was to them a verb of the "irregular," or "old," or "strong" conjugation. But for a long time there has existed in English speech a tendency to work over such verbs, abandoning their irregularly varying inflection, and reducing them to accordance with the more numerous class of the "regularly" inflected, like *love, loved;* and *fare* is one of the many that have undergone this change. The process is quite analogous with that which has turned *ear* into *ears:* that is to say, a prevailing analogy has been extended to include cases formerly treated as exceptional.

In connection with *ear* comes to light another very striking difference between the ancient and modern English: the Anglo-Saxon had grammatical gender, like the Greek and Latin and German; it regarded *ear* as neuter, but *æcer* and *dæg* as masculine, and, for instance, *tunge*, 'tongue,' and *dæd*, 'deed,' as feminine; to us, who have abolished grammatical gender in favor of natural sex, all are alike neuter.

We turn now to consider a few points relative to the meaning of the words used. In *fôr* we find a marked difference of sense as well as of form. It is part of an old Germanic verb meaning 'go,' and is traceable even back into the earliest Indo-European, as the root *par*, 'pass' (Skt. *pârayâmi*, Gk. περάω, Lat. *ex-per-ior*); now it is quite obsolete in any such sense as this, and rather unusual even in that of 'getting on,' 'making progress:' "it *fared* ill with him." Again, *æcer* meant in Anglo-Saxon a 'cultivated field,' as does the German *acker* to the present day; and here, again, we have its very ancient correlatives in Sanskrit *ajra*, Greek ἀγρός, Latin *ager;* the restriction of the word to signify a field of certain fixed dimensions, taken as a unit of measure for fields in general, is something quite peculiar and recent. It is analogous with the like treatment of *rod* and *foot* and *grain*, and so on, except that in these cases we have saved the old meaning while adding the new.

Among the striking peculiarities of the Anglo-Saxon passage is its use of the words *Hælend*, 'healing one,' *reste-dæg*, 'rest-day,' and *leorning-cnihtas*, 'learning-knights' (i. e. 'youths under instruction'), in the sense respectively of 'Savior,' 'sabbath,' and 'disciples.' Though all composed of genuine old Germanic materials, they were nevertheless recent additions to the language. The introduction of Christianity had created a necessity for them. For the new idea of the Christian Creator and Father, the old word *god*, ennobled and inspired with a new meaning, answered English purposes well enough. But there was no current name applicable to the conception of one who saved men from their sins, making them whole or *hale*; and so the present participle of the verb *hælan*, 'make hale, *heal*,' was chosen to represent *σωτήρ*, and specialized into a proper name, a title for the one Savior. It is the same word which, in German, is still current as *Heiland*. *Reste-dæg*, as name for the sabbath, needs no word of explanation or comment. As for *leorning-cnihtas*, rendering *discipuli* and *μαθηταί*, its most striking characteristic, apart from its rather lumbering awkwardness, is the peculiar meaning which it implies in *cniht*, 'knight.' Between our *knight*, a word of high chivalric significance, and the German *knecht*, 'servant, menial,' is a long distance: both show a deviation, the one in an upward and the other in a downward direction, from the indifferent 'youth, fellow,' which lies at the bottom of the use of the word in our Anglo-Saxon compound.

But a not less noteworthy point in the history of these words is that in our later usage they have all become superseded by other terms, of foreign origin. The Anglo-Saxon did not, like our English, resort freely to foreign stores of expression for the supply of new needs. It was easier then to accept the new institutions of Christianity than new names for them. We have wonderfully changed all that, under the operation of causes which will come up for notice hereafter (chapter vii.); and in place of the three new Saxon names we have put other yet newer ones: two Latin-French, *disciple* and *savior*, and one Hebrew, *sabbath*. The substitution exemplifies a capital trait in English language-history.

Our attention being thus directed to the introduction of new elements into Anglo-Saxon, we will note another case or two of the same kind of linguistic change in another department. *Sôthlîce* is an adverb, answering to our 'truly.' We recognize in the first part of it our *sooth*, a word now almost obsolete—quite so, as far as ordinary use is concerned. Its second part, *lîce*, is our *ly*. But it is also a case-form (instrumental) of an adjective *lîc*, our *like*, which was appended to the noun *sôth*, 'truth,' forming a compound adjective (or adjectival derivative) equivalent to *truth-like*, and completely analogous to *truthful*, from *truth* and *full*. Our adverbial ending *ly*, then, by which most of our adverbs are made, and which to us is only a suffix, is really the product of alteration of a case-form of a compounded adjective, a word originally independent. Instead of using, like the modern German, the base or crude-form of an adjective as adverb—that is to say, in the formal grammatical character of adaptedness to qualify a verb or adjective rather than a substantive —we have wrought out for that purpose a special form, of which the history of development may be followed step by step to its origin, and which is exclusively the property of our language among its kindred Germanic dialects.

A second case is brought before us in *hyngrede.* Its preterit ending *de* is not, like the adverbial *ly*, exclusively English; it is rather, like the adjective *lîc*, a common Germanic possession. Without dwelling here at length upon its history, we will only observe that it is, like *lîce*, traced back to an independent word, the preterit *did*, which was in remote Germanic time added to some verbal derivative, or other part of speech, to form a new style of past tense, when the yet older processes of preterit formation had become no longer manageable.

There are also changes of construction in our passage which ought not to pass without a moment's notice. The word *leorning-cnihtas* is object, not subject, of *hyngrede;* and the construction is that peculiar one in which the impersonal verb, without expressed subject, takes before it as object the person affected by the action or feeling it signifies. This is still a familiar mode of expression in German, where one freely says *mich hungerte*, 'me hungered,' for 'I hungered;' and even we have a trace of it, in the obsolescent *methinks*, German *mich dünkt*—that is, 'it seems to me.' Again, the infinitives *pluccian* and *etan*, being by origin verbal nouns and having properly the construction of nouns, are directly dependent, as objects, on the transitive verb *ongunnon*. We make the same construction with some verbs: so, *he will pluck*, *he must eat*, *see him pluck*, *let him eat;* and even after *began* shortened to *'gan* it is allowed;[1] but in the vast majority of cases we require the preposition *to* as "infinitive sign,"

[1] "Around 'gan Marmion wildly stare."—W. Scott.

saying "began *to* pluck and *to* eat." This preposition was not unknown in Anglo-Saxon; but it was used only where the connection pretty manifestly favored the insertion of such a connective; and the infinitive after it had a peculiar form: thus, *gôd to etanne*, 'good unto eating,' and so 'good to eat.' The *to* which at the period of our specimen-passage was a real word of relation has now become the stereotyped sign of a certain verbal form; it has no more independent value than the ending *an* of *pluccian* and *etan*—which, indeed, it in a manner replaces; though not, like *-ly* and *-d*, combined with the word to which it belongs, its office is analogous with theirs.

We will notice but one thing more in the passage: the almost oblivion into which *sôth*, our *sooth*, has fallen. Only a small part of the great body of English-speakers know that there is such a word; and no one but a poet, or an imitator of archaic style, ever uses it. We have put in place of it *true* and *truth*, which of old were more restricted to the expression of faithfulness, trustworthiness.

The brief sentence selected, we see, illustrates a very considerable variety of linguistic changes; in fact, there is hardly a possible mode of change which is not more or less distinctly brought to light by it. Such are, in general, the ways in which a language comes to be at a later period different from what it has been at an earlier. They are matters of individual detail; each item, or each class of accordant items, has its own time and occasion, and analogies, and secondary causes, and consequences; it is their sum and collective effect which make up the growth of language. If we are to understand how language grows, we must take them up and examine them in their individuality. This, then, is the subject which is now for some time to occupy us: an inquiry into the modes of linguistic change, and their causes, nearer and remoter.

We have already rudely made one classification of these linguistic changes, founded on the various purpose which they subserve: namely, into such as make new expression, being produced for the designation of conceptions before undesignated; and such as merely alter the form of old expression; or, into additions and alterations. It will, however, suit our purpose better to make a more external division, one depending upon the kind of change rather than upon its object. In carrying this out, it will be practicable to take everywhere sufficient notice of the object also.

We may distinguish, then:—

I. Alterations of the old material of language; change of the words which are still retained as the substance of expression; and this of two kinds or subclasses: 1. change in uttered form; 2. change in content or signification; the two, as we shall see, occurring either independently or in conjunction.

II. Losses of the old material of language, disappearance of what has been in use; and this also of two kinds: 1. loss of complete words; 2. loss of grammatical forms and distinctions.

III. Production of new material; additions to the old stock of a language, in the way of new words or new forms; external expansion of the resources of expression.

This classification is obviously exhaustive; there can be no change in any language which will not fall under one or other of the three classes here laid down

CHAPTER IV.

GROWTH OF LANGUAGE: CHANGE IN THE OUTER FORM OF WORDS.

Relation of the word to the conception it designates, as conditioning the possibility, and the mutual independence, of its changes of form and meaning. Tendency to ease or economy in changes of form. Abbreviation of words; examples; its agency in form-making; loss of endings. Substitution of one sound for another; examples of vowel and consonant change; Grimm's law; underlying causes of phonetic change; processes of utterance; physical or natural scheme of spoken alphabet; its series and classes; distinction of vowel and consonant; syllabic or articulate character of human speech. General tendencies in phonetic change. Limits to phonetic explanation. Change of form by extension of a prevailing analogy.

In this chapter we have to take up and illustrate the first division of the first class of linguistic changes, that which includes alterations of the uttered and audible forms of words. But first it will be well to call attention anew to certain general principles (already hinted at in the second chapter), which are of fundamental importance as underlying the whole subject of verbal alteration, whether in respect to shape or sense. And we shall best attain our object by discussing a selected example.

Let us take a familiar word, found in most of the languages of modern Europe, and having a well-known history—the word *bishop*. It comes, as almost every one is aware, from the Greek ἐπίσκοπος (*episkopos*). This, again, is a derivative from the root *skep*, 'see, look,' with the prefix *epi*, 'at;' and so it means by origin simply 'inspector, overseer;' in the early formative period of the Christian church, it was selected as offi cial designation of the person to whom was committed the oversight of the affairs of a little Christian community: and both word and office are still readily recognizable in our *bishop* and its use. But we have cut down the long title into a briefer one, by dropping its first and last syllables: and we have worked over into new shape most of its constituent sounds: we have changed the first *p* into a different but closely kindred sound, its corresponding sonant, *b*; the *sk*, a sibilant with following palatal mute, has been as it were fused together into the more palatal sibilant, *sh*, a simple sound, though it is written with two letters, just because of its usual derivation by fusion of two simple sounds into one; and the *o*-sound of the second syllable has been neutralized into what we usually call the "short *u*" sound—and the result is our word, with two syllables instead of four, and with five sounds instead of nine, and among those five only two, the consonant *p* and the vowel *i*, which were of the nine. The German, in its *bischof*, has altered even the final *p*. The French, again has made out of the same original a very different looking product, *évêque*, which does not contain a single sound that is found either in the English word or in the German; it comes, by another set of changes, from *evesc*, for *episk*. In Spanish, the word is made into *obispo*, by yet another process, and this is further shortened in the Portuguese *bispo*. The Danish, finally, shows the extreme of abbreviation, in the monosyllable *bisp*. While these changes have been going on, the meaning of the word has been not less altered. The official who was, when first named, merely overseer of the interests of a little band of timid proselytes to a new and proscribed faith, half-expectant martyrs, has risen immensely in dignity and power, along with the rise of the religion to importance, and to preëminence in the state; he has become a consecrated prelate, charged with spiritual and temporal authority through an entire province—a kind of ecclesiastical prince, yet still wearing his old simple title.

From this word, taken as a type, we may learn many things, which a wider induction, from innumerable examples, would only confirm.

First, the name had its origin in a need which arose at a particular time and place in the progress of human history. A new religion came into being, and required organization of its votaries; and this made a call for technical designations of its officials—which, as in all similar cases, were then without difficulty found: not *bishop* only, but *priest* and *deacon*, and so on. The words were, in fact, already in existence, as general terms, ready, like the people who should wear them, to be selected and set apart to this specific office. What should come of it further, whether the new titles should rise to importance and attain wide currency, depended on the after-fate of the system to which they belonged.

Again, the word *bishop* did not describe, either fully or accurately, the office which it was used to designate. Mere 'looking on' or 'looking over' was not what men expected of the person elected; the barest hint of his official duty is contained in the term. But, imperfect as it may have been as a description, it was sufficient as a designation. The description would have needed to be a long one, and varied to suit the circumstances of each new place and time; the title answered its desired purpose equally well in all circumstances.

Hence also, as little did the retention of the title depend upon the maintenance of just that kind and degree of relation between its etymological meaning and the office it denominated which had existed at the outset. Even what etymological appropriateness it once possessed was no longer of any account, when once it had become established in use as name of the office. It passed, with the institution to which it belonged, into the keeping and use of great communities which did not speak Greek and had no knowledge of what it originally signified, and it served its purpose with them just as well as if they had understood its whole history. From the moment when it became an accepted sign for a certain thing, its whole career was cut loose from its primitive root; it became, what it has ever since continued to be, a conventional sign, and hence an alterable sign, for a certain conception, but a variable and developing conception.

In this fundamental fact, that the uttered sign was a conventional one, bound to the conception signified by it only by a tie of mental association, lay the possibility both of its change of meaning and of its change of form. If the tie were a natural, an internal and necessary one, it would seem to follow that any change in either would have to be accompanied by a change in the other. But in the case taken, while the idea has expanded into greatness, the word has been shrinking in its proportions, and is nowhere more than a fragment of its former self. The only tendency which we can discover in its treatment is a tendency toward economy of effort in its utterance; it has been reshaped to suit better the convenience of those who used it. In the forms which it has assumed, we can plainly trace the influence of national habits. The Germanic races accent prevailingly the first syllable of their words; they have, then, while retaining the old accented syllable with its accent, cast off the one that preceded it. The French, on the other hand, accents its final syllable (which is regularly the Latin accented syllable); it, accordingly, drops all that followed the accented *-písk-*, but retains the initial syllable which the others rejected. And the other various alterations of form which the word has undergone may be paralleled with classes of similar alterations in other words of the same language; all apparently made to humor the ease of the speakers.

In treating separately, therefore, the subjects of change of form and change of meaning in words, we are not parting two necessarily connected and mutually dependent processes, but only recognizing a natural independence. A word may change its form, to any extent, without change of meaning; it may take on an entirely new meaning without change of form. As a matter of fact, the words are few or none which have not done both; and, in taking up either, we shall have to use examples which illustrate the other as well. All the material of language exhibits more or less the working of all the processes of growth; but it will not be hard to direct our attention, exclusively or especially, now to the one and now to the other of them.

And, as regards change of form, we have to recognize, as the grand tendency underlying all the innumerable and apparently heterogeneous facts which it embraces, the disposition, or at least the readiness, to give up such parts of words as can be spared without detriment to the sense, and so to work over what is left that it shall be more manageable by its users, more agreeable to their habits and preferences. The science of language has not succeeded in bringing to light any more fundamental law than this, even any other to put alongside of it; it is the grand current setting through universal language, and moving all its materials in a given direction—although, like other such currents, it has its eddies, where a counter-movement on a small scale may seem to prevail. It is another manifestation of the same tendency which leads men to use abbreviations in writing, to take a short cut instead of going around by the usual road, and other like things—in which there is no harm, unless more is lost than gained by the would-be economy: then, indeed, it becomes rather laziness than economy. Its operation, as manifested in language, is of both kinds, true economy and lazy wastefulness; for it works on with blind absence of forethought, heedless, in part, of the results to which it leads.

The character of the tendency is seen most clearly in the abbreviation of words; obviously, nothing else is needed to explain the gradual reduction of form which has ever been going on in the constituents of every language. We noticed above (p. 38) sundry examples of innocent abbreviation made by us in the words of our specimen-passage: the most striking was our *knights* (i. e. *naits*) for *cnihtas*, a loss of two pronounced elements besides the shortening by a syllable. It is easy to perceive in all these cases the tendency to ease at work; and we appreciate in the last the comparative difficulty of uttering a *k*-sound before an *n*: the class of words in which we have dropped it off is not a small one (e. g. *knife* and *knit*, *gnaw* and *gnarl*). And the German *ch*-sound (of *ich*, etc.) belonging to the *h* of *cniht*, itself coming by phonetic change from an earlier *k*, is one which English organs have taken a distaste to, and have refused longer to produce. Sometimes they have left it out altogether (with compensatory prolongation of the preceding vowel), as in the word before us; sometimes they have changed it into *f*, as in *draught* and *laugh*. In *ongunnon*, 'begun,' however, and in *pluccian* and *etan*, 'pluck' and 'eat,' we have instances of that kind of loss which is akin to wastefulness; for the lost final syllables are those which showed the grammatical form of the words, being plural ending and infinitive ending. Regrettable as they may be, the history of our language, and of the others related with it, has been from the beginning marked with such losses, whereby grammatical distinctions have been let go, along with the forms on which the speakers' consciousness of them depended. To show this more fully, we will for a moment follow the history of the *on*, the now lost ending of *ongunnon*. In the oldest form to which it can be traced, it was *anti*, probably the relic of an independent pronoun or pronouns, distinguishing the third person plural in all verbal inflection. In the Latin it is shortened to *unt*, but still perfectly distinctive. In the oldest Germanic (Mœso-Gothic), it is *and* in the present tense, but in the preterit already contracted to *un*. The corresponding ending in the first person plural was *masi*, also of pronominal derivation; this, after passing through such intermediate forms as Sanskrit *mas*, (Doric) Greek *μες*, Latin *mus*, and Slavonic *mŭ*, had become in Gothic *am* in the present, *um* in the perfect. In German, we find only *en* in both first and third person, the slight difference of *um* and *un* having been obliterated; but the second person has *et*, different from the other two; in the Anglo-Saxon, this distinction has gone the way of the rest, and we have left only a general ending *on*, separating all the plural persons alike from the singular; and finally, the English has swept away even this remnant of a former elaborate system.

Another example of the earlier effects of the same tendency in our passage is *fôr*, 'fared,' the brevity of which, like that of English monosyllables generally, is the result of a long succession of abbreviating processes. Its earliest traceable form is *papâra;* but even that shows the loss of a personal ending *ti*, which it must have had at the outset, and which is still represented to us in the present tense by the *t* of German *führt*, and the *th* or *s* of our *fareth* or *fares*.

It was pointed out above (p. 41) that in the *lîce* of *sôthlîce* we have the full case-form of a compounded adjective, out of which has been made later the adjective and adverbial suffix *ly*. Here is illustrated another department of the action of the abbreviating tendency; its aid is essential to the conversion of what was once an independent word into an affix, an appended element denoting relation. So long as the word which enters into combination with another retains its own shape unaltered, the product is a compound only; but when, by phonetic change, its origin and identity with the still subsisting independent word are hidden, the compound becomes rather a derivative. Phonetic abbreviation has made the difference between *godly*, for example—a formed word, containing a radical and a formative element—and *godlike*, a mere compound. Just so, in German, the adjective suffix *lich* has become distinct from *gleich* (which has, besides, a prefix); and in that lan guage *göttlich* and *göttergleich* stand in the same manner side by side, the one a derivative and the other a compound. At an earlier period of Germanic language-history, the same influence helped to convert the compound *hyngre-dide*, 'hunger-did,' into the grammatical form *hyngre-de*, 'hunger-ed;' and, in vastly more ancient time, to shape over certain pronominal elements into the personal endings *anti*, *masi*, and *ti*, spoken of above.

Thus the tendency to economy, in the very midst of its destructive action, is at the same time constructive. It begins with producing those very forms which it is afterward to mutilate and wear out. Without it, compound words and aggregated phrases would remain ever such. Its influence is always cast in favor of subordinating in substance what is subordinate in meaning, of integrating and unifying what would otherwise be of loose structure—in short, of disguising the derivation of linguistic signs, making them signs merely, and signs easy to manage. The point is one to which we shall have to return in discussing (in the seventh chapter) the third great class of linguistic changes, the production of new words and forms.

But while the tendency is everywhere one, the ways in which it manifests itself by abbreviation are very various, each needing for its explanation a full understanding of the habits of the language in which it appears. The Germanic languages are all characterized by a pretty strong accentual stress, laid in general on the first or radical syllable of their words, derivative or inflectional, and on the first members of compounds. This mode of accentuation is itself an example of phonetic change; for it belongs to none of the related languages, not even to the Slavonic, generally regarded as nearest of kin with the Germanic. A result of it has been that at a later time, and quite independently in the different Germanic languages, the endings or suffixes, of inflection or derivation, have generally lost their distinctive vowels, and come to be spoken with the more neutral *e:* this change belongs, for example, to the transition from Old to Middle High-German, and from Anglo-Saxon to Old English. To it is also in part due (though also to a more mental willingness to abandon distinctions formerly established and maintained) the extensive loss of endings to which these languages have been subjected, and which appears most of all in our English. In French, the history of change has been somewhat different: there has been no general shift of the place of the accent as compared with Latin; but there has been a wholesale abbreviation and loss of whatever in Latin followed the accented syllable, which has accordingly become (leaving out of account the mute *e*) the final one of every regular French word: so *peuple* from *pópulum*, *faire* from *fácere*, *prendre* from *prehéndere*, *été* from both *æstátem* and *státum*. This last example—*été* from *státum*—draws aside our attention for a moment to a class of alterations which, by a curious turn, end in the extension of a word's syllabic form. To the Gallic peoples who adopted Latin speech, the utterance of an *s* before a mute—*k*, *t*, or *p*—seemed a difficulty which should be avoided: just as to us, later, the utterance of a *g* or *k* before *n* (in *gnaw*, *knife*, etc.). But, instead of dropping the trying letter, they at first prefixed a vowel to it, to make it more manageable, producing such words as *escape* (Lat. *scapus*), *esprit* (*spiritus*), *estomac* (*stomachus*). And then, by an actual abbreviation, and a common one, the sibilant has in later times been usually dropped out, and a large class of words like *école* (*schola*), *époux* (*sponsus*), and *étude* (*studium*), is left in the French vocabulary. Another consequence of the same difference of accent is the greater mutilation of the radical part of the word in the Romanic languages (especially French) than in the Germanic; and many of its results have passed into English: thus, *preach* (Fr. *prêcher*) from *prædicare*, *cost* (Fr. *coûter*) from *constare*, *count* (Fr. *compter*) from *computare*, *blame* (Fr. *blâmer*) from *blasfemare* (Gr. *βλασφημεῖν*). Words, however, like *such* and *which* (A.-S. *swylc* and *hwylc*, Scotch *whilk*, Germ. *solch* and *welch*), from *so-like* and *who-like*, show plainly that this disguising fusion of two parts of a word is by no means limited to the French part of English.

One conspicuous result of these processes is the presence of numberless "silent letters" in the written forms of languages like French and English, in which the omission of sounds formerly uttered has been going on during the period of record by writing. Such letters are relics of modes of utterance formerly prevalent.

This must suffice by way of illustration of the tendency to ease as manifested in abbreviation. But the other mode of its action, consisting in the alteration of the retained elements of words, the substitution of one sound for another, is quite as extensive, and much more intricate and difficult. We have already noted examples of it: the abbreviated *piskop*, we saw, has been mouthed over into *bishop*; and we reviewed above (p. 37) some of the principal differences which separate our vowel-utterance from that of the Anglo-Saxon. The consistency of our vowel-system, especially, has been completely broken up by these changes, the pervading nature of which is attested by the strange names we give to our vowel-sounds. The original and proper sound of *a* is that in *far, father:* what we call "long *a*" (*fate*) is really long *ē*, the nearest correspondent in quality to the "short *e*" of *met*, which we continue to call by its right name because we have not generally altered its ancient sound; our "short *a*" (*fat*) is a new tone, intermediate between *a* (*far*) and *e* (*fate*), and none of our letters was devised for its representation. In like manner, our "long *e*" (*mete*) is really a long *ī*, and what we call "long *i*" (*pine*) is a diphthong, *ai*. And, on the other side, our "long *u*" (*pure*) is not even a diphthong, but a syllable, *yu*, composed of semivowel and vowel, and our "short *o*" (*not*) and "short *u*" (*but*) are new sounds, having nothing to do with "long *o*" and "long *u*," and, of course, possessing no hereditary and rightful representatives in our alphabet. It is somewhat as if we were to call our elms "tall lilacs," and our rose-bushes "short maples." That our written vowels have from three to nine values each, is owing to the fact that we have altered their original unitary sounds in so many different ways during the historic period; and there lies yet further back another like history of change. This kind of change has been carried on upon a larger scale in English than in almost any other known language; but its effects are found abundantly in every other: the French, for example, has given to the old Latin *u* a mixed *i* and *u* sound (the German *ü*), and has converted the old diphthong *ou* into an *u*(*oo*)-sound (being curiously paralleled in both respects by the ancient Greek); it has taken a strange fancy for the diphthongal *oi* (nearly equal to our *wa* of *was*), and substitutes it for all manner of ancient sounds: as in *moi* for *mē*, *crois* for *credo*, *mois* for *mensis*, *quoi* for *quid*, *foi* for *fides*, *loi* for *legem*, *noir* for *nigrum*, *noix* for *nucem*; and so on.

The vowels are much more liable to wholesale alteration than are the consonants, and in our specimen-passage the indications of consonantal change are rather scanty. *Ofer*, however, has become *over* with us, by the conversion of a surd into its corresponding sonant sound, a phenomenon of very wide range and great frequency in language; and the same change has passed upon the final *s* of *his* and *æceras*, making of it a *z*, though without change of spelling. But if we look further away, among the tongues kindred with ours, we shall discover signs in plenty of consonantal mutation. *Dæg* is in German *tag*, with *t* for *d*, and *hyngrede* is *hungerte*; and if we were to go through the whole vocabulary of the two languages, we should find this the prevailing relation, and be led to set up the "law" that English *d* and German *t* correspond to one another. Again, *etan* is *essen* in German, with an *s*-sound for *t*: and this, too, is a constant relation; nor is it otherwise with *thâ*, which is German *die*, with *d* for *th*. But *etan* and *essen* answer to Latin *edere*, Greek ἔδω, Sanskrit *ad*; and *thâ* and *die* are the two regular Germanic forms of the old pronominal root *ta* (Gr. το, etc., Skt. *tad*, etc.): and these, too, are general facts; insomuch that comparative grammarians are led to set up the "law" that a *t*-sound, as found in most of the languages of our family, is regularly a *th* in part of the Germanic dialects and a *d* in others; that a *d*-sound, in like manner, is a *t* or an *s*; and that to English *d* and German *t* an aspirate, *th* or *dh*, corresponds in Greek and Sanskrit. This is, indeed, the famous "Grimm's Law," of the permutation or rotation of mutes in Germanic speech. It is only an example—to be sure, an unusually curious and striking example—of what is universally true between related languages: their sounds, in corresponding words, are by no means always the same; they are diverse, rather, but diverse by a constant difference; there exists between them a fixed relation, though it is not one of identity. Hence, in the comparison of two languages, a first point to which attention has to be directed is this: what sounds in the one, vowel or consonantal, correspond to what sounds in the other. This condition of things is only a necessary result of the fact, already noted, that the mode of pronunciation of every language is all the time undergoing a change: a change now more and now less important and pervading, but never entirely intermitted; and that no two languages change after precisely the same fashion. In presence of such a phenomenon as that last instanced, the student of language has to inquire which (if any) of the sounds, *t*, *d*, *th*, *dh*, *s* is in any given case the original, through what steps of successive change each varying result has been reached, and, if within his reach, what cause has governed the course of mutation.

And, heterogeneous as the facts may at first sight appear, the student soon finds that they are very far from being a mere confusion of lawless changes; they have their own methods and rules. One sound passes into another that is physically akin with it: that is to say, that is produced by the same organs, or otherwise in a somewhat similar manner; and the movement of transition follows a general direction, or else is governed by specific causes. This has caused the processes of articulation to be profoundly studied, as part of the science of language. And such is the interest and importance of the study that we cannot avoid dwelling upon it here a little: not long enough, indeed, to penetrate to its depths, but at least until we are able to gain some idea of our spoken alphabet as of an orderly system of sounds, and of the lines and degrees of relationship which bind its members together, and help to determine their transitions.

The organs by which alphabetic sounds are produced are the lungs, the larynx, and the parts of the mouth above the larynx. The lungs are, as it were, the bellows of the organ; they simply produce a current of air, passing out through the throat, and varying in rapidity or force according to the requirements of the speaker. The larynx is a kind of box at the upper end of the windpipe, and contains what is equivalent to the reed of the organ-pipe, with the muscular apparatus for its adjustment. From the sides of the box, namely, spring forth a pair of half-valves, of which the membranous edges, the "vocal chords," are capable of being brought close together in the middle of the passage, and made tense, so that the passing current of air sets them in vibration; and this vibration, communicated to the air, is reported to our ears as sound. In ordinary breathing, the valves are relaxed and retracted, leaving a wide and rudely triangular opening for the passage of the air. Thus the larynx gives the element of tone, accompanied with variety of pitch: and how important a part of speaking this latter is, only they can fully realize who have heard the performance of an automatic speaking-machine, with its dreadful monotone. Above the vibrating reed-apparatus is set, after the fashion of a sounding-box, the cavity of the pharynx, with that of the mouth, and the nasal passage; and movements of the throat and mouth-organs under voluntary control so alter the shape and size of this box as to give to the tone produced a variety of characters, or to modify it into a variety of tones—which are the sounds of our spoken alphabet. A concise description of voice, then, is this: it is the audible result of a column of air emitted by the lungs, impressed with sonancy and variety of pitch by the larynx, and individualized by the mouth-organs.

To describe in detail the construction of the vocal apparatus, and the movements of the muscles and cartilages and membranes which cause and modify the vibrations, belongs to physiology; to determine the form and composition of the vibrations which produce the audible variety of effects upon the ear, belongs to acoustics: the part of phonetics, as a branch of linguistic science, is to follow and describe, as closely as may be, the voluntary changes of position of the mouth-organs, etc., which determine the various sounds. These are in part easy of observation, in part much more difficult; but the main points, nearly all that we need to take account of here, are within the reach of careful and continued self-observation. And no one can claim to have any proper understanding of phonetic questions, unless he has so studied that he fairly follows and understands the movements that go on in his own mouth in speaking, and can arrange his spoken alphabet into a systematic and consistent scheme. Such a scheme, for the ordinary sounds composing the English alphabet, we will attempt here to set up.

Every alphabetic system must start from the sound *a* (of *far*, *father*); for this is the fundamental tone of the human voice, the purest intonated product of lungs and throat; if we open the mouth and fauces to their widest, getting out of the way everything that should modify the issuing current, this is the sound that is heard. Upon this openest tone various modifications are produced by narrowing the oral cavity, at different points and to different degrees. The less marked modifications, which, though they alter decidedly the quality of the tone, yet leave predominant the element of tone, of material, give rise to the sounds which we call vowels. But the cavity may be so narrowed, at one and another point, that the friction of the breath, as driven out through the aperture, forms the conspicuous element in the audible product; this, then, is a sound of very different character, a fricative consonant. And the narrowing of the organs may be pushed even to the point of complete closure, the element of form, of oral modification, coming thus to prevail completely over that of material, of tone: the product, in that case, is made distinctly audible only as the contact is broken; and we call it a mute.

This brief statement suggests the plan on which the systematic arrangement of every human alphabet is to be made. It must lie between the completely open *a* (*far*) and the completely close mutes; these are its natural and necessary limits; and it may be expected to fall into classes according to the intermediate degrees of closure. But there are also other lines of relationship in it. Theoretically, an indefinite number of mute-closures are possible, all along the mouth, from the lips to as far back in the throat as the organs can be brought together; in practice, however, they are found to be prevailingly three: one in the front, made by lip against lip, the labial closure, giving *p*; one in the back of the mouth, made against the soft palate by the rear upper surface of the tongue, the palatal (or guttural) closure, giving *k*; and one intermediate between the other two, made by the point or front of the tongue against the roof of the mouth near the front teeth, the lingual (or dental) closure, giving *t*. These are the only mute-closures found in English, or French, or German; or even in the majority of tongues in the world. And the same tendency toward a triple classification, of front, back, and intermediate, appears also in the other classes of sounds, so that these arrange themselves, in the main, nearly upon the lines of gradual closure proceeding from the neutrally open *a* (*far*) to the shut *p*, *t*, *k*. This adds, then, the other element which is needed in order to convert the mass of articulate utterances into an orderly system. We have below the English alphabet arranged upon the plan described, and will go on to consider it in more detail.

	palatal series				lingual series				labial series		
sonant.					*a*					vowels.	
sonant.				*æ*		*A*				vowels.	
sonant.			*e*		*ə*		*o*			vowels.	
sonant.		*i*						*u*		vowels.	
sonant.	*y*				*r*, *l*				*w*	semivowels.	consonants.
sonant.	*ng*				*n*				*m*	nasals.	consonants.
surd.	*h*									aspiration.	consonants.
sonant.	*zh*				*z*					sibilants.	fricatives. consonants.
surd.	*sh*				*s*					sibilants.	fricatives. consonants.
sonant.					*dh*				*v*	spirants.	fricatives. consonants.
surd.					*th*				*f*	spirants.	fricatives. consonants.
sonant.	*g*				*d*				*b*	mutes.	consonants.
surd.	*k*				*t*				*p*	mutes.	consonants.

Along with *k*, *t*, *p*, in the first place, go their nearest kindred, *g*, *d*, *b*. These are their sonant (or vocal, phthongal, intonated) counterparts. In the former, namely, there is no audible utterance, but complete silence, during the continuance of the closure; the antithesis to *a* is absolute; the explosion is their whole sensible substance. In the latter there is, even while the closure lasts, a tone produced by the vibration of the vocal chords, a stream of air sufficient to support vibration for a very brief time being forced up from the lungs into the closed cavity or receiving-box of the pharynx and mouth. This is the fundamental distinction of "surd" and "sonant" sounds; anything else is merely a consequence of this and subordinate to it; the names strong and weak, hard and soft, sharp and flat, and so on, founded (with more or less of misapprehension added) upon these subordinate characteristics, are to be rejected. The difference between *pa* and *ba*, then, is that the sonant utterance begins in the former just when the contact is broken, and in the latter just before; in *ab*, it continues a moment after the contact is made; in *aba*, it is uninterrupted and continuous: and so also with *d* and *g*.

But there is a third product of the same three positions of mute-closure. By dropping, namely, the veil of the palate, which in ordinary utterance closes the passage from the pharynx into the nose, the intonated current of *b*, *d*, *g* is allowed entrance to the nose and exit there: and the result is the class of nasals (or "resonants"), *m*, *n*, and *ng* (as in *singing*). Here, though there is closure of the mouth-organs, the tone is so sonorous and continuable that the breach of contact, or explosion, is reduced to a very subordinate value, and the class belongs high up in the alphabet, toward the vowels.

As a general rule (exceptions to it are not common), any language that has either of these three products of a given mute-closure will have also the other two: thus, the presence of a *p* in the alphabet implies also that of a *b* and an *m;* and so on.

In the older tongues of our family, and even in some modern ones, both of our own and of other families, there are fourth and fifth products of the same positions, the former made by letting slip an audible bit of breath or flatus, a brief *h*, after the simple mute, turning *p* into *ph* (pronounced as written), and so on; the latter, the sonant *bh*, of more doubtful character. These are called aspirate mutes, or, briefly, aspirates.

Next to the mutes in regard to degree of closure are the class of so-called "fricatives," defined above as containing a rustling or friction of the breath through a narrowed aperture as their main element. If the lips are brought together in loose instead of close contact, and the breath forced out between them, there is heard an *f*-sound; or, if the breath be intonated, a *v*-sound. These, however, are not precisely our English or French (nor the general German) *f* and *v;* for, in the latter, the tips of the teeth are brought forward and laid upon the lower lip, and the expulsion is made between them; giving a product somewhat differently shaded, a dentilabial instead of a purely labial sound. A relaxation of the lingual contact, in like manner, gives the *s* and *z* sounds; and that of the palatal gives the German *ch* (its sonant counterpart is very rare). Practically, however, it is found convenient to divide the fricatives into two sub-classes: *s* and *z* have a peculiar quality which we call sibilant or hissing; and the same is shared by the *sh* and the *zh* (in *azure, vision*) sounds, which are produced farther back upon the roof of the mouth, or in a more palatal position. These two pairs, accordingly, we set by themselves, as lingual and palatal "sibilants." Then, along with the *f* and *v*, as akin with them, especially in their dentilabial variety, we have the two English *th*-sounds, surd in *thin* and sonant in *then* (written *dh* in the scheme), real dentilinguals, produced between the tongue and teeth. These four, with the (German) *ch*-sound, we class as "spirants." Historically, they have a special kinship in that they are all alike frequent products of the alteration of an aspirate mute; hence it is that they are so often, in various languages, written with *ph*, *th*, *ch* (=*kh*).

A like tendency to the points of oral action already defined appears in the vowels, the opener tone-sounds. An *i* (in *pīque*, *pĭck*) is a palatal vowel, made by an approach of the flat of the tongue toward the palate where its contact produces a *k*; an *u* (*rūle*, *pŭll*) involves a rounding approach of the lips, the organs whose contact makes a *p* (although not without accompanying action at the base of the tongue also). And between *a* (*far*) and *i* stands *e* (*thēy*, *thĕn*), made by a less degree of palatal approach, as *o* (*nōte*, *ŏbey*) between *a* and *u*. And again, the sound of *fat*, *man* (*æ* in the scheme) stands between *a* and *e*, as that of *ăll*, *whăt* (*ʌ* in the scheme) between *a* and *o*. Representing for the moment the pure fricatives by *kh* and *ph*, we have the palatal series *a æ e i kh k*, and the labial series *a ʌ o u ph p*, which are true series all the way through, made by gradually increasing degrees of approximation of the same parts of the mouth until complete closure is reached.

There is still one class to be noticed: that of the semivowels, or sounds which stand nearly on the division-line between vowel and consonant. *I* (*pique*) and *u* (*rule*) are the closest sounds we can make with retention of the predominant tone-quality which constitutes a vowel. But so close are they, that it is only necessary to abbreviate them sufficiently, making them merely starting-points from which to reach another vowel-sound, in order to convert them into consonants, *y* and *w*; these differ, at the utmost, only infinitesimally in articulating position from *i* and *u*. And with them belong the *r* and *l*, lingual semivowels, used in many languages also as vowels; the *l*, even in English, in *able*, *eagle*, etc. The *r* is produced between the tongue-tip and the roof of the mouth, and is so generally trilled or vibrated that trilling is apt to be given as its distinctive characteristic; the *l* sets the tip of the tongue against the roof of the mouth, but leaves the sides open for the free escape of the intonated breath.

We have one more pair of simple vowels, that in *hūrt* and *hŭt* (ə in the scheme), the specific quality of which is due to a dimming action along the whole mouth rather than an approach at a definite point or points, and which are thus a duller kind of *a*; they are put in the centre of the vowel-triangle rather because they belong nowhere else than because they belong precisely there.

The distinctions of long and short vowel, although in English they always involve differences of quality as well as of quantity, and the three compound vowel-sounds or diphthongs, *ai* ("long *i*" of *aisle*, *isle*), *au* (*out*, *how*), and *ʌi* (*oil*, *boy*), are for simplicity's sake left unnoticed in the scheme. And it remains only to find a place in it, and a definition, for the somewhat anomalous *h*. We have seen that in the classes of mutes and fricatives the sounds go in pairs, one produced by mere breath, the other by intonated breath, forced through the same position of the organs; while this is not the case with the remaining and opener classes of sounds. We may define the difference in a general way thus: after a certain degree of closeness is reached, simple breath is sufficiently characterized to give a constituent to the alphabet for every articulating position; short of that degree, only tone is fully distinctive; surd breath, though somewhat differentiated in the several positions, is not enough so to furnish a separate alphabetic element in each; the various breaths count only as one letter—namely, the *h*. The *h*, the pure aspiration, is an expulsion of *flatus* through the position of the adjacent letter, whether vowel, semivowel, or nasal; in English, it occurs only before a vowel, or before *w* and *y*, in such words as *when* and *hue*. It is, then, the common surd to the three classes of sonant sounds just mentioned.

The scheme thus drawn up and described may be taken as a general model, on the plan of which the spoken alphabet of any language may best be arranged, in order to the determination of its internal relations and to its comparison with other alphabets. Though not accurate to the very last detail, it exhibits more of the relations of alphabetic sounds, and exhibits them more truly, than any other plan that can be adopted. And, restricted as it is in number of sounds, as compared with the immense variety—not less than three or four hundred—which enter into human speech, it yet includes those sounds which make up the bulk of all human speech, and of which many of the others are slightly differentiated variations. The possible number of human articulations is theoretically infinite; but practically it is rather narrowly limited; and a system like our own, which contains about forty-four distinctly characterized sounds, is hardly excelled in richness, among tongues ancient or modern.

Our scheme is to be valued, especially, as putting in a true light the relations of vowel and consonant: which, though their distinction is of the highest importance in phonetics, are by no means separate and independent systems, but only poles, as it were, in one continuous unitary series, and with a doubtful or neutral territory between them: they are simply the opener and closer sounds of the alphabetic system. Upon their alternation and antithesis depends the syllabic or "articulate" character of human speech: the stream of utterance is broken into *articuli*, 'joints,' by the intervention of the closer sounds between the opener, connecting the latter at the same time that they separate them, giving distinctness and flexibility, and the power of endlessly variable combination. A mere succession of vowels passing into one another would be wanting in definite character; it would be rather sing-song than speech; and, on the other hand, a mere succession of consonants, though pronounceable by sufficient effort, would be an indistinct and disagreeable sputter.

Another advantage of the same arrangement consists in its illustration of the general historical development of the alphabet. The primitive language of our family had not half the sounds given in the scheme; and those which it had were the extreme members of the system: among the vowels, only *a*, *i*, and *u*, the corners of the vowel triangle; among the consonants, mainly the mutes, along with the nasals *m* and *n*, which are also mutes as concerns their mouth-position; of the whole double class of fricatives, only the *s*. The *l* was not yet distinctly separated from the *r*, nor the *w* and *y* from *u* and *i*. There has been a filling-up of the scheme by the production of such new sounds as are intermediate in character, made by less strongly dif ferentiated positions of the organs. We may fairly say that, in the process of time, with greater acquired skill in the art of utterance, men's organs have come to be able to make and use more nicely distinguished, more slightly shaded tones than at first. This is no mere loose poetic expression; nor, on the other hand, does it imply any organic change in the organs of utterance. The case is only as in any other department of effort: the higher skill is won by the advanced or adult speakers, and the shape which they give to their inherited speech becomes the norm toward which new learners have to strive, attaining it when they can.

In the process, too, is involved an evident manifestation of the tendency to ease. Not, indeed, that the new sounds are in themselves any easier than the old; on the contrary, judged by some tests, they are harder: they are not so readily learned and reproduced by children; they are not so frequently met with in the general body of human languages. But they are easier to the practised speaker, in the rapid movements of continuous utterance, when the organs are making constant quick transitions between vowel and consonant, between opener and closer positions. To reduce the length of swing of these transitions, by reducing the openness of the open sounds and the closeness of the close ones, is an economy which the articulating organs—of course, unconsciously—find out for themselves by experience and learn to practise. It is the most general kind of assimilating influence exerted by consonant and vowel upon one another: each class draws the other toward itself; the vowels become more consonantal; the consonants become more vocalic. Hence the prevailing direction of phonetic change is from the extremities toward the middle of the alphabetic scheme: the mutes become fricatives; the *a* (*far*) is changed to *e* (*they*) and *i* (*pique*), or to *o* (*note*) and *u* (*rule*). Movement in the contrary direction is by no means unknown; but it is exceptional or under special causes: it is, as we have called it above, the eddy in the current. The central classes, of nasals and semivowels, which are least exposed to this general movement, are also, on the whole, the least convertible of the alphabetic sounds. To illustrate the effects of the tendency: in Sanskrit (the least altered, phonetically, of the tongues of our family), the *a* (*far*) is full thirty per cent. of the whole utterance; and we can easily reason back to a time when *a* and the mutes were three quarters of the sounds heard in continuous speech; in English, the most altered, *a* is only about half of one per cent. of our utterance, while *i* (*pique*, *pick*) and *ə* (*hurt*, *hut*), the closest and thinnest of the vowels, are over sixteen per cent.; and the fricatives have become rather more common than the mutes (each class, about eighteen per cent.).[1]

We have called this a process of assimilation; and under the same comprehensive head may be grouped the greater part of the other phonetic changes that occur in language. The combinations of elements to form words, their contraction by the omission of light vowels, often bring into contact or into proximity sounds which cannot be so uttered without too much muscular exertion: it is eased by adapting the one to the other. For example, many combinations of surd consonant with sonant have that degree of difficulty which we call impossibility (this is only a matter of degree); and nothing is more frequent in all language

[1] See the author's "Oriental and Linguistic Studies," second series (1874), where many of the questions concerning the alphabet are more fully discussed.

than the interchange of surd and sonant utterance. There is also a more general movement here: since the sonant elements in connected speech are (including the vowels) much more numerous than the surd, the general weight of the assimilative force is in the direction of sonancy, and surds are converted into sonants more often than the reverse.

There is a degree of assimilation effected in vowels by the consonants with which they come into immediate connection; yet the cases are rather sporadic and often doubtful. The influence of vowels on other vowels, even when separated from them by consonants, is more marked, and leads to some important classes of phenomena. The difference between *man* and *men* is ultimately due only to the former presence of an *i*-vowel in the plural ending, which colored by anticipation the preceding vowel: in Icelandic, the effect is still plainly illustrated in the forms *degi* and *dögum* from *dagr*. In the Scythian languages, on the other hand, it is the final vowel of the base which assimilates that of the following suffixes, as will be noted hereafter (p. 234).

Though assimilation is the leading principle in the mutual adjustment of sounds, its opposite, dissimilation, is not altogether unknown, as the close recurrence of two acts of the same organs is felt as burdensome, and avoided by the alteration of one of them.

Not only the parts of the same words, in their combination, but also separate words, in their collocation, affect one another; and the influence expresses itself particularly in their final elements. There are various circumstances which help to condition this. In our own and the majority of other families of speech, the formative or less indispensable element comes last, and is the one least efficiently conserved by the sense of its importance. Moreover, all experience shows that an "open syllable," one ending with an open or vowel sound, is easier, more "natural" to the organs, than a closed one, ending with a consonant. A mute, indeed, is hardly audible as final, unless the contact is broken again with a puff of *flatus;* and something of the same disability clings also to the other consonants. The difficulty is one which English-speakers can hardly realize, since they allow freely every consonant in their alphabet (with the accidental exception of the *zh*-sound) at the end of a word, or of a syllable, before another consonant; but the Polynesian dialects, for example, admit no groups of consonants anywhere, and end every word with a vowel; the literary Chinese has no final consonant except a nasal; the Greek, none save *ν, σ, ρ* (*n, s, r*); the Sanskrit allows only about half a dozen, and almost never a group of more than one; the Italian rarely has any final consonant; the French silences, as a rule, all save *c, f, l, r;* the German tolerates no final sonant mutes: and so on.

But the principle of ease does not find its sole exercise in the work of assimilation. Nothing is more frequent than for a language to take a dislike, as it were, to some particular sound or class of sounds, and to get rid of it by conversion into something else. We found an example of this above in the old English *h*-sound of *cniht*, etc. Most of the tongues of our family have cast out the ancient aspirate mutes, changing them to simple mutes or to spirants. The Greek early rejected the *y*-sound, and then the *w:* the latter, as the "digamma," just prolonging its existence into the historical period. Curious caprices, discordances between different languages as to their predilections and aversions, come abundantly to light in this department of phonetic change. Yet more exceptional and puzzling are the cases of interchange between two sounds: for example, the Armenian mutual exchange of surd and sonant (*Dikran* for *Tigranes*, and so on): to which the cockney confusion of *w* and *v*, and of the presence and absence of an initial *h*, furnishes a familiar, if undignified, parallel. And of a comparative difficulty which is at least as the square of the number of elements involved is "Grimm's Law" of permutation of mutes, illustrated above (p. 57). Phonetic science is not yet far enough advanced to deal successfully with facts like this; no attempted explanation of the particular phenomenon in question does much more than ignore its real difficulties.

It must be carefully noted, indeed, that the reach of phonetics, its power to penetrate to the heart of its facts and account for them, is only limited. There is always one element in linguistic change which refuses scientific treatment: namely, the action of the human will. The work is all done by human beings, adapting means to ends, under the impulse of motives and the guidance of habits which are the resultant of causes so multifarious and obscure that they elude recognition and defy estimate. The phonetist is never able to put himself in an *à priori* position; his business is only to note the facts, to determine the relation between the later and the earlier, and to account for the change as well as he can, showing of what tendencies, in which of their forms, it may be accounted the result. The real effective reason of a given phonetic change is that a community, which might have chosen otherwise, willed it to be thus; showing thereby the predominance of this or that one among the motives which a careful induction from the facts of universal language proves to govern men in this department of their action.

The tendency of phonetic change is so decidedly toward the abbreviation and mutilation of words and forms that it has been, suitably enough, termed "phonetic decay." Under the impulse to ease, the component elements of speech are first unified, then unbuilt and destroyed. It is the processes of combination (to be treated of in the seventh chapter) that open a wide field for the action of the tendency; if language had always remained in its original simple state, the sphere of change would have been a greatly restricted one, and the effects far less comparable to decay.

Before quitting the subject of changes of external form, we must give a moment's attention to a class of changes which bear a very different character, although their cause has its points of analogy with those which we have been considering: the class, namely, of which we found instances in our modern *ears* and *fared* (p. 38), as compared with the earlier *ear* and *fôr*. When phonetic corruption has disguised too much, or has swept away, the characteristics of a form, so that it becomes an exceptional or anomalous case, there is an inclination to remodel it on a prevailing norm. The greater mass of cases exerts an assimilative influence upon the smaller. Or, we may say, it is a case of mental economy: an avoidance of the effort of memory involved in remembering exceptions and observing them accurately in practice. The formal distinction of plural from singular was one which our language was never minded to give up. Of all the plural signs, the one which had the most distinctive character was *s*. The attention of the language-users became centred upon this as an affix by which the plural modification of sense was made, and they proceeded to apply it in words where it had not before been used; and the movement, once started, gathered force in its progress, until it swept in nearly all the nouns of the language. So with the verb. By the numerical predominance of forms like *loved* from *love*, the addition of a *d* got itself more conspicuously associated with the designation of past time; and men began to overlook the cases which by right of former usage ought to be made exceptions. Considerable numbers of verbs, in the middle age of our tongue, thus changed, like *fare*, their old mode of conjugation for a new. But the tendency is ever at work, and on a small scale as well as a large; and, of course, especially among those whose acquisition of their language has not been made complete and accurate. Children, above all others, are all the time blundering in this direction—saying *gooder* and *badder*, *mans* and *foots*, *goed* and *comed*, even *brang* and *thunk*—and items of such products creep not seldom into cultivated speech. *Its* was made in this way, in the sixteenth and seventeenth centuries; we have gained thus the double comparatives *lesser* and *worser;* many are led to say *plĕad* (like *rĕad*) instead of *pleaded*, and even to fabricate such unsupported anomalies as *proven* for *proved*. And the principle is often appealed to in explaining the processes of earlier language-making. The force of analogy is, in fact, one of the most potent in all language-history; as it makes whole classes of forms, so it has power to change their limits.

CHAPTER V.

GROWTH OF LANGUAGE: CHANGE IN THE INNER CONTENT OF WORDS.

Wide reach and variety of this change; underlying principles: looseness of tie between word and meaning; principle of economy; class-names and proper names. Illustrations: the *planets* and their kin. Restriction of general terms to specific use; extension of specific terms to wider use. Figurative extension; illustrations, *head*, etc.; forgetfulness of derivation. Growth of intellectual vocabulary from physical terms; of means of formal expression from material terms; auxiliaries, formal parts of speech; phrases.

WE come next to consider the other grand department of change in the existing material of language—namely, that of the inner content or meaning of words. This is just as vast a subject as the preceding; and, if possible, even more irreducible in its immensity and infinite variety to the dimensions of a chapter. The processes of phonetic change have been worked out with great industry by numerous students of language and brought into order and system, and the comparatively restricted and sensible movements of the organs of speech investigated in order to form a concrete basis for their explanation; but no one has ever attempted to classify the processes of significant change, and the movements of the human mind under the variety of circumstances defy cataloguing. Yet we may hope within reasonable space to lay out at least the foundations of the subject, and to trace some of the chief directions of movement.

It has been already pointed out that the separate possibility of external and internal change rests upon the nature of the tie, as a merely extraneous and unessential one, which connects the meaning of a word with its form. Were the case otherwise, the two kinds of change would be mutually dependent and inseparable; as it is, each runs its own course and is determined by its own causes; even though the history of the two may often touch, or go on for a time in close connection. We also saw that words were assigned to their specific uses (so far as it is possible to trace their history) each at some definite time in the past, and for reasons which were satisfactory to the nomenclators, though they did not make the name either a definition or a description of the conception; and that the name, once given, formed a new and closer tie with the thing named than with its own etymological ancestor. We took as illustration of this the word *bishop*, originally simply 'overseer;' claiming that it was only a specimen of the way things regularly go on in language. It is just so, for example, with *priest*, formerly πρεσβύτερος, presbyter, elder, literally 'older person;' so with *volume*, though no longer 'rolled,' as when the name was given; with *book*, though not now a block of 'beech'-wood; with *paper*, now made of other material than *papyrus;* with *gazette*, which has ceased to be sold for a Venetian 'penny;' with *bank*, which has infinitely outgrown the simple 'bench' of the money-changer in the market-place, while the *bankrupt* has vastly worse trials to endure than having his 'bench broken;' with *candidate*, though one in such a position is no longer expected to be 'dressed in white;' with *copper* and *muslin*, which come now from other quarters than Cyprus and Mosul; with *lunatic*, even if we discredit the moon's influence on the disorder; with *Indian*, though the error of the Spanish navigators, who thought they had discovered 'the Indies' in America, was detected a good while ago—and so on indefinitely.

We may see in all this something of the same principle of ease or economy which we found to underlie the changes of form. Were it altogether as easy, when the shape of one's conception alters a little, or more than a little, to fling away its old name and make a new one; were it as easy, when a new conception presents itself, to give it an appellation before unheard-of, as to stretch a familiar term a little to cover it, then might there perhaps be no such thing as significant change in human speech; as it is, the old material of language is constantly suffering extension and transferral to new uses, obstructed by no too intrusive sense of original meaning. Again, in virtue of the same principle, our words are, almost universally, class-names. There is, if narrowly enough regarded, a degree of individuality about every being, thing, act, quality, which would justify it in laying claim to a separate appellation; but language would be utterly unmanageable if it were made up of such appellations; and, in practice, having named an individual thing, we apply the same name to whatever other things are enough like it to form a class with it. And thus, as we noted in the second chapter, the acquisition of language is the adoption of certain classifications; herein consists a large share of its value as a means of training. The classes, to be sure, are of very different extent: there are even some—as *sun*, *moon*, *God*, *world*—which have a natural restriction to a single member. Then, again, there are classes of which the individuals in their separateness rise to such importance for us that we give each in addition a name belonging to it as an individual only, or a "proper name," as we call it: such are the persons of our community, our pet animals, streets, towns, and other localities, the planets, months, week-days, and the like. In this class-use is an additional facilitation of significant change; for every class is liable to revision, in consequence of increased knowledge, keener insight, and consequent change of criteria.

We shall best establish these fundamental principles, and win suggestion of a classification for the modes of change, by glancing over a series of illustrations.

In the olden time, certain heavenly bodies which, as they circled daily about the earth from east to west, had also a slower and more irregular movement in the opposite direction among their fellows, were by a little community in the eastern Mediterranean called *planêtês*, because the word in their language meant 'wanderer.' From their use, we imported it into our own tongue in the form *planet*, mutilated in shape and having no etymological connection with any other of our words. The class included the sun and moon not one whit less than Jupiter and Mars; it did not include the earth. But within two or three centuries past, we have acquired new knowledge which has led us to alter this classification, and give a new value to its nomenclature. We see now that, in a truer sense, the sun is not a planet, but that the earth is one; and *planet* has been changed to mean, not a 'wandering star' as viewed from earth, but a body that moves about a central sun.

The moon is no longer precisely a planet, but a secondary planet, a satellite. Having thus altered the conception designated by *moon*, we are ready, when the telescope discloses to us like satellites of other planets, to convert this unique appellation into a class-name, calling them all alike *moons*. So also with *sun:* having found that the sun is essentially akin with the fixed stars rather than with the planets, we put him into the linguistic class of fixed stars, or we call the fixed stars *suns*.

The class of planets is one of those already referred to, of which each separate member calls for an individual designation, or "proper name." Apart from the sun and moon, however, they did not so impress the popular mind as to receive popular titles, and it fell to the learned, the astronomo-astrologers, to christen them. These, though they did their work reflectively, were not altogether arbitrary in their selection; they took the names of gods, since Sun and Moon were already names of gods as well as of luminaries; and they distributed the names—Jupiter, Saturn, Mercury, Mars, Venus—under the guidance of motives which we can at least in part recognize: Mercury, for example, the swift messenger of the divinities, had the most rapidly moving and changeful of the class called after him. Then, by a like transfer, the alchemists gave the god- and planet-name to the most mobile of the metals. And now, though the god Mercury is only a memory of a state of things long gone by, *Mercury* and *mercury* are still words of familiar use in our vocabulary; we even shut up *mercury* in a tube and bid him, as Jupiter used to do, go up and down, to tell us what the weather is. Again, the Frenchman calls the middle day of his week 'Mercury's day' (*Mercredi*), though without being well aware of it, and yet less comprehending why: it is because, in the distribution by the astrologers of the hours through the whole week to the planets in their order, the first hour of that day fell to the regency of Mercury. Then, once upon a time, these Latin day-names were mechanically turned into German shape for the use of Germanic peoples, and *Mercurii dies* became *Woden's day*, our *Wednesday:* and so with the rest. Certainly a most curious history of transfer, which brings out of a series of reflective acts of nomenclature made by learned heathen—and not without Christian aid, since the planetary day-names would have remained to Europe, as to India, a mere astrologers' fancy, but for Christianity and its inheritance of the Jewish seven-day period as a leading measure of time—a little group of some of the commonest and most truly popular terms in our language! The same words, moreover, have been made to answer other purposes: the astrologers held that a person born under the special influence of a certain planet was characterized by a corresponding disposition; and those dispositions we still call *mercurial*, *jovial*, *saturnine*; *martial* and *venereal*, on the other hand, come from the office of the divinities themselves.

Again, we use *sun* and *moon* to designate 'day' and 'month,' saying "so many *suns*," "so many *moons*." Here is simply a striking ellipsis: we mean really "so many [revolutions of] sun or moon"—counting, however, the revolutions on different principles; else a *sun* would be a 'year.' Then *month*, which is only a derivative form of *moon*, has been transferred to designate an arbitrary period of twenty-eight to thirty-one days, having nothing whatever to do with the moon's movement. Further, a *moon* (or *lune*) is in fortification a crescent-shaped outwork: an analogy, this time, of shape merely. Nor is it meant to imply that the moon is always, or usually, of this shape; but only that she is the most conspicuous object in nature that ever assumes the shape. If we want to be more precise, we say "*crescent*-shaped." But here also is an ellipsis, and of the most striking kind; for *crescent* literally means simply 'growing,' and does not contain even a hint of the moon. Moreover, the moon does not have this shape all the time she is "growing," but only at a particular period, and she has it just as much when decreasing as when increasing; so that *crescent* really means '[resembling the moon at a certain stage of her] *growing* [as also of her waning].' It is good English, too, to talk of a *moon*-struck idler as *mooning* around, although we should indignantly deny the belief in lunar influences which suggested the expressions.

This may seem like an aimless roaming through one department of our vocabulary; but its heterogeneousness is due to the character of the facts with which we have to deal, and is an important part of the value of the illustration. It is simply impossible to exhaust the variety of significant change in linguistic growth: there is no conceivable direction in which a transfer may not be made; there is no assignable distance to which a word may not wander from its primitive meaning. There is no such thing as a concise and exhaustive classification of such variety; all we can do is to point out some of the main divisions, the leading directions in which the movement goes on, neglecting the unclassified and perhaps in part unclassifiable residue.

One of the largest classes (already more than once hinted at) has a striking example in *crescent*. *Crescent*, 'growing,' is a word of the widest application; a young child or tree, an aggregating crystal, a new-built fire, a beginning reputation, an evolving cosmos, are really as much *crescent* as a young (so, by a figure, we call it) moon. To seize upon the word as specific title of the growing moon, then, is to commit a very bold and arbitrary act of restriction. But the act is also open to objection on another side. It takes account of only a single, and that a very trivial, characteristic of an object which has many others. All we can say in reply is that nomenclature is a free and easy process, and that such objections count for nothing as against the demands of convenient expression. The case was the same with *bishop*, 'overseer,' as we saw above; it was the same with *green*, 'growing;' it was the same with *planet*, 'wanderer.' It is believed by the etymologists that *moon* itself comes in a similar way from a root meaning 'measure;' our satellite having been thus designated, in remote ages, because of her office in measuring the longer intervals of time: "so many *moons*." Certainly, her Latin name *luna* is for *lucna*, and related with *lux*, and so describes her simply as a 'shiner.' And *sun* goes back, it is believed, to an equivalent source. Comparative philology claims to have shown (as will be noticed hereafter) that the earliest appellations of specific things were in general won in precisely this way, the germs of speech being expressions for acts and qualities. However that may be, it is certain that, through the whole history of language since, the method has been in constant use: epithets of things, representing some one of their various attributes, become the names of things, through every department of nomenclature. Our etymologies are apt to bring us back finally to some so general, comprehensive, colorless idea, that we almost wonder how it can have given birth to such strongly-marked progeny. All the varied and definite meanings of *post* (to take a further example or two) go back to the sense of 'put, placed.' The idea of *rolling* is specialized into the muster *roll* and the breakfast *roll*, the *roll* of the drum and *rolls* of fat; by a longer route, it comes to us in the form of the actor's *rôle;* and a slight addition makes of it *control*, of which the connection with its original escapes all but skilled and curious eyes.

Another leading principle, of the first order of importance, is somewhat contrary in its effects to that which we have been considering: it is the principle of extension, as opposed to restriction, of the sphere of meaning of a term. A name won by specialization begins an independent career, which ends in its gaining the position of head of a tribe. Mr. Miller, named by the specializing process from his vocation, becomes the father of a multitude of Millers, so named from their relation to him, without the least regard to their vocations. And he may turn out the founder of a sect, who shall call themselves Millerites after him, and make his name as conspicuous an element in the nomenclature of theology as is already that of Arius or Nestorius. The *butterflies* were first named in the species which showed itself *butter*-colored as it *flew:* the title is extended, heedless of the differences of color, to every other kindred species. Our recent examples showed us *sun* and *moon* made class-names. *Crescent* develops a group of new uses out of the fortuitous presence of the figure on the Mohammedan standard. No one knows precisely why the *rose* was so entitled: the botanist has made it the type of a whole order of quite diverse plants, which he terms *rosaceæ*, 'rose-like.' A great part of our acquisitions of new knowledge go to swell old established classes, expending themselves, so far as language is concerned, in the extension of existing class-names. To take an example of the most obvious kind: the discovery of every new animal or plant or mineral stretches a little not only the scope of those widest terms, but also of a whole series of subordinate ones. And sometimes the change rises to conspicuous value. The zoologist's conception of *horse*, for example, has undergone no slight modification by the recent discovery in the American West of numerous fossil species, of greatly varying size and structure. Every exploring naturalist, in fact, is all the time illustrating, in an openly reflective way, in his naming of species, the two principles which direct a great part of the world's less conscious nomenclature. Having in his hands a new plant, he at once proceeds to classify it: that is to say, to determine of what current class-names it must swell the content: he finds it, we will suppose, a plant, and a phenogamous, a dicotyledonous, a rose-like plant, and finally a *rubus* or 'blackberry.' But it has peculiarities which entitle it to a specific designation; and this must be gained by the other method: the nomenclator selects the quality which he will describe, and christens it *megalocarpus*, 'big-fruited,' *gracilis*, 'elegant,' or the like; or he gets a suggestion from the locality, the situation, the circumstances of discovery; or he connects it with some still more extraneous matter: so, for instance, he compliments his friend Smith by naming it *Smithii*

The extension of a name's application, however, involves a great deal that is far less plain and legitimate than all this. Not only a true accordance in generic character, but relations of an infinitely looser kind, are used to tie together the classes that go under one name. We saw lately a heathen god, a planet, a metal, a temperament, and a day of the week, all forced into unnatural union under the title *mercury*. Since fruit is apt to be green when not fully ripe, *green* becomes a synonym for 'unripe' (and so we can commit the familiar linguistic paradox that *black*berries are *red* when they are *green*); and then, in less elegant diction, it is again shifted to signify 'immature, not versed in the ways of the world.' Such transfers we are wont to call figurative; they rest upon an apprehended analogy, but one generally so distant, subjective, fanciful, that we can hardly regard it as sufficient to make a connected class. Instances of this kind lie all about us, in our most familiar words; and this department of change is of so conspicuous importance in language-history that we must dwell upon it a little longer. Our minds delight in the discovery of resemblances, near and remote, obvious and obscure, and are always ready to make them the foundation of an association that involves the addition of a new use to an old name. Thus, not only an animal has a *head*, but also a pin, a cabbage. A bed has one, where the head of its occupant usually lies—and it has a *foot* for the same reason, besides the four *feet* it stands on by another figure, and the six *feet* it measures by yet another. More remarkable still, a river has a *head:* its highest point, namely, where it *heads* among the highlands—and so it has *arms;* or, by another figure, *branches;* or, by another, *feeders;* or, by another, *tributaries;* and it has a right and left *side;* and it has a *bed*, in which, by an unfortunate mixture of metaphors, it *runs* instead of lying still; and then, at the farthest extremity from the head, we find, not its *foot*, but its *mouth*. Further, an army, a school, a sect, has its *head*. A class has its *head* and its *tail;* and so has a coin, though in quite a different way. A sermon has its *heads*, as divided by their different *headings;* and we can beg to be spared anything more "on that *head.*" A sore comes to a *head;* and so, by one step further away from literalness, a conspiracy or other disorder in the state, the *body* politic, does the same. We give a horse his *head*, which he had before our donation; and then we treat in the same way our passions—that is to say, if by their overmastering violence we lose our *heads*. And so on, *ad infinitum*.

These side or figurative uses of a word do not perplex us; they do not even strike us as anything out of the way; they are part and parcel of the sphere of application of the word. For it is an important item in this process of transfer that we gradually lose our sense of the figure implied, and come to employ each sign as if it had always been the simple and downright representative of its idea. Here we see again the willingness, which has been already pointed out, and which is essential to the prosperous development of a language, to forget the origin of a name when once it is won, to let drop the old associations and suggestions which belonged to it in virtue of its etymology, and invest it with a new set appertaining to its present use. Perhaps there is in English hardly a more striking example of this than our word *butterfly*, a name of utterly prosaic and trivial origin, but which has become truly poetic and elegant, as we think in connection with it of the beautiful creatures it designates, and not one in a thousand has ever had come into his head the idea that it literally means 'a *fly* of *butter*-color.' The relics of forgotten derivations, of faded metaphors, are scattered thickly through every part of our vocabulary. It is, to our apprehension, in the nature of a word to have its figurative as well as its literal uses and applications; we inherited our vocabulary in that condition; and, by new discoveries of analogies and new transfers of meaning, we are all the time adding to the confusion—if it were a confusion. Sometimes the connection between the different senses is obvious on the least reflection; sometimes, again, it is so obscure that we cannot find it, or that we conceive it wrongly; ordinarily, we do not concern ourselves about the matter; we use each word as we have learned it, leaving to the lexicographer to follow up the ramifications to their source in its primitive or etymological meaning.

A conspicuous branch of the department of figurative transfer, and one of indispensable importance in the history of language, is the application of terms having a physical, sensible meaning, to the designation of intellectual and moral conceptions and their relations. It is almost useless to attempt to illustrate this; the examples would come crowding in too numerously to be dealt with: we will merely notice a few of those which happen to be offered in the preceding paragraph. *Perplex* means 'braid together, intertwine.' *Simple* is 'without fold,' as distinguished from what is *double*, or 'two-fold;' in *simplicity* and *duplicity* we have a moral contrast more distinctly brought to view; *application* contains the same root, and denotes an actual physical 'folding or bending to' anything, so as to fit it closely; while *imply* intimates a 'folding in.' *Important*, means 'bringing in, *importing*, having conferred *import* or consequence.' *Apprehension* signifies literally the 'taking hold' of a thing. *Relation* is a 'carrying back,' as *transfer* is a 'carrying across' in Latin, and *metaphor* nearly the same thing in Greek. To *invest* is to 'put into clothes;' to *develop* is to 'unwrap.' *Trivial* is what is found 'at the street-crossings;' anything is *obvious* which meets us 'in the way,' which *occurs* to, or 'runs against' us. *Derivation* involves the curiously special idea of drawing off streams of water from a *river*, for irrigation or the like. To *suggest* is to 'carry under,' or supply, as it were, from beneath, not conspicuously—and so on. All these are from the Latin part of our language, which furnishes examples in the greatest abundance, because our philosophical and scientific vocabulary comes mainly from that source; but there is plenty like it in the Saxon part also. *Wrong* is '*wrung*' or 'twisted,' as its opposite *right* is 'straight;' and *downright* involves the same figure as *upright*, as having nothing oblique or indirect about it. A *striking* example needs no comment. To *forget* is the opposite of to *get*, but signifies only a mental loss. We *see* things that never come before our bodily eyes. And *point out*, *let drop*, *follow up*, *lay down*, *come into the head*, *out of the way*, are instances of phrases that show plainly a similar shift of application. In fact, our whole mental and moral vocabulary has been gained precisely in this way; the etymologist feels that he has not finished tracing out the history of any one of its terms until he has hunted it back to the physical conception in which, by the general analogies of language, it must have had its origin.

Thus, as the general movement of human knowledge is from the recognition of sensible objects to an ever finer analysis of their qualities and determination of their relations, and to the apprehension of more recondite existences, objects of thought, so, as the accompaniment and necessary consequence, there is a movement in the whole vocabulary of language from the designation of what is coarser, grosser, more material, to the designation of what is finer, more abstract and conceptional, more formal. Considered with reference to the ends rather than the methods of expression, there is no grander phenomenon than this in all language-history. But the evolution of the intellectual vocabulary is only one division of the movement; there is another to which a few moments' attention must be given.

We have a verb, *be*, bearing the purely formal grammatical office of connecting a subject with its predicate. Such a connective is wanting in many languages, which are obliged simply to set the two elements side by side, leaving their relation to be supplied by the mind. Its conjugation is made up of various discordant parts; which, however, agree in the quality of derivation from roots having a distinct physical meaning: *am*, *is*, *are*, come from *as*, which signified either 'breathe' or 'sit;' *was*, *were*, from *vas*, 'abide;' *be*, *been*, from *bhû*, 'grow.' The French has filled up its scheme of the same verb from the Latin *stare*, 'stand.' The development of meaning here is analogous with what we have been considering, a case of transfer and extension—extension so wide that it has effaced all that was distinctive in the words; we may call it an attenuation, a fading-out, a complete formalizing, of what was before solid, positive, substantial.

The same general connective *be*, when used with the past participle of a transitive verb, becomes an "auxiliary," making a whole conjugation of what we call "passive" forms—"I *am* loved," etc.; with a present participle, it makes a like scheme of "continuous" or "imperfect" tenses—"I *am* loving," etc. It thus enters just as fully into the service of formal grammatical expression as the formative endings of languages of other habit than ours. We have many other words of which the history and present application are nearly the same. There is *do*, which, from the original physical notion of 'set, place,' has been extended and formalized into expressing efficient action of every kind—*do* good, *do* one's best, *do* to death, and so on; and which also *does* service as verbal auxiliary—I *do* love, *did* I love? etc. Again, the Latin root *cap* (*capere*) means 'seize, grasp.' Its Germanic correspondent is *hab*, in Gothic *haban*, German *haben*, our *have*. But here the more physical sense of 'grasp' has almost disappeared (we have it in Germ. *handhabe*, our *haft*, the part of an instrument that is 'grasped' by the hand); in its place has come the more conceptional one of 'possess.' So also with the Latin *habere*, the relation of which to *capere* on the one hand and *haben* on the other is a puzzle to the etymologists. Finally, this too has been turned to use in verbal expression, and by a transfer which, though illustrated in the history of many languages, must be called a very remarkable one. Present possession often implies past action: *habeo cultellum inventum*, *habeo virgulam fissam*, *habeo digitum vulneratum*, 'I possess my knife found (recovered after loss), I possess a twig that is split, I have a wounded finger:' here the several conditions have been preceded by the several acts, of finding, splitting, wounding. On this absurdly narrow basis is built up the whole immense structure of the "perfect"-tense expression: the phrase shifts its centre of gravity from the expressed condition to the implied antecedent act; and *I have found the knife*, *ich habe das Messer gefunden*, *j'ai trouvé le couteau*, become indicators of a peculiar variety of past action contemplated as completed: further examples are the Sanskrit *kritavân*, '[I am] possessing [something] done,' i. e. 'I have done;' and Turkish *dogd-um*, 'striking mine,' i. e. 'I have struck.'

The next step is to forget how *have* came by its "perfect" meaning, and to use it with all sorts of verbs, where an etymological analysis would make nonsense: as in *I have lost the knife*, *I have lived* (German and French the same); and, in English, even *I have come*, where the other languages still say, more properly, 'I *am* come.'

But the same verb has other auxiliary work to do. The phrases *habeo virgulam ad findendum*, *j'ai une verge à fendre*, *ich habe ein Aestchen zu spalten*, *I have a twig to split* (*for splitting*), as plainly imply a contemplated future action. They become formal verbal expressions when, by a like shift of emphasis and apprehended connection with that noted above, the construction is changed to *I have to cut a twig*, and the noun is viewed no longer as object of the *have*, but rather of the other verb, the infinitive; and yet more completely when (again as above) the construction is so extended that we say *I have to strike*, *I have to go*, *I have to be careful*. We thus have a phrase denoting obligation to future action, developed out of the same expression for 'seizing' which is also used to denote past action. The French has gone still further. Not emphasizing, as we do, the idea of obligation, it uses the same phrase as simple expression of futurity; and more, it combines the auxiliary into one word with the other verb—*je fendrai* (for *je fendre ai*, i. e. *j'ai à fendre*); in which no French speaker, unless philologically educated, ever recognizes the elements of the combination.

Once more, the English is peculiar in expressing a causative sense by the same agency: *I had my horse shod*, *I will have the book bound*, point to a different aspect of the action, setting it forth as something brought about, though not executed, by the actor. It is merely a turning-up to view of another of the many implications involved in the state of possession.

All our verbal auxiliaries come after a like fashion. Behind our *shall* and *will*, as signs of future action, lies a history of transfers and extensions. One step back, *I shall* means 'I owe, am under obligation;' *I will*, 'I intend, purpose.' Both are examples of that important little class of Germanic verbs called "preterito-presential," because (by a change just the opposite of that which we noticed above) they have won their present meaning through a "perfect" one. And *shall*, it is claimed, goes back finally to 'I have offended,' and hence 'am under penalty;' *will*, to 'I have selected' (yet more primitively, 'have enclosed or surrounded'). The Greek *κέκτημαι*, 'I have acquired' (colloquial English, *I have got*), for 'I possess,' is a parallel here: indeed, both Greek and Sanskrit have one of the very verbs that compose the Germanic class: Skt. *véda*, Gr. *οἶδα*, Goth. *wait*, Germ. *weiss*, 'I *wot* or know:' literally, 'I have seen.' And the Latin furnishes a very notable parallel to the shifts of construction we have been instancing, in its use of the accusative as "subject" of an infinitive: it all grew out of an inorganic extension of such constructions as *dicit te errare*, 'he declares you to err.' Toward this we have in English at least a near approach in phrases like "for him to err is a rare thing," where we have almost forgotten that *for* logically connects *him* with *rare:* "to err is a thing rare for him." Another kindred case is the infinitive in passive sense in German causative phrases: *er liess sich nicht halten*, 'he did not let himself be held;' literally, 'did not let [any one] hold him.'

This kind of change is by no means limited to verbal constructions, as a few examples from other parts of the grammar will show. In Anglo-Saxon there was no such word as *of*, as distinguished from *off*; their separation, in form and meaning, is a piece of very recent word-history. *Off* is the earlier sense, as the more material: though itself, as preposition, a sign of relation, and therefore formal as compared with our general vocabulary. But in *of* we have all limited and definable relation extinguished; the word is a token of the most indefinite appurtenance, the absolute equivalent of a genitive case-ending, a link between a noun and its modifying noun, sign of the adjective relation of one noun to another. The French *de* has a history not unlike this. Almost as striking an example is our *for*, originally the same word with *fore*, 'before, in front of;' in German the word has taken on a threefold form for its various offices, in *vor*, *für*, and the inseparable prefix *ver*—each of more attenuated quality than its predecessor. *To* retains in general its ancient office as designating approach; but as "sign of the infinitive" it is as purely formal as *of* itself; in *to have*, for example, it is nothing more than a kind of modern substitute for the old ending *an* of *haban:* we have absolutely lost from memory its real value, as that of a preposition governing a verbal noun.

But there is another shift of construction lying back of the whole class of prepositions. The oldest of them were originally—as many of them still continue also to be—adverbs, modifiers of verbal action, only aiding to determine the noun-case which that action should take as its further adjunct. Here is a whole part of speech, of an especially formal character, developed from those of more material aspect and office. The conjunctions are another case of the same kind, though into the details of their history we have no time here to enter. And the articles, sometimes ranked as a separate part of speech, are likewise altered and faded words: their originals, to be sure, were formal enough; but they are etherealized formals: the definite article is a demonstrative, from which the full demonstrative force has been withdrawn; the indefinite article comes by a similar process of attenuation from the numeral 'one.'

The great variety and prominent importance of this department of change of meaning tempt to protracted illustration; and no brief array of examples can do it justice: but we must content ourselves with only one more. Alongside the conjunctions, the relative pronouns are by far the most important of the connectives by which we bind together separate assertions, making a period out of what would otherwise be a loose aggregation of phrases. They are pronouns with conjunctive force; they fasten distinctly to their antecedent an assertion which would otherwise be connected with it only by implication. There are plenty of languages in the world which have no such syntactical apparatus; and we, too, could make shift to get on well enough without it. To say "my friend had had a fever; he was not quite recovered; he was looking pale and ill," is fully sufficient to enable the hearer to combine the circumstances in their proper relations. We only put into expression the necessarily implied mental act when we say "my friend, who had had a fever from which he was not quite recovered, was looking ill;" and we have no small variety of other ways of putting the same thing: "he was looking ill because (or, for) he had had" etc.; or, "my friend, being not yet recovered from a recent fever, was looking ill;" and so on.

The various modes of statement are devices for presenting to more special attention one and another aspect of a fact and its causes; their possibility is an added decoration rather than a substantial resource of speech; they serve a rhetorical purpose. But the relatives, which, though not indispensable, are an agency we could hardly afford to miss, are only a comparatively recent acquisition. They are demonstratives and interrogatives put to a new use; employed first with pregnant allusion to an antecedent, then gaining such allusion as an essential element. The construction was in a forming and doubtful state in our earliest English, and *who* and *which* won their relative force only considerably later.

It is by no means only in verbal phrases and other examples of the reduction of terms of independent meaning to formal value that language exhibits its characteristic tendency toward oblivion of original meaning and disregard of etymological concinnity. Most tongues are full of idiomatic phrases, which, when we attempt to analyze them, are often obscure or meaningless or absurd, and which nevertheless constitute no small part of the strength and charm of expression. *Take place* is a fair English example; the same expression in German, *Platz nehmen*, means 'sit down,' while to represent our meaning the German says rather *Statt finden*, 'find stead.' In French we may instance *avoir beau*, literally 'to have beautiful,' used to intimate the uselessness of an action: *il a beau s'excuser*, 'he tries in vain to excuse himself;' or *en vouloir*, literally 'wish about it,' but meaning 'bear a grudge.' And between the three equivalent expressions *there is*, *il y a*, literally 'it has there,' and *es gibt*, 'it gives,' it is hard to choose the one which implies the most curious twist of meaning. The very abundance and heterogeneousness of the material here discourage more extended illustration.

It is, as has been already said, impossible to exhaust the variety of significant change in linguistic growth. Whole volumes, full of interest and instruction, have been produced upon this subject alone; and if our object were general interest and instruction, we should not quit the theme here. We should dwell, for instance, upon the curious fate which, while some words fade to the thinnest skeleton, almost shadow, of substantial value, crowds others with pregnancy and force —like *home*, *comfort*, *tact* (literally '*touch*'), *taste*, *humor* ('moisture'); upon the contrast between words which from a low or an indifferent origin rise to dignity, and those which from a respectable origin sink into contempt (we had above, p. 40, an example of both these changes in the same word, our *knight* and the German *knecht*); between words which become so conventionally inexpressive that we seek for newer and more positive phraseology, and those which, dealing with delicate subjects, become too directly suggestive, and are replaced in refined usage by others which hint more remotely at the intended sense; between words which for no assignable reason become the fashion, and others which as causelessly come to be looked askance at and avoided. Some of these cases will call for remark farther on, in other connections: for the present we must be satisfied with having noticed at least the principal tendencies, those which have most influence on the growth of language.

CHAPTER VI

GROWTH OF LANGUAGE: LOSS OF WORDS AND FORMS.

Loss of words; its causes; obsolescent and obsolete words. Loss of meanings. Loss of grammatical forms and the distinctions conveyed by them; examples; excess of this loss in English.

WE saw above (in the third chapter) that loss of what had constituted the material of a language was an appreciable element in that constant change and development which we called its growth. Even such a process of subtraction is fairly enough to be reckoned as a part of growth; just as the growth of organic beings consists in removal as well as in resupply. And our preliminary illustrations showed us that the loss might consist either in the disappearance of complete words from a vocabulary, or in the disappearance of the signs of grammatical distinction.

The reduction of a vocabulary by loss of its words is a matter so simple that we shall not need to spend much time upon it.

As all the items of a given language are kept in existence only by being taught and learned, it is evident enough that the cessation of this process of tradition with regard to any item will bring about its annihilation. Existence, in speech, is use; and disuse is destruction. Whatever leads to disuse leads to loss; and there is nothing else that can have that effect. And there are, accordingly, two principal ways in which loss can occur.

In the first place, the disappearance from before the attention of a community of the conceptions designated by certain words occasions the disappearance of those words. If anything that people once thought and talked about comes to concern them no longer, its phraseology goes into oblivion—unless, of course, it be preserved, as a memory of the past, by some of those means which culture supplies. It has been so, for example, with the old heathen religion of our Germanic ancestors. Once, the names of Thor and Woden, of Tuis and Freya, and the rest of them, were as common on English lips as those of Christ and the Virgin Mary, of St. Peter and St. Paul, are nowadays; but, save for their fortuitous and generally unrecognized retention in the names of the days of the week, they have become extinct in the speech of common life, and are known only to curious students of antiquity. The same thing is true of a host of words belonging to the vocabulary of the ancient arts and sciences, the ancient institutions and customs. The technical terms of chivalry mostly fell out as those of modern warfare came in; those of astrology, as this was crowded from existence by astronomical science. Only, we have here and there, not always consciously, in our present speech, reminiscences of the old order of things, in the shape of words transferred to new uses. Even so common and indispensable a term as *influence* is said to be of astrological origin, denoting in its early use only the bearing of the heavenly bodies on human affairs; *disaster* is etymologically a mishap due to a baleful stellar aspect; and we have already noted *jovial*, *saturnine*, *mercurial*, as names for dispositions that were regarded as produced by the *influence* of planets. In like manner, part of the vocabulary of hawking, when that mode of securing game went out of use, was transferred to the new apparatus: as an especially noticeable instance, *musket* was the name of a certain small hawk.

But, in the second place, words are crowded out of use, and so out of life, by the coming into use of other words which mean the same thing, and which for some cause, definable or not, win the popular favor, and supplant their predecessors. Of this process we found examples in our specimen-passage: the honest Saxon derivatives or compounds *Hælend*, *reste-dæg*, *leorning-cnihtas*, are replaced in our usage by the outlandish terms *Savior*, *sabbath*, *disciple*, and have themselves disappeared. And this is but a specimen of a process of wide reach and abundant results in English. In consequence of the Norman conquest, a considerable body of French words was poured in upon our language, and gradually accepted and put to service as an integral part of it. To no small degree, indeed, as a direct enrichment of English speech, by furnishing expression for new ideas, or French synonyms for Saxon words, each useful in its own style and connection: like *brotherly* and *fraternal*, *outlandish* and *foreign*, *forgive* and *pardon*, *rot* and *decay*, *hue* and *color*, *stench* and *odor*, *foresight* and *providence*. But to a considerable extent also there was an over-enrichment, which the requirements of practical use did not justify; and the intrusion of the new caused an extrusion of the old. Thus a host of Saxon words gave place to substitutes of foreign origin: nothing would be easier than to add to the examples given above numberless others, like *wanhope* displaced by *despair*, *ayenbite* by *remorse*, *inwit* by *conscience*, and so on.

Nor is it by foreign importation alone that words of native growth become superfluous, and are dropped out of a language. There are cases in abundance of a word's simply going out of fashion, becoming obsolescent and then obsolete, by an act of supersession attributable only to what we call chance or caprice. We have one or two fair examples of it in our specimen-passage, as already pointed out (pp. 39, 43): namely *fôr* and *sôth.* In Anglo-Saxon, the verb *faran*, 'fare,' was in frequent and familiar use in the simple sense of 'go' or 'pass.' *Gân*, 'go,' was also good English, with its irregular preterit *eode*, 'went;' likewise *gangan*, 'gang,' with *gêng*, 'ganged;' and *wendan*, 'turn, wend,' with *wende*, 'turned, went.' Out of this, as it was found, somewhat wasteful provision of words for 'going,' our later English has made arbitrary selection of *go* and *went*, dropping the rest—or else, as in the case of *fare*, restricting them to special uses. In a similar way, *equus* has gone out of use as name for 'horse' in all the descendants of the Latin, and has been replaced by *caballus*, which was originally a word of inferior dignity, like our *nag;* although, in *chivalry*, etc., it has since come to honor enough: so *magnus* has been superseded by *grandis*, and *pulcher* by *bellus;* and so, in French, *vulpes* has been given up for *renard*, which is the German *Reinhart*, a proper name, by which a fox was at one time popularly called, much as we call a dog "Tray." It may even happen that an important word dies out, without provision of any full substitute: so the Anglo-Saxon *weorthan*, corresponding to the German *werden*, 'become.' Doubtless the transfer to its present meaning of *become* (literally 'come by, get at, get') caused the oblivion of the older and more legitimate synonym; and with this went the possibility of such distinctions as the German makes abundantly by means of *werden:* especially, that of the true passive *es wird gebrochen*, 'it is getting broken,' i. e. 'is undergoing fracture,' as against *es ist gebrochen*, 'it is broken,' i. e. 'has undergone fracture;' whence, further, the necessity for such awkward, but naturally formed and really unavoidable phrases as *it is being broken*.

By these means, there is in every language a certain amount of obsolescent material, in various stages: some words that are only unusual, or restricted to particular phrases (like *stead*, in *in stead* alone); some that belong to a particular style, archaic or poetical; some that have become strange and unintelligible to ordinary speakers, though formerly in every-day use; some that survive only in local dialects. And the older records of any tongue, if preserved, show words in greater or less number that are gone past recovery.

It is hardly necessary even to spend, in passing, a single word upon the somewhat analogous loss, by words and phrases, of their old meanings, although this may also involve, in its manner and degree, a reduction of the resources of expression. The examples of transfer of meaning given in the last chapter have shown also sufficiently that the process is not always, though it may be usually, an addition of new meanings without an abandonment of the old. It may be, too, that the substantial sense of a word remains to it, while its accessory suggestiveness is altered; so when Milton speaks of ladies who "from their eyes rain *influence*," we miss the whole poetic significance of the line if we do not know the astrological allusion it involves. In reading older authors, we are constantly liable to this loss or misunderstanding, often skimming a mere surface com prehension off that which has a profound meaning, or deluding ourselves with a belief that we understand where the real sense escapes us.

A subject of greater consequence and deeper reach in language-history is the loss of old distinctions of grammatical form. Of this, our illustrative sentence brought to light several striking examples, already briefly noticed by us. By the wearing off, under the prevalent phonetic tendency, of the old infinitive ending *an* (Middle English and German *en*), our infinitive as a verbal form is no longer different from the root of verbal inflection. And yet we do not fail to appreciate distinctly enough the idea of the form, and have even (as we saw) fabricated a new sign *to* as a kind of substitute for the obliterated suffix. Again, having lost all such signs of plurality as the final *on* of *ongunnon*, we no longer distinguish the plural of a verbal tense formally from the singular except in *am* and *are*, *was* and *were*: yet here, also, the difference made by us between singular and plural nouns and pronouns, scantily supplemented by the absence of a personal ending in *they love* as compared with *he loves*, seems still to keep up in full life the old distinction. The *se* and *thâ*, however, as singular and plural respectively, and the former of them as specifically masculine (the feminine was *seo*, and the neuter *thæt*), are examples of a class of grammatical distinctions which have gone by the board, swept clean away, so that we have forgotten that they ever existed: namely, the variation of an adjective word for gender and number and case. The Anglo-Saxon adjective had a fuller inflection than the German, almost as full a one as the Greek or Latin; it even had a double one, definite and indefinite, like the German; and the language still retained the old system of concord, of formal correspondence between a substantive and its qualifier or representative, which, founded on the original identity of substantive and adjective, is one of the glories of a completely inflective language; but since we have lost it, we have never thought of missing or regretting it; and no one of us would be easy to convince that, when we say *good men*, there would be anything gained by giving the word *good* a different form from that which it has in *good man*. And yet less, from that which it has in *good women*. For the distinctions of gender have been extirpated even in our nouns. To us, the name or appellation of a person is masculine or feminine only according as the person is male or female; and of sex in the lower animals we make very small account; while our Anglo-Saxon ancestors were as much under the dominion of that old artificial grammatical distinction of all the objects of thought as masculine, feminine, and neuter, on a basis only in small part coinciding with actual sex, as are the Germans now, or as were the Greeks and Latins of old: it was one of the original and characteristic features of that language from which all these, and most of the other tongues of Europe, are descended. The French has suffered the same loss only partially, having saved the distinction of masculine from feminine, but confounded neuter and masculine together by the obliteration of their respective marks of difference. But also the old scheme of cases in our nouns has become a wreck and a remnant, although the distinctions on which it is founded are just as necessary a part of language as ever. The English has no dative, and no accusative except in a few pronouns (*him*, *them*, *whom*, etc.); the French is still poorer, having not even a possessive; although it makes in a few pronominal words a somewhat evanescent distinction of subject and object. We have also nearly parted with our subjunc tive, which in German is as rich in forms as is the indicative.

The English is, in truth, of all the languages of its kindred, the one which most remarkably illustrates that mode of linguistic change consisting in the loss of formal grammatical distinction by synthetic means; there is no other known tongue which, from having been so rich in them, has become so poor; none which has so nearly stripped its root-syllables of the apparatus of suffixes with which they were formerly clothed, and left them monosyllabic. All this has come about mainly through the instrumentality of the tendency to ease and abbreviation, a tendency which in this department of its working, especially, makes truly for decay; the conservative force, the strictness of traditional transmission, has not been sufficient to resist its inroads. Much of the loss has been the work of the last few centuries; and there is no difficulty in pointing out causes which have at least quickened it. When men learn a strange language, by a practical process, they are apt especially to make bad work with its endings; if they get the body of the word, its main significant part, intelligibly correct, they will be content to leave the relations to be understood from the connection. This was what helped the decay of the Latin tongue, and its reduction, in the mouths of Italians, Celts, Iberians, and others, into the corrupted and abbreviated shape of the modern Romanic dialects; and the irruption into England of the French-speaking Normans, and their fusion with the Saxon-speaking English, added an appreciable element of force to a tendency which was perhaps already sufficiently marked in the later Anglo-Saxon.

But it is only in degree that the English differs herein from the other languages of its family, and from those of other families. The tendency to abbreviation for ease, for economy of effort in expression, is a universal and a blind one; destruction lies everywhere in its path. The same process which, by a disguising fusion and integration of elements once independent, makes a word or form, goes straight on to its contraction and mutilation—and in early language as certainly, though not necessarily so rapidly, as in later. There is believed to be hardly anything, if anything at all, earlier in the structure of our language than the first-personal endings, *mi* in the singular, *masi* in the plural. Yet these are already economized alterations of something still more primitive; the *masi*, especially, so changed that the comparative philologists dispute as to its derivation. All that we have left of either of them in English is the solitary *m* of *am* (for *as-mi*). And every language related with ours has something of the same loss to show; and like losses in every other department of inflection and of derivation.

The forms, even of the richest known languages, embody and bring to distinct consciousness only a small part of the infinity of relations which subsist among the objects of thought, and which the mind impliedly recognizes, even when it does not direct attention to them by expression. Not one of those which are expressed, any more than those which have not found embodiment, is absolutely essential to successful speech. When it has attained expression, the mind which contemplates it is not dependent upon its audible sign, but may even be made carelessly secure by this, and, while realizing the idea, permit itself to drop the sign as not indispensable. But we may note for our consolation that, unless a people is undergoing actual degradation in quantity and quality of mental work, it does not lose what it once possessed in the way of inflectional apparatus without providing some other and on the whole equivalent means of expression. The style of expression may become very much changed, without any real loss of expressiveness. The downfall of the case-system was accompanied by the uprise of the class of prepositions; the loss of pronominal elements in the form of personal endings led only to their more extended use as independent words; the impoverishment of the scheme of moods and tenses was compensated by the introduction of a rich apparatus of auxiliaries, capable of expressing nearly all the old distinctions, along with a host of new ones.

This brings us, however, as we have already been repeatedly brought, to face the remaining department of change of language—namely, the addition of new resources of expression; and to that we now turn.

CHAPTER VII.

GROWTH OF LANGUAGE: PRODUCTION OF NEW WORDS AND FORMS.

Special importance of this mode of linguistic change; objects attained by it. These objects partly gained without external additions; enrichment, definition, multiplication of meaning in old words. Provision of new styles of expression. External additions; borrowing from other languages; its kind and degree; excess of it in English. Invention of new words; onomatopœia. New words made by combination of old ones; production of forms by this method; its wide reach and importance; internal formative changes really the result of external additions. Differentiation of the form of a word in different uses. Multiplication of the uses of a word by derivative apparatus; conversion of one part of speech into another.

In our examination of the methods of change or growth in language, we have finally to consider the subject of acquisition of new material, of the means whereby the waste incident to phonetic decay is made up, and expression for new thought and knowledge provided. These means have been already in part set forth or alluded to; for all the modes of linguistic growth so intertwine and interact that it is impossible to discuss any one of them, however succinctly, without taking more or less account of the others.

This last mode of change, it may be remarked in introduction, constitutes in a higher and more essential sense than any of the others the growth of language, and ought to bring most distinctly to light the forces actually concerned in that growth.

The general object attained by additions to language is obviously the extension and the improvement of expression, supply of representative signs for new knowledge, amendment in the representation of old knowledge. But, as we must first observe, these ends are to no small extent gained without any apparent change in language. In part, by new syntactical combinations of the old materials of speech, by putting together old words into new sentences: and this is plainly a department of the use of language by which great results are won; hosts of new cognitions and deductions are thus provided for. And yet, this work cannot go on without more or less affecting the inner content of the terms we use, changing the limits and even the whole character of the conceptions which they represent. If, for example, we say "the sun rises, shedding light and heat on the earth," the sentence is one which (or its equivalent in other languages) might have been uttered, so far as concerns the items of which it is made up, at any time since the infancy of speech and knowledge: but how different the real meaning which it stands for as employed by us, and by a modern boor or an ancient sage! *Rise* to us, as applied to the sun, is only a concession to appearances; we do not care to take the trouble to say that the earth has been rolling over till now our spot of it comes within reach of the sun's rays; and as to *rising* and *falling*, it is only since Newton discovered the great cosmic law of gravitation that we really know what the words denote. It is a much shorter time since we learned that *light* and *heat* are modes of motion of matter, apprehended by certain effects which they produce on our sensitive organization. And the transformation which *sun* and *earth* have undergone in our minds needs no more than an allusion. The example is, no doubt, an extreme one; yet it is a perfectly fair, even normal, illustration of what becomes in speech of one most important part of the new knowledge we acquire. This kind of change is ever operating like a ferment through the whole material of language, incorporating without outward show the changed apprehensions, the clearer cognitions, the sharpened distinctions, which are the result of gradual intellectual growth. It is, as we have called it before, the mind of the community all the time at work beneath the framework of its old language, improving its instruments of expression by adapting them to new uses.

In fact, all the ground over which we went in the fifth chapter, treating the alterations of meaning as individual changes, of various kind and direction, we might properly enough here go over again, having in view the purposes which the changes are made to subserve. That, however, would take too much time; and we must content ourselves with briefly pointing out certain aspects of the subject.

How great, in the first place, is the sum of enrichment of language by this means, may be seen by observing the variety of meanings belonging to our words. If each of them were like a scientific term, limited to a definite class of strictly similar things, the number which the cultivated speaker now uses would be very far from answering his purposes. But it is the customary office of a word to cover, not a point, but a territory, and a territory that is irregular, heterogeneous, and variable. A certain noted English lexicographer thought he had performed a great feat when he had reduced the uses of *good* to forty varieties, besides an insoluble residue of a dozen or two of phrases; and, though we need not accept all his distinctions as valuable, their number at any rate indicates a real condition of things. No student who remembers his occasional despair as (in early stages of his studies) he has glanced over the lists of meanings of Greek and Latin words in his dictionaries, trying to find the one that fitted the case in hand, will question that foreign words, at any rate, have a perplexing variety of signification; but the case is precisely the same with the foreigner who uses an English dictionary. It is the duty of the competent lexicographer, in any language, to reduce the apparent confusion to order by discovering the nucleus, the natural etymological meaning from which all the rest have come by change and transfer, and by drawing out the others in proper relation to their original and to one another, so as to suggest the tie of association by which each was added to the rest—if he do not find (as is not very rarely the fact) that the tie is doubtful or undiscoverable. If we were to count in our words only those degrees of difference of meaning for which in other cases separate provision of expression is made, the 100,000 English words would doubtless be found equivalent to a million or two. As an extreme example of what this mode of enrichment can do, there is in existence one highly cultivated tongue, the Chinese, all the growth of which has had to be by differentiation of meaning, since it rejects all external additions; and it has only about 1,500 words: what a host of discordant and hardly connectable meanings each word is compelled to bear may be easily imagined.

The particular mode of transfer by which new expression is most abundantly won is the figurative (as set forth and illustrated in the last chapter but one). But, rich as are its contributions to the absolute needs of expression, especially in the department of intellectual and relational language, they are by no means limited to that. The mind not only has a wonderful facility in catching resemblances and turning them to account, but it takes a real creative pleasure in the exercise, and derives from it desirable variety and liveliness of style. The power is strikingly illustrated in the case of men whose life-occupations run in restricted lines, and who have little general culture; when they come to talk upon matters less familiar, they see constant analogies between these and their staple subjects of thought, and their discourse is redolent of the "shop." So especially the sailor talks as if all the world were a ship, and with a piquancy and raciness which, as illustrated in the nautical stories, is full of charm to us land-lubbers; and many a term or phrase of this origin has passed into our general English tongue. And if we would see how far the phraseology of the mine and the card-table can be made to go in figurative substitution for ordinary speech, we may read, in Mark Twain's "Roughing It" (chap. xlvii.), that amusing (and, in this aspect, instructive) account of the interview between the preacher and the gambler who wants to get his late exemplary partner decently buried. For a more dignified example, take the constant recurrence of the Vedic poets to the cattle-yard and the pasture for the staple of their comparisons, and for the suggestion of many a term used later, without any sense of a figure involved in it, to express human conditions. So far as this is odd or undignified, it forms the largest element of what we call "slang," and we frown upon it; and properly enough; but yet it is only the excess and abuse of a tendency which is wholly legitimate, and of the highest value, in the history of speech. It seeks relief from the often oppressive conventionality, even insipidity, of words worn out by the use of persons who have put neither knowledge nor feeling into them, and which seem incapable of expressing anything that is real. In the exuberance of mental activity, and the natural delight of language-making, slang is a necessary evil; and there are grades and uses of slang whose charm no one need be ashamed to feel and confess; it is like reading a narrative in a series of rude but telling pictures, instead of in words.

A meaningless conventionality, to be sure, has also its special uses, as in the forms of social intercourse, where we are sometimes called upon to disguise instead of disclosing our thoughts by speech. To take an example or two of the simplest kind—we say "how do you do?" to an acquaintance, but should feel imposed upon if he answered by detailing all the symptoms of his health; we begin a letter to one whom we really detest with "my dear sir," and at the end declare ourselves his "obedient servant," though we should resent a single word from him which bore the semblance of a command. And so in many other cases: to devise more sincere phrases would seem blunt and odd, an unbecoming intrusion of our personality. Then, again, there are subjects of decency or delicacy, with reference to which we have to pick our expressions very carefully, if we would not offend or disgust. It is one of the most striking illustrations possible of the dominion which words have won over our thoughts, that we will tolerate in indirect, figurative, merely suggestive expression what would be repulsive in direct statement. Here, by an effect contrary to that which we noticed above, a term perhaps becomes after a time, by frequent use, too directly significant, and we have to devise a new one, less lively.

Thus, independently of any marked increase of knowledge and multiplication of conceptions, as well as in connection with this, the instrument of expression is continually undergoing alteration for the better, by being applied to more varied and defter modes of use. The same methods of increase serve both the one purpose and the other. We have perhaps already given sufficient attention, in the fifth chapter, to that most general and grandest of movements of signification, which carries words over from a more material and substantial value toward one that is more conceptual and formal, in its two departments of the making of intellectual expression and the production of form-words—in the former, turning more to the uses of new thought; in the latter, more toward the completion of the expression of old thought; and we may proceed to take up the other and more conspicuous part of growth, consisting in external additions to language, the accession of new words to the vocabulary.

And we may best begin with that particular mode of external increase which is the most extraneous of all—namely, the bringing into a language of words borrowed out of other languages. Borrowing, in greater or less degree, is well-nigh universally resorted to; there is hardly a dialect in the world, of which the speakers ever come in contact with those of another dialect, which has not taken something out of that other. What comes most easily after this fashion is names for articles and institutions of foreign growth, which, on making their acquaintance, and deeming them worthy of introduction or adoption, we often find it convenient to call by the names given them by their former possessors

So the *banana* is a tropical fruit, with its own tropical title; and the nations of continental Europe mostly call *anana*, for the same reason, the fruit for which we have chosen to provide the more native appellation of *pine-apple*—i. e. such an apple as, judging from its cones, a pine might bear if it tried to be an apple-tree. So also with the institution of the *tabu*, of which the Polynesian name has fairly won a place in more than one European tongue. A language like ours—since we come in contact with nearly all the nations of the world, and draw in to ourselves whatever we find of theirs that can be made useful to us, and since even our culture derives from various sources—comes to contain specimens from dialects of very diverse origin. Thus, we have religious words from the Hebrew, as *sabbath*, *seraph*, *jubilee*; certain old-style scientific terms from the Arabic, as *algebra*, *alkali*, *zenith*, *cipher*, besides a considerable heterogeneous list, like *lemon*, *sugar* (ultimately Sanskrit), *sherbet*, *magazine*; from the Persian, *caravan*, *chess*, *shawl*, and even a word which has won so familiar and varied use as *check*; from Hindî, *calico* and *chintz*, *punch* and *toddy*; from Chinese, *tea* and *nankeen*; from American Indian languages, *canoe* and *moccasin*, *guano* and *potato*, *sachem* and *caucus*. Some of these are specimens out of tolerably long lists; and there are yet longer from sundry of the modern European languages, as the Spanish and Italian. All together, they do not make up any considerable proportion of English speech; but they have for us a high theoretical importance, as casting light upon the general process of names-giving, of which we shall treat more particularly in the next chapter. It is by no process of organic growth, assuredly, that we put a certain title upon a certain thing because some far-off community, of which we know little and for which we care less, gave it that title; yet this makes, when once in use, just as good English as the words that belong to the very oldest Saxon families, or that "came in with the Conqueror."

This last expression, however, reminds us that there is another kind and rate of borrowing in which our language indulges, more or less in common with others. All the leading nations of Europe have received their culture and their religion, directly or indirectly, from Greece and Rome. Some of them, indeed—as the various tribes of Italy, the Celts of Gaul, the Celtiberians of the Spanish peninsula—took so much from Rome that, along with the rest, they accepted also her speech, in mass, and now talk a nearly pure Latinic dialect. With the others, there followed only a result akin with that which we have been noticing above; in connection with new ideas and institutions, they took the names by which these were known to their more original possessors. Thus there came to be numerous Latin and Greek words in the Germanic, the Slavonic, and the Celtic tongues. Not a few of them occur in the oldest Anglo-Saxon; and they abound in the German vocabulary, even in those parts of it which have an original aspect. The dependence of Europe on the classical sources for knowledge, arts, and sciences, continued long. Latin was everywhere read and written by the learned, almost as the only language worthy of such high uses; and even now its study is a pervading element in education. This kept fully alive the habit of resorting to the stores of Latin expression to satisfy all those needs of the learned which the more regular growth of the popular speech did not supply. In a certain way, it was easier for those modern tongues which are themselves derived from the Latin to do this than for others; but we must not estimate their advantage too highly, observing how little we ourselves borrow from the Anglo-Saxon, or from any other Germanic language. The Latin and Greek alone have occupied such a position that all Europe could resort to them for the enrichment of its multifarious speech. In other parts of the world, other languages have stood in a like place. To the scores of tribes and nations of discordant speech in India, the Sanskrit has long been the sacred and literary dialect, and its literature the fountain of higher thought and knowledge; and all the cultivated tongues of modern India have come to be full of Sanskrit words, as the European tongues are of Latin. The Persians, a thousand years and more ago, were forced to receive a new religion and constitution at the hands of their Arab conquerors, and modern Persian is almost more Arabic than Persian. The Turks burst into Persia as a wild uncultivated horde, with nearly everything to learn save war and plunder; and their present written style is more crowded with Persian and Arabic than the most extreme Johnsonese with Latin. The Japanese made themselves, fifteen centuries since, the pupils of the Chinese; and they have absorbed the Chinese vocabulary almost bodily into their own language.

The English, then, is not at all peculiar in its borrowing freely from other tongues to enrich its vocabulary; it is merely peculiar among European languages for the extent of its borrowing from tongues only remotely akin with itself. A trustworthy estimate of the derivation of the words found in our great dictionaries makes nearly five sevenths of them to be of classical derivation, and only about two sevenths native Germanic: the sum of derivatives from other quarters—

only a thousand or two—being of no account in such an estimate. Of course, the words do not enter into the ordinary combinations of practical use in any such proportion as this, because our commonest terms, the bulk of the material of ordinary speech and nearly all its machinery, are Germanic. In the list of words used by Milton, for example, full two thirds are classical; but in a page anywhere of Milton's poetry the classical element is only ten to thirty per cent.; and even in Johnson's style its proportion is but little greater.

For this preponderance, in one aspect, of the borrowed material in English speech, there are easily assignable reasons. The Norman invasion, leading to a long antagonism and final fusion of a French-speaking with a Saxon-speaking race, brought in by violence, as it were, a great store of French words, of Latin origin, and thus made it comparatively easy to bring in without violence a great many more. And the deadening of the native processes of composition and derivation and inflection, caused in part by the same great historical event, made the language more incapable of meeting out of its own resources any great call for new expression. So, when the pressing exigencies of the last century or two, almost unexampled in their urgency, arose, the resource of borrowing, already much availed of, was drawn upon almost to excess. When a community is living quietly on, with no marked accumulation of the fruits of mental activity, ruminating its old conceptions and slowly elaborating new, the purely natural increase, proceeding slowly and unconsciously from the great body of speakers, will be likely to serve all needs. But when science and art and philosophy are making rapid advances, when new branches of knowledge are springing up, one after another, each calling for a whole vocabulary of new terms, when infinite numbers of new facts and new objects are coming to notice, then the native modes of growth, of even the most fertile language, will be taxed beyond their capacity to provide a nomenclature for all. The call is in very great part for technical vocabularies, words for learned use; and the learned find what they want most conveniently in the learned languages. They gain in addition the practical advantage that all the inheritors and continuers of a common civilization thus possess something like a common dialect, in which to denominate those conceptions in which they have a joint interest closer than that which they have with the mass of their countrymen. Our five sevenths of classical material are mainly words of learned use only, which the young child does not acquire in order to "speak English," and which the uneducated man never learns; a host of them are of rare occurrence even in books. But any one of them may come, under the conditions of practical life, to be as familiar as material of less artificial origin: cases of this kind are *gas*, *Thursday* and its kin, *dahlia*, *petroleum*, *telegraph*, *photograph*.

There are degrees of kind as well as of extent in the process of borrowing. What is most easily taken out of the stores of one language to be added to those of another is the names and epithets of things, nouns and adjectives; verbs, much less easily; particles, hardly at all; apparatus of derivation, prefixes and suffixes, very sparingly; and apparatus of inflection, endings of declension and conjugation, least of all. Even English is nearly unmixed in its grammar; its articulating parts, the elements that bind ideas together and show their relations, that make sentences, are almost exclusively of Anglo-Saxon origin. For this reason, notwithstanding the preponderance of classical material in its wider vocabulary, the English is still rightly reckoned a Germanic language.

Of the out-and-out invention of new words, language in the course of its recorded history (for we do not now speak of its initial stage) presents only rare examples. Sometimes, however, a case occurs like that of *gas*, already noticed as having been devised by an ancient chemist, as artificial appellation for a condition of existence of matter which had not before been so distinctly apprehended as to seem to require a name. Along with it, he proposed *blas* for that property of the heavenly bodies whereby they regulate the changes of time: this, however, was too purely fanciful to recommend itself to general use, and it dropped out of sight and was forgotten, while the other came to honor.

More frequent than such words as this, which only by a lucky hit gain life and a career, are those in which the attempt has been made in a rude way to imitate the sounds of nature: as when the *cuckoo* and the *pewee* and the *toucan* were named from their notes; or as in some of the descriptive words like *crack* and *crash*, *hiss* and *buzz*, which are by no means all old, but have been made, or shaped over into a pictorial form, within no long time. We call such words *onomatopœias*, literally 'name-makings,' because the Greeks did so: they could conceive of no way in which absolutely new language-material should be produced except by such imitation.

We pass now to notice another process, whereby there comes into being for the uses of expression material which is only in a certain sense new, but which nevertheless furnishes notable enrichment to speech, and in more than one department; a process which the general history of language shows to be more important than any other. It is the composition of words, the putting two independent elements together to form a single designation. Our illustrative passage furnished us one or two examples of it: namely, *reste-dæg*, 'rest-day,' and *leorning-cnihtas*, 'learning-knights,' i. e. 'pupils.' Such a word is logically an abbreviated descriptive phrase, with the signs of relation, the ordinary inflections or connectives, omitted; the two main ideas are put side by side, and the mind left to infer their relation to one another from the known circumstances of the case. It is so far an abnegation, for the sake of brevity and convenience, of the advantages of a language which has formative elements and form-words. The undefined relation may be of every variety: thus, a *headache* is a pain *in* the head; a *head-dress*, a dress *for* the head; a *headland*, a point of land *comparable to* a head; a *headsman*, a man for *cutting off* heads; *headway*, motion *in the direction of* the head (of any animal but man); thus, also, a *steamboat* is a boat *propelled by the force of* steam; a *railroad* or *railway* is a road *laid with* rails; a *buttercup* or *butterfly* is a cup or fly *having the color of* butter: and so forth. Such a word, again, is formally characterized by a unity of accent; this is the chief outer sign of combination, binding the word together—although it is not enough of itself to make a compound; else *the man* and *have gone* and *shall go* and their like would be compounds also. Nothing is simpler or more common than for a language to form such compounds. Yet their frequency is very different in different languages: the Sanskrit abuses the liberty of making them; the Greek, the Latin, the German, are examples of tongues which use them abundantly, yet with wise moderation; the French has most nearly lost the power of their production.

Though in English they are far from being as numerous as in German, our speech is pretty full of them; the words quoted above may serve as examples of what is done in this way to increase the resources of expression. How ready the language-users are to forget the source of the compound, to lose the separate impression of its constituent words, to use it as a unitary sign for the conception to which it is attached, and then to disguise and integrate it by phonetic change, has been already pointed out, and need not be here further dwelt on or exemplified. But a most important department of its action is in a direction which calls for a little additional illustration.

Among the many adjectives which we sometimes combine with nouns to form compound adjectives, there are those which, in virtue of their meaning and consequent wide applicability, we use with special frequency, forming considerable classes of compounds with a common final element. A typical instance is *full*, German *voll*, which is added to nouns enough, and in a sufficiently general sense, to be made a kind of suffix, its own specific force being lost: *dutiful* and *plentiful* are equivalent to *duteous* and *plenteous*. Its opposite is *less*, German *los*; not our adjective *less*, but, as the German indicates and as the older forms of our language prove, *loose*; here the originally independent word has been so disguised by phonetic change as to have become absolutely an adjective suffix. *Ly* (of *godly*, *homely*, etc.) has been already fully enough explained (p. 41), as coming, by a different sort of phonetic change, from *like*. And a certain case-form of this compounded adjective, we saw, was by a change of office converted into a nearly universal adverbial suffix: thus, *truly*, *plentifully*. The French adverbial ending *ment* is in like manner from the Latin ablative *mente: grandement*, 'grandly,' is by origin *grandi mente*, 'with great mind.' Our *some* in *wholesome* (German *sam* in *heilsam*) is altered from older *sam*, and identical with *same* in the sense of 'like.' There are noun-forming suffixes, also, which own a like origin. The plainest cases among them, perhaps, are *ship*, German *schaft*, in *lordship*, *herrschaft*, and their like; and *dom*, German *thum*, in *kingdom*, *wisdom*, *königthum*, *weisthum*: the former comes from *shape*, the latter from *doom*. We have glanced above at a case or two of verbal tense-making after the same fashion. The *don* of *hyngredon* (plural of *hyngrede*, p. 42) was in Gothic *dêdum*, an evident auxiliary, our *did*, which, at a time very early in the common history of the Germanic dialects (for it is found in them all, though not in any even of their nearest relatives), was added to some verbal word to make a verbal form, with the final result that the two became fused together into one, even as we now add it to a verbal word, the infinitive, to make a verbal phrase, *I do love*, *I did love*, only without fusion. Quite parallel with this is the fusion of the present of the verb 'to have' with the infinitive in the Romanic languages, to make their modern future, as *donner-ai*, 'I shall give,' when compared with our verbal phrase *I have to give*, its unfused equivalent. Abundant traces of the same sort of composition, fusion, and resulting production of a new verbal form, are to be seen in the Latin, whose imperfect in *bam*, future in *bo*, and perfect in *ui* or *vi*, are generally acknowledged to contain as their endings certain forms of the verb which in our language is the substantive verb *to be*. And even the Greek and Sanskrit have like compound forms to show, of earlier and later date: one, the future in Skt. *syâmi*, Gr. *σω*, is believed to go back to the primitive period of linguistic growth in our family of languages.

These are some of the plainest among the numerous examples which might be brought forward, going to show that suffixes of derivation and inflection are made out of independent words, which, first entering into union with other words by the ordinary process of composition, then gradually lose their independent character, and finally come to be, in a more or less mutilated and disguised form, mere subordinate elements, or indicators of relation, in more elaborate structures. The auxiliary processes of oblivion and attenuation and transfer of meaning, and of disguise and abbreviation of form, are simply the same here as in all the other cases we have treated; they are essential parts of the making of forms; for so long as the independent word, in its individual shape and meaning, is plainly recognized in the combination, so long does this remain a compound rather than a form: our *ful*, for example (German *voll*), is not so truly a suffix as *ly* (*lich*), because the independent adjective is too apparent in it; a disguising alteration is needed to help make an affix—a "formative element," as it is properly termed, in distinction from the "radical element," the root or base, or the crude-form, to which it is appended.

Now it is by no means all, or even the largest part, of our existing formative elements, suffixes of derivation and inflection, of which the origin in this method can be actually proved; and if we are to believe nothing respecting language which does not rest on positive evidence, we shall never make the principle of combination go far toward explaining the growth of language. But it would be highly unreasonable to demand everywhere such proof. The disguising effect of the two principles of change which bear their part in every new formation is such that after a time we may be able only to guess, or not even that, at its origin. We could not explain the *ly* from modern English alone; we could not be certain as to the *d* of *loved* without the help of the Gothic; nor as to the σω of the Greek future without the Sanskrit. Every period of linguistic life, with its constantly progressing changes of form and meaning, wipes out a part of the intermediates which connect a derived element with its original. There are a plenty of items of word-formation in even the modern Romanic languages which completely elude explanation. Mere absence of evidence, then, will not in the least justify us in assuming the genesis of an obscure form to be of a wholly different character from that which is obvious or demonstrable in other forms. The presumption is wholly in favor of the accordance of the one with the other; it can only be repelled by direct and convincing evidence. And, in actual fact, linguistic study does not bring to light any such evidence; its trustworthy results go rather to prove that the combination of independent element with element has been from the beginning, in the languages of our family, the fertile and the sufficient method of new external growth. has furnished the needed supply of fresh material, which then, under the action of the other processes, has been applied to meet the needs of expression. We shall have, by and by, to review in brief the history of early development of these languages, as explained by the comparative philologists upon the principle here stated.

But a part of our forms, derivative and inflectional, appear to be made by internal modification rather than external addition. We say *boy* and *boys*, indeed, but we also say *man* and *men*; we say *love* and *loved*, but also *rēad* and *rĕad;* and then there is that wide-reaching and most important phenomenon in Germanic language, the variation of radical vowel, in large classes of words like *sing*, *sang*, *sung*, and *song;* like *break*, *broke*, and *breach;* like *bind*, *bound*, *bond*, and *band*. The Greek has a kindred but less conspicuous change in a considerable body of verbs and verbal derivatives like *λείπω, ἔλιπον, λέλοιπα;* like *τρέπω, ἔτραπον, τέτροφα, τρεπτός, τράπηξ, τρόπος;* etc. These are seeming violations of the principle of new growth by external addition, by combination; if, however, they can be shown to be, after all, its results, they will rather lend it a strong support.

Let us begin with *rēad rĕad*, as the most recent and the plainest case. In the Anglo-Saxon, this verb and the little class that go like it had no such difference of vowel between present and preterit; and they had in the preterit the same added ending as other "regular" or new verbs: the forms were *rædan*, 'rēad,' *rædde*, 'rĕad.' But here came in the phonetic principle of easy utterance: the penult of *rædde* had a long vowel before a doubled consonant; it was lightened by shortening the vowel—a proceeding so customary in all Germanic speech that it has led to the frequent orthographic device of marking a vowel as short by doubling the consonant after it. When, then, in the further course of abbreviation, by loss of final vowels, both forms were reduced to monosyllables, the double pronunciation of the final consonant was lost, and the difference of vowels was left alone to mark the difference of tense. The case is, on the one hand, analogous with *lēave lĕft*, *feel fĕlt*, etc., where there is a shortening of the vowel for a like cause, the occurrence of two consonants after it, but where the consonant group has been preserved;

and, on the other hand, it is analogous with *set*, *put*, and their like, which have also lost their preterit ending, but, having a short vowel in the present, never established a difference between the two tenses, and so have the same form in both. The distinction of *rēad rĕad*, *lēad lĕd*, etc., is thus a mere phonetic accident; a final turning to account, for the purposes of grammatical expression, of a difference which arose secondarily, as the unforeseen consequence of an external addition, when that addition had been lost by phonetic decay. Such a distinction is wont to be termed "inorganic," as distinguished from one like *loved* from *love*, which answers just the purpose for which it was at first intended.

As for *man men*, that is a case of what in German is termed *umlaut*, or "modification of vowel," a phenomenon of wide range in Germanic language, but of which the results are reduced almost to a minimum in English. It was originally the alteration of an *a*-sound to an *e*-sound by the assimilating influence of a following *i* (see above, p. 71): a change, therefore, which depended on the character of the case-ending, and had nothing whatever to do with the distinction of plural from singular; it was even the fact in Anglo-Saxon that one of the singular cases (dative) had *e*, and two of the plural cases (genitive and dative) had *a*. But, after exercising their assimilative influence, the endings were lost (like the second *d* which had shortened the long vowel of *read*); and the dative and genitive (plural) were lost as separate forms; and so *man* and *men* were left to stand over against one another as singular and plural. And because this difference of vowel was sufficient to distinguish the two numbers, linguistic usage did not go on, as in a multitude of other cases (e. g. in *ears* for *ear*: see p. 38), to add an *s* for the same purpose. Here, again, is an application to the purposes of grammatical distinction of a difference which was accidental, inorganic, in its origin.

To enter into a full discussion and explanation of the remaining case, the *ablaut*, or variation of radical vowel, in *bind, bound, band, bond*, and their like, would take a great deal more time than we can afford to it, and would bring up some obscure and difficult points, as to which the opinions of investigators are still at variance. But we should find in it nothing different, as regards the essential principles involved, from what the other two examples have furnished us. The preterit, the participle, the derivative noun, had originally their external formative elements—the first its reduplication, as in *cano cecini, τρέπω τέτροφα, haldan haihald;* the other two their endings of derivation—there was no difference of vowel. And when the difference first appeared, it was not significant, any more than that of *felt* from *feel*, of (German) *männer* from *mann;* it was developed under purely euphonic influences; it involves, in its various manifestations, the weakening and varying of original root-vowels, under accentual and other influences, and a fusion of the preterit reduplication with the root. There is nothing here to call for the admission of an exception to the general rule that, in our languages, forms are made by an external accretion of elements which were at first independent words.

The fact, however, is here brought to light, and constitutes an addition of some importance to the means of enrichment of language, that accidental differences are seized upon and turned to account by being put to new uses. A word thus, as it were, divides into two or more, each of which then leads an independent life

Some notable examples of this we have seen already: the Anglo-Saxon *ân* has become in English the numeral *one* and the article *an* or *a*; *of* has become *off* and *of*; *also* and *as*, like German *also* and *als*, are representatives of one original; so *fore* and *for*, like German *vor*, *für*, *ver*; *through* and *thorough* are a very peculiar divorcement, with accompanying conversion of an adverb into an adjective; *outer* and *utter* are two sides of one word and one idea; *cónduct* and *condúct* are specimens of a large class of couplets, distinguished by accent alone; *minúte* and *mínute* (*mínit*) are a convenient distinction, which we might wish we had also for the two uses of *second*; and *genteel*, *gentle*, and *gentile* are all alike the Latin *gentilis*, and in their variety of meaning, as well as in their common derivation from a root signifying simply 'to be born,' are a striking example of the possibilities of linguistic mutation.

The method of growth out of the native resources of a language, by putting its materials together into new combinations, and so making new names for things, and sometimes new forms, is of course one of much slower operation than the importation of learned and technical terms from abroad, especially when this is pushed to such an extreme as in our speech. Above all, in the making of forms, its progress is almost insensibly gradual, and its results are few. It cannot well take less than generations to pass an element originally independent through those changes of shape and meaning which it must undergo in order to become a suffix. As a set-off against this, to be sure, the results, once attained, are of very wide application. When, for example, *did* is worked down into a preterit ending, we apply it to make past tenses for all our new verbs, however many they may be; and there are few adjectives in the language which may not form their corresponding adverb with *ly*, little as most of them would endure composition with *like*. But if we take into consideration the whole long course of life of a language, extending through thousands of years, and also the sum of human languages in all parts of the world, few of which, comparatively, are placed in circumstances to derive much advantage from borrowing, it is of the utmost importance. It is capable of providing, along with variation of meaning, and variation of form under phonetic change, all the new material which is needed for the ordinary development of expression; it is also able, with the same help, to transform by degrees the grammatical character of a language, adding new distinctions, and supplying the place of those that are lost by the wearing-out processes.

In connection with this, we have to note one more important department of the means of enrichment of a language: namely, the capacity, belonging to every tongue that has any share of an inflective character, of multiplying the applicabilities, and so the usefulness, of its material, new or old, by adding formative elements to it, by putting it through the processes of inflection and derivation. By no means all the formative apparatus which a language possesses can be turned to use in this way; the English distinctions, for example, of *he* and *him* and *they* and *them*, of *man* and *men*, of *give* and *gave*, of *sit* and *set*, of *true* and *truth*, of *land* and *landscape*, though inflective, are dead, and we can no longer make new forms by their help. But to any noun which we import we may add an *s* for the possessive and plural, as *telegraphs;* from any verb we can make a little scheme of inflectional forms, as *telegraphest, telegraphs, telegraphed* (pret. and part.), *telegraphing* (part.

and infin.). Then we have our suffixes for turning a noun into an adjective, as *telegraphic;* a number of these, as *ful*, *less*, *ous*, *ish*, *y*, are still sufficiently alive to admit of practical application. Then, besides that we can turn any adjective, on occasion, into a noun—as *the good*, *the beautiful*, and *the true*—we have a suffix *ness*, of very wide applicability, for abstracts. And the *ly* will convert almost any adjective into an adverb, as *telegraphically*. The verb, too, has its instruments of mutation: *telegraph*, for instance, makes *telegrapher* and *telegraphist* and *telegraphy*. And, on the other hand, there are means of turning nouns and adjectives into verbs: we say *harden* and *roughen*, and *revolutionize* and *demoralize*, and so on. This last is in all languages the principal means whereby the stock of verbal expression is increased, and new starting-points are obtained for further development: such "denominative" verbs, as they are called, abound in every member of our family, in every period of its history. All depends upon the power which language has of treating its stock of formative elements in the same way as its more material elements. Let a certain modificatory syllable, however reduced to formative value, once come to occur in forms enough to get itself distinctly associated in the minds of speakers with a certain modification of meaning, and it is further applied when that modification needs to be expressed, just as naturally as a connective or an auxiliary is similarly used. A notable example of how an element of extraneous origin can come into a language, and by slow extension finally work its way up to such a use, is afforded by *ize* and *ism* and *ist*, which, though ultimately of Greek origin, and imported by us through the French, have made themselves part of our living apparatus of derivation, and are even abused, in a half-artificial and affected way, by low speakers and writers, to the formation of such monstrosities as *walkist, hair-cuttist.*

It is of high importance, if we would understand the structure of any language, to distinguish its living apparatus of inflection and derivation from that which is only recognizable in its older words as having been formerly alive. And it is in great part by the deadening of such means of multiplication of expression that a language like ours gains its peculiar character, as a prevailingly analytical speech. Each tongue has its own way in this regard: the French is poorer even than English in apparatus of derivation; the Slavonic tongues, as the Russian, are vastly richer than either Germanic or Romanic.

The English retains a peculiar relic of its former capacities as an inflective language, in its power to turn one part of speech directly into another, without using any external sign of the transfer. The tongues of our family had in old time a formal means of making "denominative" verbs out of nouns and adjectives; we have mainly worn out and lost the means, but we make the verbs almost more freely than ever: thus, to *head* an army, to *foot* a stocking, to *hand* a plate, to *toe* a mark, to *mind* a command, to *eye* a foe, to *book* a passenger, to *chair* a candidate, to *table* a resolution, to *stone* a martyr, to *scalp* an enemy: and so on indefinitely. The examples show that the relation of the action to the conception expressed by the noun is of the greatest possible variety, determined in each case only by its known conditions, as apprehended by the mind of speaker and hearer. An equally peculiar capacity is that of transmuting without ceremony a noun into an adjective: thus we say a *gold* watch, while the French man must say 'a watch of gold,' and the German 'a golden watch,' or else, by actual composition, 'a gold-watch;' so also, a *steam* mill, as against the French 'a mill by steam' and the German 'a steam-mill;' so a *China* rose; and so on. This comes from a relaxation of the bonds of composition; the division, as it were, of a loose compound like *gold-mine* into its parts, and an attribution to the name itself in separate use of an office rightfully belonging to it only when it loses its independence by union with another. This changeableness of office is something very different from the original indefiniteness of uninflected languages. Our apprehension of the different office of verb, noun, and adjective is kept clear enough by the numerous words which have only one and not another of these characters; we preserve the distinction even after abandoning its sign; and thus have by inheritance more of the power of increasing the resources of expression than makes any outward show in our language.

CHAPTER VIII.

SUMMARY: THE NAME-MAKING PROCESS.

Review of the processes of change; their contribution to name-making. Degrees of reflectiveness in name-making. Antecedence of the conception to its sign; illustrations; examination of arguments used against this view. Sources of the material of names; artificiality of the tie between name and idea. Etymological inquiries; character of the reasons for names; a science of morphology. Force concerned in name-making; the linguistic faculty; false views and their grounds examined. Part taken by the community in the process; its relation to the action of individuals.

WE have now finished our compendious review of the individual processes—at least, the leading ones—of which is made up the growth of languages like ours. In order to understand the historical movement of any language at a given period, we need to analyze it into such parts as these, and to see how, separately and together, they are working; to note the kind and degree of activity of each, and trace, if possible, the causes that determine their difference. In our exposition and illustration, we have had in view especially their agency in the recent and present growth of English; and we cannot spend the time, nor is it necessary, to take any more notice of their different operation in other languages than we have already incidentally done, and shall have occasion in the same way to do hereafter.

We go on, rather, to consider certain general principles, mainly derivable in the way of inference from the details we have had before us, and bearing upon the general process of name-giving, or the provision of signs for conceptions. The other departments of linguistic change, as we have already seen, are of comparatively subordinate importance and not difficult of explanation; but to understand fully the means whereby language compasses the expression of whatever calls for expression is to comprehend the essential nature of linguistic growth, and even that of language itself.

We will begin by noticing that a part of the name-giving process, at any rate, is easy enough to understand; it goes on in the broadest daylight. When a human being is born into the world, custom, founded in convenience, requires that he have a name; and those who are responsible for his existence furnish the required adjunct, according to their individual tastes, which are virtually a reflection of those of the community in which they live. English-speaking parents do not give a Chinese or a Sioux name, nor *vice versâ*; the saint to whom his natal or christening day is sacred, a conspicuous public character, a relation from whom expectations are entertained, or something else equally unessential, directs their choice; no matter what, so long as the individual is named, and with such a name that neither the community who call him by it, nor he himself later, shall revolt and insist on another appellation. Such an act as this may seem to have little to do with general language; but that depends upon circumstances: the proper name *Julius* has ended in our calling a month *July*; the nickname *Cæsar* has given the title to the heads of two great nations, Germany and Russia (*kaiser*, *czar*); the christening of the baby Vespucci as *Amerigo* has led to *America* and *American.* So also with a planet: Herschel had the naming of Uranus, and Leverrier of Neptune; only they too were guided by the already established usages of language and the consequent preferences of the community; the name of *Georgium sidus*, with which, in the former case, it was unworthily sought to flatter a monarch, was frowned upon, and dropped out of sight. The discoverers of the asteroids enjoy the same privilege; and under the same conditions. So with all scientific discoverers; they exercise a prerogative, yet under limitations; they must respect the prejudices of their fellows, and they must prove their right as nomenclators: in the scientific community, as every one knows, the claims of rival name-makers are very sharply discussed, under government of nicely-established rules. So with inventors likewise: to each is conceded a limited right to give a name, or to determine the acceptance of a name given by some one else, to what he has produced. Nor is the case different anywhere in the technical vocabularies of art, of science, of philosophy. The metaphysician who draws a new distinction denominates it; he is even allowed—always with restrictions—to recast the whole vocabulary of his department, for his own special convenience; and if the other philosophers are convinced of the usefulness of the change, they ratify it.

All this is done under the full review of consciousness. There is first the apprehension of something as calling for expression, or for better expression, and then the reaching out after, and the obtaining in some way, the means of expression.

But just this, only with variety in the degree of consciousness involved, is the nature of the process of name-making in all its varieties. If it were not so, language would consist of two discordant parts, one made in this way, and one in some other. Let us consider it a little more particularly, with reference to some of the principles involved.

First, there is always and everywhere an antecedency of the conception to the expression. In common phrase, we first have our idea, and then get a name for it. This is so palpably true of all the more reflective processes that no one would think of denying it; to do so would be to maintain that the planet, or plant, or animal, could not be found and recognized as something yet unnamed until a title had been selected and made ready for clapping upon it; that the child could not be born until the christening bowl was ready. But it is equally true, only not so palpable, in all the less conscious acts, all the way down the scale to the most instinctive. The principle of life, for example, was called *animus*, 'blowing,' or *spiritus*, 'breathing,' because the nomenclators had a dim, to us a wholly insufficient, apprehension of something within the bodily frame, distinct from it, though governing and directing it—something which could come to an end while the body continued in existence; and because the breath seemed a pecular manifestation of this something, its stoppage being the most conspicuous sign of the latter's death: they seized the expression for an already formed conception as undeniably as did the anatomist who, by an equally bold figure, first applied *inosculation* to the observed connection of the arteries and veins. Every figurative transfer which ever made a successful designation for some non-sensible act or relation, before undesignated, rested upon a previous perception of analogy between the one thing and the other: no one said *apprehend* of an idea until he had felt the resemblance between the reaching-out of the bodily organs after a physical object they want to handle and the striving of the mental powers toward a like end; we repeat the act when we say "you don't *get hold of* my meaning." No one said "a thought *strikes* me," or "*occurs* to me" (i. e. 'runs against me'), or "*comes into* my head" (German, *fällt mir ein*, 'falls in to me'), except as result of an analogy which his mind had discovered between the intellectual and the physical action. When a certain new shade of red had been produced by the creative ingenuity of modern chemistry, the next thing was to give it a name; and *magenta* was pitched upon, by a perfectly conscious process, because historical causes had at about that time given a celebrity to the town Magenta: the name was not a whit more indispensable to the conception of the color than, at a period so much more ancient that we cannot get back to it, the name *green* had been to the conception of its color: men said *green* when they had observed the distinction of this from other colors, and its especial appurtenance to 'growing' things. And if we were to trace the etymology of any other similar word, we should find it of the same character. Nor is the genesis of form-words and forms unlike this. *Off* was changed to a (virtual) sign of the genitive case, and *to* to an infinitive sign, by a long succession of steps, each of which was a putting of the word to a use slightly different from that which it had served before, in order to answer a felt need of expression; and nothing other than this is implied in the making of *loved*, of *donnerai*, of *amabam*, of δώσω, of *asmi* (*am*).

We might go over the whole list of illustrations given in the preceding chapters, and as many more as we chose to take, without finding a case different from these. The doctrine that a conception is impossible without a word to express it is an indefensible paradox —indefensible, that is to say, except by misapprehensions and false arguments. One or two of these it may be worth while to notice more particularly.

It is wont to be assumed by those who oppose the antecedence of the idea to the sign, that this opinion implies the elaboration by thinkers of a store of thoughts in advance, and then the turning back and naming them by a conscious after-thought. Here is an inexcusably gross misrepresentation. There is implied, rather, that each act of nomenclature is preceded by its own act of conception; the naming follows as soon as the call for it is felt: even, it may be, before the need is realized; the forward step in mental action may be so small in each particular case that only after many have been taken in the same direction is the removal noticed, when reflection chances to be applied to it. Every conceptual act is so immediately followed as to seem accompanied by a nomenclatory one. Or, an inkling of an idea is won; it floats obscurely in the mind of the community until some one grasps it clearly enough to give it a name; and it at once takes shape (perhaps only a delusive shape), after his example, in the minds of others. The immense gain in clearness of apprehension, in facility of handling, conferred upon a conception by its naming, is not for a moment to be denied: only those are in error who would transform this advantage into an absolute necessity. Not less is their error by whom the acknowledged impossibility that the mind should do without language the work which it actually does is transferred to each single minute mental action. It might just as well be claimed that a man cannot ascend to the summit of St. Peter's, or go from Rome to Constantinople, because in each case the distance is vastly greater than the length of his legs. In point of fact, he takes one step, upward or onward, at a time, and makes each newly-won position a starting-point for further motion; and in this way he can go just as far as circumstances and his natural powers allow. Just so with the mind; every item of knowledge and of self-command that it conquers it fixes in assured possession by means of language; and it is always reaching out for more knowledge, and gaining additional control of its powers, and fixing them in the same way. It is, as we have repeatedly seen already, always at work under the surface of speech, recasting and amending the classifications involved in words, acquiring new control of conceptions once faintly grasped and awkwardly wielded, crowding new knowledge into its old terms—all, on the whole, by and with the help of language, and yet in each individual item independently of language: and there is nothing in the production of new signs that is different from the rest. The mind not only remodels and sharpens its old instruments, but also makes its new ones as it works on.

Again, in making provision of expression for new conceptions, the names-giving faculty gets its material simply where it can most conveniently, not inquiring too curiously whence it comes. Virtually, the object aimed at is to find a sign which may henceforth be linked by association closely to the conception, and used to represent it in communication and in the processes of mental action. To attempt more than this would be useless indeed, when the tie by which each individual holds and uses his whole body of expression is only this same one of association. As we saw abundantly in the second chapter, the child gets his words by learning them from others' lips, and connecting them with the same conceptions that others do. Questions of etymology are naught to him, as even the question what language he shall acquire at all. But those questions are not really anything more to the adult; nay, not even to the learned etymologist, so far as concerns his practical use of speech. The most learned of the guild can only follow for a brief distance backward the history of most words; and, near or far, he comes to a reason identical with that of the peasant: "It was the usage:" a certain community, at a certain time, used such and such a sign thus and so; and hence, by this and that succession of partly traceable historical changes, our own usage has come to be what it is. We have had to notice over and over again, above, the readiness on the part of language-users to forget origins, to cast aside as cumbrous rubbish the etymological suggestiveness of a term, and concentrate force upon the new and more adventitious tie. This is one of the most fundamental and valuable tendencies in name-making; it constitutes an essential part of the practical availability of language.

Even when there is no conspicuous transfer, when the changes of use are so slight and gradual that each new application stands closely connected with its predecessor, there is no real persistency of original value, and the point finally reached is often enough so far off from the place of starting that the one cannot be seen from the other—as when, in one of our examples above, a word (*have*) of which the ultimate radical idea is 'seize, grasp,' has become in one and the same language a sign of possession in every kind, physical and moral, and likewise of past action, of future obligation, and of causation. There is nothing in the least abnormal about such a case; every language has a plenty like it to show. But every language has also cases in abundance of a more summary distant transfer, making the reasons that underlie the current use of words so trivial or so preposterous that, if use were heedful of incongruities, the words could not stand a moment. Two forms, for example, of the great forces that govern matter, *electricity* and *magnetism*, are named, the one from a Greek word for 'amber,' the other from an obscure province of Thessaly; merely because the first electric phenomena observed by the founders of our civilization appeared in connection with the rubbing of a bit of amber, and because the stones that exhibited to them the magnetic force came from Magnesia. *Galvanism* seems more worthy, because there is a certain propriety in our honoring the man who initiated our acquaintance with this department of phenomena; yet, after all, it is rather petty to link such an element to the name of an Italian doctor. *Tragic*, *tragedy*, and all their train, come, by some tie of connection not yet fully understood, from the Greek word for a 'he-goat;' *comic* and *comedy*, probably from that for 'village,' the same with our *home*. Many of the examples already used in other connections might well be recalled here, as equally suiting our present purpose; but it is surely unnecessary to go further; our thesis is already sufficiently proved. If a direct and necessary tie had to be established even at the outset between idea and sign, new inventions would be constantly coming into speech, instead of showing themselves, as at present, the rarest of phenomena. The reason why we resort instead to the store of old material is, like all the rest, simply one of convenience. And perhaps, after all, the most telling fact of wide range is that the stores of expression of a wholly strange language are, when once the way is opened, drawn upon without stint; and we English-speakers come to call things innumerable by certain names for the very unphilosophical reason that certain communities in southeastern Europe, a long time ago, called things more or less resembling these by names somewhat similar.

Our doctrine must not at all be understood as implying that there is no reason why anything is called as it is: there is in every case a reason; only the present use of the name is not dependent on it; it cannot always be found out; and, if found, it is grounded on convenience, not on necessity of any kind. It amounts to this: the conception in question is thus designated because that other was formerly so and so designated; and the same is true of the latter also; another earlier designation of a more or less kindred conception lay back of it —and so on, as far back toward the beginning as our limited vision can reach. Our tracing of the etymology of a word is the following-up of a series of acts of name-making, consisting chiefly in the new applications of old material—with the accompanying, but independent, changes of form. And every one of those acts was one of choice, involving the free working of the human will; only under the government, as always and everywhere, of conditions and motives. In order completely to understand and judge it, we need to put ourselves precisely in the nomenclator's place, apprehending just his acquired resources of expression and his habits of thought and speech as founded on them; realizing just his insight of the new conception and his impulse to express it. But this, of course, is wholly out of our power; the *à priori* position is one we can never assume; we can only deal with the case *à posteriori*, reasoning back toward the mental condition from the act in which it is manifested.

Hence it is evident in what sense alone there can be a science of morphology, or of the adaptations and re-adaptations of articulate signs to the uses and changes of thought. As implying the existence of necessary laws of significant development, which are to be traced out and made to explain the phenomena underlain by them, no such science is possible; as classifying and arranging the infinite variety of actual facts, and pointing out the directions in which the movement takes place more than in others, it has a most useful work to do. What has been done above, in the fifth chapter, is only a beginning; the subject is one which would reward a deep and comprehensive investigation, embracing the languages of many or all families.

Once more, there is nothing in the whole complicated process of name-making which calls for the admission of any other efficient force than the reasonable action, the action for a definable purpose, of the speakers of language: their purpose being, as abundantly shown above, the adaptation of their means of expression to their constantly changing needs and shifting preferences. This great and most important institution, though carried forward from step to step of its existence in its condition as heretofore existing, by the incessant process of teaching and learning, is at the same time in no part or particle out of reach of the altering action of those who learn and use it. If convenience require that the word learned and hitherto only used in a certain sense or group of senses, and having a certain form, be applied to an additional sense, or change its application from the old to a new, and be shaped a little differently, the thing is done, and no one can hinder it; if practical use is for any reason no longer served by a word, it drops out of use and is no more; if practical need, again, call for provision of new expression, it is in one way or another obtained, the particular way depending on the conditions of the particular case. Nor is there any peculiar faculty of the mind, any linguistic instinct, or language-sense, or whatever else it may be called, involved in the process; this is simply the exercise in a particular direction of that great and composite faculty, than which no other is more characteristic of human reason, the faculty of adapting means to ends, of apprehending a desirable purpose and attaining it. It is different only in its accidents—namely, the kind of object aimed at and the kind of material used—and not in its essential nature, from that other process, not less characteristic of human reason, the making and using of instruments. No exercises of reason, in fact, as we have already once or twice remarked, are so closely and instructively parallel as these two.

This point is obviously one of the most fundamental and vital importance in the philosophy of language. There are those still who hold that words get themselves attributed to things by a kind of mysterious natural process, in which men have no part; that there are organic forces in speech itself which—by fermentation, or digestion, or crystallization, or something of the sort—produce new material and alter old. No one, however, has ever managed, if indeed any one has ever attempted, to show these forces in actual operation, or to analyze and set forth their way of working and the results it produces in detail, exhibiting their product item by item. Take any individual bit of linguistic growth, and it is found and acknowledged to be the act of a human being, working toward definable ends under the government of recognizable motives, even though without any reflective consciousness of what he is accomplishing: and it is manifestly absurd to recognize one force in action in the items and another in their sum. If we refuse to examine the items when forming an estimate of the force, and only gaze with admiration at the great whole, there is no theory so false that we may not for a time rest in it with satisfaction. But we might with the same reason regard the pyramids, in our wonder at their immensity and grandeur, as great crystals, produced by the infinite organizing forces of Nature, as ascribe language to organic powers contained within itself; the moment we come to examine their component parts, we find everywhere the marks of human workmanship; and we ourselves are all the time building similar structures, even if not upon so grand a scale as the men of old. The general laws or general tendencies of language, well enough called by that name if we do not let ourselves be deceived by the terms we use, are really only laws of human action, under the joint guidance of habit and circumstance. As for setting them up as efficient causes, that is sheer mythology; we might as well erect into forces the laws which govern the development of political institutions, or the tendencies which in any country, at a given time, are leading to the victory of one party over another: it all resolves itself at last into the action of individual minds, capable of choice, under wide-reaching motives and inducements, which are recognizable in their general operations, though not in the detail of their working upon each mind.

One great reason why men are led to deny the agency of the human will in the changes of speech is that they see so clearly that it does not work consciously toward that purpose. No one says to himself, or to others: "Our language is defective in this and that particular; go to now, and let us change it;" any more than he says: "All things carefully considered, this particular word in our speech can well enough be spared; let us cast it out." The end aimed at—and not even that with full consciousness—is the supply of a need of expression, or the attainment of a more satisfactory expression. An exigency arises, a conjuncture in which the existing available resources are not sufficient for the speaker's ends; and, in one or other of the various ways described above, he adds to them to answer his present purpose. Or the opportunity offers itself, and is seized, for a short cut, a new and more attractive path, to a point accessible enough in old ways. A person commits thus an addition to language without ever being aware of it; any more than the parents who name their son reflect that they are thus virtually making an addition to the city directory. If he will well understand it to be in this sense, every one is welcome to hold that alterations of speech are not made by the human will; there is no will to alter speech; there is only will to use speech in a way which is new; and the alteration comes of itself as a result. So it was not by the exertion of his will that the reptile, creeping over the muddy surface of a Permian or Jurassic shore, made a record of himself for the human geologist to study, a few million years later; and yet, if he had not voluntarily taken the steps, under sufficient inducement, there would have been no record.

We must not, indeed, commit the error of ascribing too much consciousness even to the act of satisfying the momentary impulse which produces the alteration. Thus, for example, in phonetic change. A word is produced by a highly intricate succession of acts on the part of the vocal organs; a careless and unheeded omission of any one of them results in a mutilation of the word, or a slight relaxation of the energy of articulation affects the character of one of the sounds in the compound; and as the word answers its purpose just as well as before, it passes without notice, and the act is repeated, and becomes first customary, then constant. This is, in fact, the normal method of phonetic corruption; yet no sensible person would ever think of recognizing any other agency at work than the speaker himself, acting voluntarily—any more than he would attribute it to some force operating from outside if a man, on coming to a ditch which he had been used to leap every day, should some time put forth an insufficient exertion of force, and should fall in. If there were penalties of this sort following slips in utterance, the subject of phonetic change would make but a small figure in our comparative grammars. And this is not the only way in which careless or slovenly handling of language leads to change. A very large department of alterations has no other source, but is due to the omission of distinctions, the blunders of mistaken analogy, on the part of those who have not carefully studied and do not bear accurately in mind the proper uses of the words they employ. And yet, here just as much as in the case of the naturalist who cons his Greek and Latin dictionaries in search of a name for a new mineral or plant, the act of change is the work of the speaker, and of him alone.

Another reason for holding the false view which we are now combating is that every person is conscious of his inability to effect a change in language by his own authority and arbitrarily; and what he cannot do, he is sure that nobody can do. And that is true enough; in a sense, it is not the individual, but the community, that makes and changes language. We must be careful, however, to see clearly in what sense, lest we fail signally to understand the subject we are examining. There is implied here a point of high importance in linguistic philosophy, one which we have already had more or less in view, but have not taken up for direct consideration: namely, the part which the community of speakers, as distinguished from the individual speaker, have to play in language-making.

The community's share in the work is dependent on and conditioned by the simple fact that language is not an individual possession, but a social. It exists (as we shall notice more particularly in the fourteenth chapter), not only partly, but primarily, for the purpose of communication; its other uses come after and in the train of this. To the great mass of its speakers, it exists consciously for communication alone; this is the use that exhibits and commends itself to every mind. That would have no right to be called a language which only one person understood and could use; and there is not, nor has ever been, any such in existence. Acceptance by some community, though but a limited one, is absolutely necessary in order to convert any one's utterances into speech. Hence arise the influences which guide and restrain individual action on language. In the first place, an individual's alterations and additions, if not adopted by others and kept up in their tradition, die with him, and never come to light at all. But again, even if he were careless of offending the prejudices or shocking the taste of his fellows, he would not, at any rate, pass the limit of being intelligible to them; and this would be by itself a powerful brake to check his arbitrary action. But such a brake is unnecessary, because, in the third place, each individual feels, in the main, the governing force of the same motives which sway the minds of his fellows. He does not himself incline, any more than they would incline to allow him, to abandon the established habits of speech and go off upon a tangent, toward some new and strange mode of expression. Everything in language goes by analogy; what a language is in the habit of doing, it can do, but nothing else; and habits are of very slow growth; a lost habit cannot be revived; a new one cannot be formed except gradually, and almost or quite unconsciously. And the reason of this lies in the common preferences of the speakers. We signify the fact popularly by saying that such and such a thing is opposed to the "genius of the language;" but that is merely a mythological term; the German calls the same thing the *Sprachgefühl*, 'speech-feeling,' or 'linguistic instinct:' both are expressions of a convenient dimness, under which inexact thinkers often hide an abundance of indefinite or erroneous conceptions. What is really meant is the sum, or resultant, of the preferences of the language-users, as determined by the already existing material and usages of their speech; outside of certain narrow limits of variation, they are not themselves tempted to suggest, nor will they ratify and accept as suggested by any one, new meanings, new phrases, new words.

Our recognition of the community as final tribunal which decides whether anything shall be language or not, does not, then, in the least contravene what has been claimed above respecting individual agency. Some one must lead the way for the rest to follow; if they do not follow, he falls back or stands alone. The community cannot act save by the initiative of its single members; they can accomplish nothing save by its coöperation. Every new item in speech has its own time and occasion and place of origination; it spreads from one to another until it wins general currency, or else it is stifled by general neglect. Only, of course, it is not necessary that every single change should start from a single point. There are some toward which the general mind so distinctly inclines, which lie so close outside of and within reach from the present boundaries of usage, that they are made independently by many persons, in many places, and thus have a variety of starting-points from which to strive after currency. Probably it was thus with *its*, when, two or three centuries ago, it was crowded into English speech, against the outspoken opposition of educated and "correct" speakers, by the force of its apparent analogy with the general store of English possessives; probably the same was the case with *is being done*, the corresponding passive form to the continuous active *is doing*, as *is done* corresponds to *does*—a phrase which, against a like opposition, has not yet made its place entirely good in the best English usage. Phonetic changes are especially likely to be thus general, instead of solitarily individual, in their origin. A very notable example is seen in the Germanic *umlaut*, or modification of vowel (see above, p. 71); which, since it is wanting in the Gothic, cannot have belonged to the Germanic branches before their separation, but was later developed independently in the High-German, the Low-German, and the Scandinavian dialects, doubtless as the final and accordant working-out of habits of utterance which were already present in the unitary Germanic dialect.

Having thus recognized the nature of the force which, notwithstanding the strictness of linguistic tradition, is all the time altering the traditionary material, and seen in what ways and under what inducements it acts, we have next to view the same force, in the same modes of action, as causing not only the variation of a single language from age to age of its existence, but also, under the government of external circumstances, its variation in space, its divarication into dialects.

CHAPTER IX.

LOCAL AND CLASS VARIATION OF LANGUAGE: DIALECTS.

Dialectic differences within the limits of a single language; individual, class, and local peculiarities of speech. What makes a language one. Influences favoring or restraining dialectic differences; effect of culture. Illustration: Germanic language-history; Romanic. Centripetal and centrifugal forces; separate growth causes dialectic division; examples. Verbal correspondences prove common descent of words and languages; cautions as to applying this principle. Degrees of relationship. Constitution of Indo-European family and evidences of its unity. Universality of families and dialectic relations. Relation of terms "language" and "dialect."

Our inquiries into the phenomena of speech have thus far shown us that the mass of each one's language is acquired by him by a process of learning, of direct acquisition of what is put before his mind by others; that, however, each one is at the same time a partner in the work of changing the language: contributing, indeed, only an infinitesimal quota toward it, in exact proportion to his importance in the aggregate of speakers by whom the language is kept in existence, yet doing his part in a sum which is all made up of such infinitesimal parts, and would not exist without them. The tradition of speech is carried on by him and such as he is; its modification is due to no other agency. Every item of difference between new speech and old, whether in the way of alteration or of addition, has its separate origin, beginning in the usage of individuals, and spreading and seeking that wider acceptance which alone makes language of it; and it has its time of probation, during which it is trying to establish itself.

But if this is true, then there must be in every existing language, at any time, processes of differentiation not yet fully carried out, words and forms of words in a state of transition, altering but not altered; words and phrases under trial, introduced but not general; words obsolescent but not yet obsolete; old modes of pronunciation beginning to seem strange and affected, new modes coming into vogue—and so on, through the whole catalogue of possible linguistic changes.

And this is, in fact, precisely the state of things, in every language under the sun: a state of things only explainable by the causes which we have been considering. It exists even in our own speech; although here, for reasons to be presently adverted to, the conditions are more opposed to it than almost anywhere else in the world. We must be careful not to overrate the uniformity of existing languages; it is far enough from being absolute. In a true and defensible sense, every individual speaks a language different from every other. The capacities and the opportunities of each have been such that he has acquired command of a part of English speech not precisely identical with any one else's: the peculiarity may be slight, but it is certainly there. Then, what is yet more obvious and yet more important, the form of each one's conceptions, represented by his use of words, is different from any other person's; all his individuality of character, of knowledge, education, feeling, enters into this difference. And yet again, few if any escape the taint of local and personal peculiarities of pronunciation and phraseology, peculiarities which, because more conspicuous than the others, are more often noticed by us and called dialectic. This last shades off into the more wide-spread and deeper differences of district and class; every separate part of a great country of one speech has its local form, more or less strongly marked—even where, as in America, there are no old inherited dialects, of long standing, such as prevail in Britain, in Germany, in France: in short, almost everywhere. Every class, however constituted, has its dialectic differences: so, especially, the classes determined by occupation; each trade, calling, profession, department of study, has its technical vocabulary, its words and phrases unintelligible to outsiders; the carpenter, the iron-maker, the machinist, the miner, not less than the physician, the geologist, or the metaphysician, has occasion every day to say many things which would not be understood by a man of any of the other classes mentioned, if not exceptionally well-informed. Then there are the differences in grade of education; the highly cultivated have a diction which is not in all its parts at the command of the vulgar; they have hosts of names for objects and ideas of educated knowledge, which (like *dahlia*, *petroleum*, *telegraph*, instanced above) may perhaps some time work their way down into the lower rank, becoming universal, like *is* and *head*, and *long* and *short*, instead of class-words only; and, yet more especially, the uncultivated have current in their dialect a host of inaccuracies, offenses against the correctness of speech—as ungrammatical forms, mispronunciations, blunders of application, slang words, vulgarities; all of these, perhaps, analogous with alterations which the cultivated speech, as compared with its predecessors, has under gone, and some of them destined to become at a future time the established usage of the whole language; but as yet kept down in the category of errors by the resistance of the higher classes to their acceptance and use. Finally, there are the differences of age: the nursery, in particular, has its dialect, offensive to the ears of old bachelors; and older children have their language at least characterized by limited vocabulary.

Every one of all these differences is essentially dialectic: that is to say, they differ not at all in kind, but only in degree, from those which hold apart acknowledged dialects. They all fall, as regards their origin, under the classes of change already laid down: they are deviations from a former standard of speech which have hitherto acquired only a partial currency, within the limits of a class or district; or they are retentions of a former standard, which the generality of good speakers have now abandoned. In illustration of this latter class, we may note in passing that no small number of what the English stigmatize as Americanisms are cases of survival from former good usage, and that, on the other hand, much of what we regard as the peculiarities of Irish pronunciation is also old English, more faithfully preserved by the Irish than by the more native speakers. Of course, it is as wrong to be lagging in the rear of the great moving body of the usages of a language as to be rushing on in advance, or flying off to one side. When the speech of the best speakers changes, those who do not conform have to be ranked in a lower class.

And yet, despite all these varieties, the language is one; and one for the simple reason that, though the various individuals who speak it may talk so as to be unintelligible to one another, they may also, on matters of the most familiar common interest, understand one another. As the direct object of language is communication, the possibility of communication makes the unity of a language. No one can define, in the proper sense of that term, a language; for it is a great concrete institution, a body of usages prevailing in a certain community, and it can only be shown and described. You have it in its dictionary, you have it in its grammar; as also, in the material and usages which never get into either dictionary or grammar; and you can trace the geographical limits within which it is used, in all its varieties.

It is an obvious corollary from the view we have taken of the forces governing the growth of language, and of the way in which they act, that the *quasi*-dialectic discordances existing within the limits of the same language in the same community will be greatest where the separation of classes and sections is greatest. The necessity of communication is the restraint upon the alterative processes, and communication is the means whereby any alteration actually made is adopted by all: whatever, then, makes communication most lively and penetrating, through all regions and all ranks, will tend to preserve the unity of speech most strictly through the whole community. On the other hand, all that dulls the forces of communication, and lets a people break up into tribes, or into widely-sundered castes or classes, tends to increase the discordance of the forms comprehended together in the general language.

Different causes exert in this way a different influence. On the one hand, in a barbarous condition of society the discordances of class and occupation are at their lowest. All members of the same community stand substantially upon the same level; with but insignificant exceptions, they have the same knowledge, the same skill, the same habits; the collective wealth of thought and its expression is not too great for each person to grasp and wield the whole of it. On the other hand, local differences are at their highest point, since it is only civilization and culture that can bind together into one the parts of a great community. The influences of barbarism, beyond narrow limits, are prevailingly segregative; a wild race that multiplies and spreads widely breaks up into mutually jealous and hostile divisions, within each of which linguistic changes run their own independent course. Every element of culture that finds its way in exercises a conservative influence, tending both to preserve the language from change and to preserve its unity throughout the territory it occupies. The rise of a national feeling of so high an order that it reverences the deeds and the words of past generations, and leads to the production of a national literature, is obviously conservative, because it amounts to setting up a norm of correct speech, by which men's minds shall be influenced in judging, for acceptance or rejection, the individual proposals of change. A written literature, the habit of recording and reading, the prevalence of actual instruction, work yet more powerfully in the same direction; and when such forces have reached the degree of strength which they show in our modern enlightened communities, they fairly dominate the history of speech. The language is stabilized, especially as regards all those alterations which proceed from inaccuracy; local differences are not only restrained from arising, but are even wiped out, so far as the effect of education extends. There is also a state of things intermediate between the two extremes of barbarism and all-pervading culture: namely, where there is culture which reaches only a particular class, a minority, of the community, its conserving influences being mainly limited to that class. This alone possesses the records of the language, and, using them as models, propagates its speech nearly unaltered, while the language of the mass goes on changing unchecked. There comes thus to be a separation of the originally unitary speech into two parts: a learned dialect, which is the old common language preserved, and a popular dialect, which is its altered descendant; and the latter, perhaps, finally crowds the former out of existence, and becomes, in its turn, the cultivated speech of a new order of things. Such has been, for example, the history of the Latin, and of the later dialects descended from it, and now become the vehicles of great and noble literatures; such, also, that of the now cultivated languages of modern Aryan India, in their relations to the Sanskrit.

Let us suppose, then, that there is a definite community X, of one speech. It is divided—not, of course, by definite or fixed lines—into the various local parts A, B, C, etc., and into the classes, whether social, vocational, or educational, *A*, *B*, *C*, etc., and *a*, *b*, *c*, etc.; the various divisions variously overlapping and overlying one another. The common speech is, like all living speech, in a condition of constant growth and change; this change being possible, and actually occurring, only by such acts of alteration as we have considered in detail above, each arising at a point or points in one or more divisions, and spreading thence by communication to the rest. What arises thus in A, or B, or C, becomes at length the possession of all—if, indeed, it does not continue within certain limits, as a merely local dialectic word or mode of expression. So what arises in *A* or *a* goes through the rest—unless it remain within the boundaries of a class, as a technical term, a high-caste expression, a popular blunder or vulgarism, or something of the sort. And the amount and value of these various *residua*, constituting the minor discordances which may consist with general agreement and unity, is various according to such determining circumstances as we reviewed briefly in the paragraph next preceding: no language is or can be without them, but they are very different in different languages.

This whole state of things is dependent on historical conditions, as concerns its continuance and changes. Let us take our hypothetical case to represent the German language as it was at and after the beginning of our era. Here, while the divisions of class and occupation were comparatively unimportant, those of locality, A, B, C, etc., were very marked: so much so, indeed, as to make it improper to speak of the whole as one language; besides innumerable minor discordances, there were sections the speech of each of which was not intelligible to the rest; and if no new force had been introduced, things might have gone on thus to the end of time, the local discordances constantly deepening and widening. But a new and controlling force was introduced: that of Greco-Roman, soon to become European, civilization: this led the way to institutional and political unity. But not for a long time did it win the predominance in the domain of language. At first, each local division had its own separate culture; the beginnings of literature were produced, and are in part still extant, in one and another local form of speech, fully intelligible only within limits. But at length, early in the sixteenth century, the fullness of time was come; political and educational conditions had reached a point where a movement toward an educated—and so, in a certain sense, an artificial—unity of speech could be made with success. A certain local form of speech, A—which, to be sure, had already gained a degree of currency as a class-form also—was definitely adopted by the educated as their dialect, *A*, the style of German which should thenceforth alone be written, and looked up to as a model, and taught in the schools. And its authority has ever since gone on increasing, with the extension of the power of civilization and education, till now an outsider almost looks upon it as the sole German speech. That, however, it is far enough from being; it is still only *A*, the German of a class, though of a class which the conditions of modern civilization have made the dominant and the growing one. B, C, and D, etc., still subsist; there are whole regions of Germany where the local dialect is unintelligible to him who is versed only in the literary language; but they divide among them, for the most part, only the classes of lower education, *E* and *F*, etc.; and they, as well as the classes of vocation, *a* and *b* and *c*, etc., feel profoundly and in various ways the influence of the learned speech. *A* is the predominant speech, modifying and shaping everything else in German usage, and even promising, if the forces of education should ever attain that overwhelming degree of importance, to sweep out of existence all the other varieties, save those of occupation.

Not, however, as we must next notice, over the whole territory occupied by High or Low German tribes. There were at least two local varieties—we may call them E and F—which did not fall under the unifying influences that brought all the rest within the dominion of *A*. One, E, the English, was cut off by distance and inaccessibility, and consequent independence.

The Germanic Angles and Saxons, who carried a German dialect across the North Sea into Britain, and with it displaced the old Celtic speech, have passed, in their separateness, through a series of changes analogous with those of their former fellow-countrymen. Their own secondary divisions, of whatever kind—whether local, as E′, E″, E‴, etc., or of class, as *E′*, *E″*, etc.—have been in a similar manner brought under the controlling influence of another literary dialect, of like origin with that of Germany. And in the northeastern district of continental Germany, the Netherlands, political independence, with the consequent isolation of general interests, had a kindred result; while the rest of Low Germany, speaking by local division forms of German speech not less peculiar than those of the Anglo-Saxons and Dutch, uses the High-German literary dialect as its learned speech, the corner Holland and the colony England have given an equivalent literary value to their separate Low-German dialects. No matter how the local varieties A and B and C become separated, so that what passes in each is not participated in by the others, their development will take a different course, and they will in time become separate tongues.

The same forces, in like modes of action, but with abundant differences of detail, are seen at work in producing the modern Romanic languages, descendants of the Latin. When the arms and civilization and polity of Rome carried her speech all through Italy, and over great regions outside of Italy, it was already divided by education into class-varieties. All were transmitted together; and the learned dialect—*A*, as we may call it, in accordance with our use of this sign above—has been kept up in its complete purity even to the present day, by appropriate and adequate means, though in a con stantly diminishing class. The lower forms of speech, *B*, *C*, etc., had their full influence in laying the foundations of the new history. The changes of Latin went on, all the more rapidly for its having passed into the keeping of races who had learned it at second hand, by an outside pressure; and, as the forces of communication were very far from being sufficient to keep the immensely extended community one, it broke up, by differentiation within geographical limits, into a correspondingly numerous array of local forms, for which it would take several alphabets to provide sufficient symbols; and historical circumstances, which in their main character and influence admit of being distinctly pointed out, led to one here and another there—as C, and F, and I, and P, and S, and W—being adopted as the learned dialects of great regions, and used for literary and educational purposes, not only by their own native speakers, but also by those of the rest—which, like the German dialects, still subsist as the uneducated *patois* each of its own district.

It would be very easy to push this illustration indefinitely, but to carry it further is quite needless. The methods of linguistic change detailed above, and governed in their historical workings by the antithesis between the initiatory action of the individual, and the regulating action of the community in accepting or rejecting his proposals—this has been all we have needed to explain the historical phenomena instanced; and this, and this only, is sufficient to explain all the rest. It may be fairly and confidently claimed that there is no known case which cannot thus be solved. Individuals are the diversifying or centrifugal force in the growth of speech; for, as there are no two persons absolutely alike in countenance, so there are no two identical in character and education, and the shaping influence exerted by each on the speech he has learned will be slightly different from that of every one else. But just so far as communication extends, like the centripetal force, which dominates the other, and keeps the moving body upon a certain track never too far remote from the centre, the individualities are curbed and restrained, and their jarring action forced into and held in accordance. Or, in terms of our recent hypothesis, just so long as every change which arises in the local parts A and B and C, and so on, works its way through all the rest, passing the ordeal of their acceptance or rejection, so long will the language X remain one. It may and will alter from age to age; it may even become so changed in two or three centuries (as English has actually become in a thousand years) that its speakers at one and the other end of that period would not, if they could be brought together, understand one another at all; yet, at every period, all the community would understand each other, because it would have changed alike in the minds and mouths of all. But separate, in any way you please, the parts A and B and C from one another, so that the changes in each are made in that alone, and do not extend into the rest, and the peculiarities of each will begin to be confined to itself; what we call dialectic growth will set in; the process of divarication into diverse languages will have begun. A brick wall, high enough and long enough, between the sections, would perfectly accomplish their division, and initiate dialectic divergence; only, of course, if the separation takes place by local removal, so that the sections are brought into different external circumstances of nature and occupation, and under different historical influences, the process of linguistic divergence will be quickened.

This cutting off, by cessation of communication, of a common regulative influence over the never-ending changes of speech, may seem a very slight cause of divergence; and so in truth it is; but it is fully sufficient to account for all the phenomena of dialectic growth. No matter how small the angle may be between two lines starting from the same point; if they are protracted far enough, their extremities may be found any given distance apart. And the angle of dialectic divergence is practically an increasing one; the two lines of development curve asunder. At the outset, namely, the sum of guiding analogies in each is almost precisely the same; identity of material, and of habits of its use, is, as it were, a continuance of the common momentum, carrying the two on in almost the same direction; and independent accordant results of this community of original habit may, as we have more than once seen above, continue to appear for a long time, even indefinitely. But each bit of difference that creeps in lessens the accordance; new habits arise, special disturbing influences set in, and the distance comes at last, perhaps, to be rapidly instead of slowly increased. The history of our English, as compared with the Low-German dialects from which it sheered off in the fifth and sixth centuries, is as striking an example of this as could be desired.

Again, as dialectic discordance only arises in consequence of linguistic growth, and as the maintenance of an original condition of speech unchanged would do away with all possibility of difference of speech among the separated parts of the community which formerly spoke it as one together, it is evident that the rate of divergence must depend in great degree upon the general rate of growth. And, as we have seen, the influences of barbarism and of civilization are directly opposed to one another in this regard, although they are by no means the only determining influences which quicken or retard the alterative processes. It is the predominant forces of civilization which, by a two-fold action, have kept the language of the two great divisions of English-speakers nearly accordant, notwithstanding the broad ocean that rolls between them: first, by making actual communication between them easier and closer than between two tribes of rude people separated only by a few miles of mountain or of plain, by a forest or a river; indeed, even by giving them, as it were, in their common literature, a great body of speakers who are all the time communicating with both; and, in the second place, by so restraining the activity of the alterative processes that their results have time to reach and permeate both divisions. Absence of the same conserving influences causes the French of the *habitans* of Canada and the German of the colony in Pennsylvania to differ far more widely from the dialects of the countries whence these colonists came.

The most instructive attainable example of dialectic growth, on the whole, is that presented us in the Romanic languages, because we have there a most important and widely-spread body of highly cultivated languages, each with its legion of subsidiary dialectic forms; and also—what is nowhere else to be had in anything like the same measure—the very mother, the Latin, from which they have all sprung. The student of language finds in them a whole world of facts to study and compare, to trace out in their origin and in the laws which have produced them. And his task, though in part simple and easy, is also in no small part difficult and baffling; for even here, under the eyes of history, as it were, though hidden from them, have gone on changes which seem to defy investigation, producing results which cannot be carried back to their sources. Let us look at a specimen or two of the process of divarication, as it has passed upon some of the materials of the Latin original.

The Latin had a word for 'brother,' *frater*. In French, the word, in the abbreviated form *frère*, still bears the old office. But in Italian and Spanish, the same word, having undergone still greater mutilation—as Spanish *fray*, Italian *frate* and *fra*—signifies only a 'brother' of some ecclesiastical order, a *friar*, as we call it, by yet another form of the same name. So, for 'brother' in its original and proper sense, each language has had to provide a new word: the Italian takes the diminutive *fratello*; the Spanish puts to use the Latin *germanus*, 'nearly related,' and says *hermano*. Again, the Latin had the name *mulier* for a 'woman,' distinctively as woman, besides *femina* for 'female,' woman or other. In Spanish, now, the former is still retained, altered to *muger*, in nearly its ancient meaning; but in Italian, as *moglie*, it signifies only 'wife' or 'spouse;' and in French it has utterly disappeared. In French, *femme*, the representative of the other Latin word, has become the general name for 'woman,' adding also the meaning of 'wife;' while for 'female' has come to be used *femelle* (like Italian *fratello* for Latin *frater*). For 'woman,' the Italian has shaped a new word, *donna*, out of later Latin *domina*, 'mistress;' and the Spanish uses for 'lady' the same word *donna*, besides *señora*, a feminine of modern make to *senior*, 'older person.' These are fair specimens of how the original material of a language gets worked over, in form and in meaning, in the keeping of the severed descendants of that language. If we looked into the class of verbs, we should find the same condition of things. The verb 'be,' for example, is made up of a remnant of the forms of the Latin *esse*, pieced out in all the dialects with parts of *stare*, 'stand:' so the French *étais*, *été*, are *stabam*, *status*, with remarkable alterations of form, one of which has been commented on above (p. 54). And the French verb 'go' is put together by adding parts of Latin *ire*, 'go,' and parts of *vadere*, 'walk,' to a main stock of very obscure origin, representing Latin *adnare*, 'arrive by water,' or *aditare*, 'make one's *adit*, or arrival,' or something of the sort.

Turning now to the Germanic dialects, our own nearest relatives, we find the same kind of resemblance in difference everywhere prevailing. The Germanic words for 'brother'—as Netherlandish *broeder*, German *bruder*, Icelandic *brodhir*, Swedish and Danish *broder* and *bror* —are not less obviously the variations of one original than are the Romanic products of *frater*. The old Germanic *weib*, 'woman,' is found in most of the modern languages, in easily recognizable forms, with its former value; but in modern English its representative *wife* has become restricted (like Italian *moglie*) to a married woman. And there is another ancient word, Gothic *quens* and *quinon*, which in some dialects is the accepted name for 'woman,' instead of the other, but which in English has undergone the curious fate of being divided into two terms, of lofty and humble meaning, *queen* and *quean*. Our verbs *be* and *go*, too, like their Romanic equivalents, are made up of fragments from various roots, pieced together partly in more ancient, partly in more modern times. Both we have already noticed elsewhere in passing (pp. 90, 101); it is unnecessary here to enter into any further detail respecting them.

From these and all the other innumerable correspondences of the Germanic dialects we cannot possibly help drawing the same conclusion which is taught us by a comparison of the Latin with its descendants. It is not one whit less certain that *wife* and *weib* and *vif* and the rest are the variously altered representatives of a single primitive Germanic vocable, than that *moglie* and *muger* come from the Latin *mulier*. We may not always, or often, be able to restore by inference the Germanic word with a certainty equal to that inspired by the actually preserved Latin word; but that makes no difference. We believe in the former existence of the grandfather of a group of cousins, whom we have never seen because he died long ago, just as thoroughly as in the present existence of one whom we find still living in the midst of another group. According to our experience of how things go on in the world of human beings and in that of words, there is no other possibility. The processes of linguistic change, working regularly on in the way in which we see them working in the present and the recently past historic periods, are fully sufficient to account for the existence in certain languages of groups of words more or less resembling one another yet not identical; and there is no need that we resort to adventurous hypotheses for its explanation.

This, legitimately generalized, gives us the great principle that genuine correspondences, of whatever degree, between the words of different languages, are to be interpreted as the result of derivation from one original: relationship, in words as in men, implies descent from a common ancestor. And what is true of the words of two languages is true of the languages themselves: languages made up of related words must be descended from a single common language.

Only, to this principle need to be applied certain cautions and corrections. Two sources of error require to be guarded against in its use. First, words are borrowed out of one language into another, as was fully explained and illustrated in the seventh chapter. Certain elements in English are of common descent with elements in the Romanic and in many other of the world's languages; they have been handed over from the tradition of one people into that of another: and though there is so far a community of tradition, it does not imply general relationship of the languages. Secondly, accidental correspondences occur between words which have no historical connection: so, for example, between Greek ὅλος and our *whole*, between Sanskrit *loka* and Latin *locus*, between Mod. Greek *ματι*, 'eye,' and Polynesian *mata*, 'see,' and so on. These two difficulties impose upon the comparer of languages the necessity of increased caution in his work, and warn him against over-hasty conclusions. An instance or two, or a few instances, of verbal correspondence are not sufficient to prove anything. But accidental resemblances have their limit; and it is in general possible to distinguish borrowed material, so as not to be misled by it into false inferences. The linguist looks to see both how many and how close the asserted correspondences are, and in what part of the vocabulary they are found. If we did not know by external information the history of English, we could still recognize it beyond all question as essentially a Germanic dialect, by noticing what parts of its material accord with the Germanic tongues, and what part with the Romanic.

But relationship in language, as in genealogy, is a thing of degrees, and for the same reason. The French, Spanish, and Italian are cousins, on grounds which we have already sufficiently noticed; but each is a group of yet more closely related dialects. And so also among the Germanic languages: the English belongs to a Low-German group, still occupying the northern shores of Germany, whence the ancestors of the English came; there is likewise a High-German group, occupying the central and southern part of Germany; and there is a Scandinavian group, holding in possession Denmark, Sweden and Norway, and Iceland; moreover, there is a single dialect, the Mœso-Gothic, of which limited records are saved from extinction, and which represents alone yet another group, of unknown extent. From these minor groupings precisely the same inference is to be drawn as from the larger ones: they represent historical centres of more recent divergence, of the same kind and by the same means as the others.

Nor does the finding of correspondences and tracing of relationships end here. Between the Germanic *brothar* and the Latin *frater* there is a pretty evident resemblance, which becomes still more evident when we put alongside of them other words of the same class, as German *mothar*, *fathar*, and Latin *mater*, *pater*. But there are yet other groups of languages which show similar signs of relationship: we find in Greek φρατήρ (meaning, to be sure, only a member of a confraternity, like *fray* and *fra*, as noticed above) and μήτηρ and πατήρ; and, in Sanskrit, *bhrâtar* and *mâtar* and *pitar*; and the Persian and Celtic and Slavonic tongues have in the same words correspondences which are like these, though not quite so striking. These are telling indications of an original relationship among all the groups of languages mentioned: outcroppings, as it were, of a vein which invites further exploration. For, in the first place, the correspondences are too numerous and wide-spread and close to be explained with the slightest show of plausibility as the result of chance; and then, there appears to be equally small hope of accounting for them by borrowing. How should all these widely-sundered tribes of men, found at the dawn of history in every variety of cultural condition, have obtained from a common source, or by transmission from one to another, names for conceptions like these, the formation of which must have accompanied the first development of family life? Plainly, all probabilities are against it.

No confident conclusion, however, as to so important a fact should be built on narrow foundations; and we look further, into other classes of words. There are no savages in the world so undeveloped that they cannot count 'one, two, three'—even though there are those who have gone no further than that by their own powers, but are either destitute of the higher numbers, or have borrowed them from races more advanced. If we find these numerals accordant in the languages we have named, it will be a very strong piece of evidence corroborative of that furnished by the names of relationship. And the accordance exists, and is of the most striking character, not only in these numerals, but in all that follow: *dwa* is the common basis of the various words for 'two,' and *tri* of those for 'three,' through the whole great mass of dialects. The pronouns, again, are a class of words in which the suspicion of borrowing is, if possible, even less to be entertained; and here also, in such words as those for 'thou' (*twa*) and 'me' (*ma*), in the demonstrative *ta* and the interrogative *kwa*, we find a degree of agreement which is quite beyond the power of accident to have produced.

Yet once more, we have seen (p. 119) that inflectional

apparatus, grammatical structure, is most of all out of the reach of a language that is borrowing from another. But through all the grammatical apparatus of these groups of dialects, when we can reach far enough back in their history to find it preserved in a distinct form, we discover an accordance not less convincing. Thus, in the verbal inflection, there are the various alterations of an original ending *mi* for the first person singular, and of *masi* for the first plural; of *si* and *tasi* for the second person, and of *ti* and *anti* for the third; of a reduplication forming a perfect tense, of a sign of the optative mood, and so on. In noun declension the traces are more obscure and scanty, but still perceptible enough. The comparison of adjectives is everywhere by the same means. Participles and other derivative words show the same suffixes of derivation.

In short, there is a superabundance of evidence going to prove that the speech of all the peoples we have mentioned, filling most of Europe, ancient and modern, and an important tract of Asia, is related, in the sense in which we have used that word above. There is no theoretic reason against such a fact; rather, every conclusion drawn from the phenomena of existing speech makes directly in its favor. We know that the separation and isolation of the different parts of a once unitary community must necessarily bring about a separation of its language into different dialects; and we know that this process may go on repeating itself, over and over again; and that, at the end, those dialects which parted latest will (apart from special altering forces), though unlike, be least unlike and most like one another, while those which parted earliest will be least like and most unlike one another: and we know of no other way in which this likeness in unlikeness can be brought about. We infer, then, that all the languages in question are the divaricated representatives of a single tongue, spoken somewhere and somewhen in the past by a single limited community, by the spread and dispersion of which all its discordances have in the course of time grown up. Such a grand congeries of related languages, in different degrees, we are accustomed to call a "family:" a name taken, by an allowable figurative transfer, from the vocabulary of genealogy.

This is an example of the way we are to proceed to examine and classify all the various languages which the earth contains. The first steps in it are easy enough. It takes no conjurer to discover that London English and Yorkshire English and Scotch English and negro English, even, are all one language; and no observant person, probably, who learns German or Dutch or Swedish, fails to see that he has in hand a tongue akin with his own. But it takes a more penetrating and enlightened study to pick out the signs of original unity amid the greatly more conspicuous differences of English, French, Welsh, Russian, Romaic, Persian, and Hindî; and it requires especially a resort, in the case of each language, to the older tongues of its own nearer kindred, which have preserved the ancient common material with less change. Only the learned and experienced investigator, therefore, can be trusted to push the work of classification safely to its extreme limits; and the classification of all human tongues is only attainable by the labors of a great number of investigators, each earned in his own special department. Nor has it been even thus by any means finished; yet much has been done toward it: the vast majority of languages have been grouped together by their affinities into families and branches of families; and the results of this classification have to be briefly reviewed by us in the following chapters.

For, as might be expected to follow from the principles laid down above as determining dialectic growth, there is not a language in the world which does not exist in the condition of dialectic division, so that the speech of each community is the member of a more or less extended family—unless, indeed, there may be here and there an isolated language so nearly extinct as to be used only by the narrowest possible community: by a few families, or a single village. Even languages of so limited area as the Basque in the Pyrenees, as some of the tongues in the Caucasus, have their well-marked dialectic forms; because an uncivilized people can hardly break up even into camps, and still maintain that communication which alone can keep their speech a unit.

This linguistic condition of the earth runs parallel, in the closest manner, with its social and political condition. At the very beginning of history, and even as far beyond as archæological science can penetrate, the earth is all peopled, more or less thickly, with a seemingly heterogeneous mass of clans and tribes and nations. But not even the most heterodox naturalist who holds to a variety of origins for the human race believes these all to have sprung out of the ground, as it were, where they stand: they come from the multiplication and dispersion of a certain limited number of primitive families, if not, as many think, from that of a single family. So with language: at the first attainable period of our knowledge of it, whether by actual record or by the inferences of the comparative student, it is in a state of almost endless subdivision; and yet every sound linguist holds, and knows that he has the most satisfactory reasons for holding, that this apparent confusion is a result of the extension and divarication of a certain limited number of primitive dialects—whether of a single one, is a question which we shall have later to consider our right to determine. At the earliest historical period, too, the darkness of barbarism covers the earth in general; the centres of culture are but two or three, and their light spreads but a very little way, and is even in constant danger of being extinguished by the greatly superior brute force of the uncultivated masses around. Hence the divaricating forces in linguistic growth are also in the ascendant; dialects go on multiplying, by the action of the same causes that had already produced them. But wherever civilization is at work, an opposite influence, in linguistic as in political affairs, is powerfully operating. Out of the congeries of jarring tribes are growing great nations; out of the Babel of discordant dialects are growing languages of wider and constantly extending unity. The two kinds of change go hand in hand, simply because the one of them is dependent on the other: nothing can make wide unity of speech except extended community; nothing but civilization can make extended community. As, through the ages of recorded history, the power as well as the degree of civilization has been constantly growing, till now it is the predominant force, and the uncivilized races subsist only by the toleration of the civilized—if even that; so, by external forces, every act and influence of which is clearly definable, the cultivated languages have been and are extending their sway, crowding out of existence the *patois* which had grown up under the old order of things, gaining such advantage that men are beginning to dream of a time when one language may be spoken all over the earth. And, though the dream may be Utopian, there is not an element of the theoretically impossible in it; only a certain condition of external circumstances is needed to render it inevitable.

It is possible so to misunderstand these facts in the wide history of human speech as to believe that language actually began in a condition of infinite dialectic division, and has been from the outset tending toward concentration and final unity. But that is possible only by a total failure to comprehend the forces that are at work in the growth of language, and the modes of their interaction. Tell the ethnologist that the beginnings of the human race were an indefinite number of unconnected individuals, who first coalesced into families, and these into clans and tribes, and these into confederacies, whence came nations, and whence may yet come, by the same natural tendency to unity out of diversity, a single homogeneous race all over the earth—and he will hardly pay the theory the compliment even of laughing at it. And the corresponding linguistic view is really just as absurd; only, from the greater obscurity or unfamiliarity of the conditions involved, not so palpably absurd, and therefore not so ludicrous.

Before closing this chapter, we must notice for a moment the meaning of the terms *language* and *dialect*, in their relation to one another. They are only two names for the same thing, as looked at from different points of view. Any body of expressions used by a community, however limited and humble, for the purposes of communication and as the instrument of thought, is a language; no one would think of crediting its speakers with the gift of dialect but not of language. On the other hand, there is no tongue in the world to which we should not with perfect freedom and perfect propriety apply the name of dialect, when considering it as one of a body of related forms of speech. The science of language has democratized our views on such points as these; it has taught us that one man's speech is just as much a language as another man's; that even the most cultivated tongue that exists is only the dialect of a certain class in a certain locality—both class and locality limited, though the limits may be wide ones. The written English is one of the forms of English, used by the educated class for certain purposes, having dialectic characters by which it is distinguished from the colloquial speech of the same class, and yet more from the speech of other classes or sections of the English-speaking community—and each one of these is as valuable to the comparative student of language as their alleged superior. But English and Dutch and German and Swedish, and so on, are the dialects of Germanic speech; and the same, along with French and Irish and Bohemian, and the rest, are the dialects of the wider family whose limits we have drawn above. This is the scientific use of the terms; in the looseness of popular parlance, an attempt is made at the distinction of degrees of dignity and importance by means of the same words, as when the literary language of a community is alone allowed the name of language, and the rest are styled dialects. For ordinary purposes the usage is convenient enough; but it has no acceptableness on other grounds; it forms no part of linguistic science.

CHAPTER X.

INDO-EUROPEAN LANGUAGE.

Genetic classification. Indo-European family; its names; its branches and their earliest records: Germanic, Slavo-Lettic, Celtic, Italic, Greek, Iranian, and Indian; doubtful members. Importance of this family; value of its study to the science of language. Time and place of original community impossible to determine. Scientific method of studying its structural history; form-making by composition and integration; sufficiency of the principle. Resulting doctrine of original radical monosyllabism; Indo-European roots. Development of forms: structure of verb, of noun; pronouns; adverbs and particles; interjections, their analogy with roots. Question of order of development, and time occupied. Synthetic and analytic structure.

HAVING examined, with all the fullness which the space at our command allows, the foundation on which a genetic classification of the languages of the world reposes, we are ready to undertake a brief view of that classification, as established by the researches of linguistic scholars. We have seen that correspondence in the material of different languages, if existing in measure and kind beyond what can be accounted for as the result of accident or of borrowing, is explainable only as due to the separate tradition of an originally common tongue, a tradition which preserved a part of the original usages, while it modified or discarded other parts, or introduced what was new, to such an extent as to obscure, and perhaps even to hide, the evidences of former connection. As an example, we glanced at an outline of the great family of related tongues to which our own belongs, and noticed a limited but sufficient specimen of the evidence on which is founded the general belief in its unity as a family. We have now to go on and lay down more definitely the constitution of this family, and to sketch its structure and its structural history.

It is called, in the first place, by a variety of names, no one of which has fully established itself in general use. We will employ "Indo-European," as having on the whole the best claim; it was deliberately adopted by Bopp, the great expounder of the relations of the family, and is as widely used as any of the others. Most of Bopp's countrymen now prefer "Indo-Germanic," for no other assignable reason than that it contains the foreign appellation of their own particular branch, as given by their conquerors and teachers, the Romans. Others, rejecting both these titles as cumbrously long, say instead "Aryan," which also has a wide and perhaps a growing currency; the chief objection is, that it properly belongs only to the Asiatic division, composed of the Iranian and Indian branches, and is still needed and widely used to designate that division. "Sanskritic," from the oldest and in some respects the leading language of the family, and "Japhetic," from the son of Noah to whom are attributed as descendants in the Genesis some of the people speaking its various dialects, are terms of limited and now obsolescent employment.

The Indo-European family, then, is composed of seven great branches: the Indian, the Iranian or Per sian, the Greek, the Italic, the Celtic, the Slavonic or Slavo-Lettic, and the Germanic or Teutonic.

Taking these up in their inverse order, we have first the Germanic branch, in the four principal divisions already noted: 1. The Mœso-Gothic, or dialect of the Goths of Mœsia, preserved only in parts of a Bible-version made by their bishop Ulfilas in the fourth century of our era, being long ago extinct as a spoken language. 2. The Low-German languages, still spoken in the north of Germany, from Holstein to Flanders, and across in the neighboring England, and including two important cultivated tongues, the Netherlandish and the English. English literary monuments go back to the seventh century, Netherlandish to the thirteenth; and there is an "Old-Saxon" poem, the *Heliand*, or 'Savior,' from the ninth, and Frisian literature from the fourteenth. 3. The High-German body of dialects, represented at the present day by only a single literary language, the so-called German, of which the literature begins with the Reformation, in the sixteenth century; back of this, the New High-German period, lie a Middle and an Old High-German period, with their literatures in various somewhat discordant dialects, reaching back into the eighth century. 4. The Scandinavian division, written in the forms of Danish, Swedish, Norwegian, and Icelandic. The Icelandic monuments go back to the twelfth and thirteenth centuries, and are in point of style and content older than anything in High or Low German: the Edda is the purest and most abundant source of knowledge for primitive Germanic conditions. The Icelandic is also, especially in its phonetic state, the most antique of living Germanic dialects. Besides these literary remains, there are brief Runic inscriptions, generally of but a word or two, going back, it is believed, even to the third or second century.

The Slavonic branch has always lain in close proximity to the Germanic, on the east; it has been the last of all to gain historical prominence. Its eastern division includes the Russian, Bulgarian, Servian and Croatian, and Slovenian. The Bulgarian has the oldest records; its version of the Bible, made in the ninth century, in the same region where the Gothic version had been made five centuries earlier, has become the accepted version, and its dialect the church language, throughout the Slavonic division of the Greek church. The Russian is by far the most important language of the whole branch; it has remains from the eleventh century; some of the southern dialects present specimens from a yet remoter date. To the western division belong the Polish, the Bohemian, of which the Moravian and Slovakian are closely kindred dialects, the Sorbian, and the Polabian. There is nothing in Polish earlier than the fourteenth century; Bohemian records are believed to go back to the tenth.

This branch is often called the Slavo-Lettic, because it is made to include another sub-branch, the Lettic or Lithuanic, which, though considerably further removed from the Slavonic than any of these from the rest, is yet too nearly related to rank as a separate branch. It is composed of three main dialects: the Old-Prussian, extinct during the past two centuries, the Lithuanian, and the Livonian or Lettish; all clustered about the great bend of the Baltic. The Lithuanian is the most important and the oldest, having records from the middle of the sixteenth century. It exhibits in some respects a remarkable conservation of ancient material and form.

The Celtic branch is one which from the beginning of history has been shrinking in extent, till it now occupies only the remotest western edges of the immense region of western and central Europe which it formerly possessed. Not enough is known of the ancient Celtic dialects of northern Italy, of Gaul, of Spain, to show what was their place in the sub-classification of the branch. The preserved dialects compose two groups, usually called the Cymric and Gadhelic. The Cymric includes the Welsh, with "glosses" from the ninth century or thereabouts, and a literature from the twelfth, but of which part of the substance is probably older, even up to the sixth; the Cornish, which became extinct as a vernacular about the end of the last century, leaving a considerable literature nearly as old as the Welsh; and the Armorican of Brittany, so nearly allied to the Cornish that it is believed to belong to fugitives from that part of England; its earliest records are of the fourteenth century. The Gadhelic group includes the Irish, which has monuments going back to the end of the eighth century, the Scotch Gaelic, of which the earliest remains are attributed to the sixteenth, and the insignificant dialect of the Isle of Man.

The Italic branch is represented among living languages only by the Romanic dialects, so called as being all descended from the dialect of Rome, the Latin. We have already noticed some particulars affecting their history and their importance. They all rose at not far from the same period—namely, the eleventh to the thirteenth centuries—out of the condition of local *patois*, products of the corruption of the popular speech while the Latin continued the language of the learned. Fragments of French are oldest, coming from the tenth century; its literature begins one or two centuries later;

the earliest Italian, Spanish, Portuguese, are from the twelfth, or hardly earlier. These four are the conspicuous modern members of the group. But there was also, in the eleventh to the fourteenth centuries, a rich literature of the chief dialect of southern France, the Provençal, which, except for a recent sporadic effort or two, has been ever since unused as a cultivated tongue. There exists, too, in the northern provinces of Turkey, in Wallachia and Moldavia, a broad region of less cultivated Romanic speech, witness to the spread of Roman supremacy eastward: it is destitute of a proper literature. Moreover, certain dialects of southern Switzerland are enough unlike Italian to be ordinarily ranked as an independent tongue, under the name of Rhæto-Romanic, or Rumansh, or Ladine.

The ancient members of the Italic branch, coördinate with the Latin, were long ago crowded out of existence; but a few remains of them are still left, especially of the Umbrian, north from Rome beyond the Apennines, and of the Oscan of southern Italy. The Latin itself, in its oldest monuments, reaches hardly three centuries beyond the Christian era, appearing there in a form which seems very strange, and is hardly intelligible, to those who have learned only the cultivated dialect of the last century B. C.

The Greek branch attains a much greater age, those masterpieces of human genius, the poems of Homer, being nearly or quite a thousand years older than our era. From about 300 B. C., all Greek is written in the Attic or Athenian dialect, as all modern German literature in the New High-German; but before that time, as in the Old High-German period, each author used more or less distinctly his own local dialect; and in this way, as well as, more widely but less abundantly, by inscriptions and the like, we have a tolerably full representation of the local varieties into which the Greek had divided in prehistoric times. There is, of course, a similar variety of dialects now; but only one is written, and it is called Modern Greek, or Romaic; it is less altered from the classic Greek than is the Italian from the Latin. Notwithstanding the wide sway of Greek civilization, the spread of Greek empire under Alexander and his successors, and the unexcelled character of the language, the latter has had a limited and inconspicuous career as compared with the Latin: out of Greece itself, it is spoken only on the islands and shores of the Ægean, and along the northern and southern edges of Asia Minor.

The next branch is the Persian, or properly Iranian, since Persia is only one among the many provinces constituting the territory of Iran (*Airyana*, the home of the western Aryans). It has two ancient representatives: the Old Persian, or Achæmenidan Persian, of Darius and his successors; and the language of the Avesta, the so-called Zend, or Avestan, or Old Bactrian. The former, of determinate date (five centuries B. C.), is read in the cuneiform inscriptions, recently deciphered; of the other, the date is unknown; it may be older or younger. The Avesta is the Bible of the Zoroastrian faith, of which the date and place of origin are obscure; it is believed to reach beyond 1000 B. C.; and if parts of the record are, as they claim to be, from Zoroaster himself, they have this antiquity. The modern votaries of the religion, and the keepers of its sacred books, are the Parsis of western India, fugitives from Mohammedan persecution in their native land. With the Avesta, they have preserved a version of it in the Huzvâresh or Pehlevî, of the time of the Sassanids, a dialect of poculiar and problematical character. The Modern Persian literature, abundant and rich, begins from about A. D. 1000, after the country had been ground over in the Mohammedan mill.

These are the languages composing the main body of Iranian speech. The Kurdish is only a strongly-marked dialect of Persian; and nearly the same thing may be said of the Beluchi, the leading language of Beluchistan. The Ossetic, in a little district of the Caucasus, is plainly, but more distantly, related. The Afghan, or Pushto, near the passes that lead from Iran into India, is of Iranian kindred. Finally, the Armenian, of which the considerable literature goes back to the fifth century, is generally, though not without recent question by certain authorities, regarded as Iranian in fundamental type.

The branch of Indo-European language in India does not cover the whole of that vast territory; the Dravidian race, which was doubtless crowded out by the intrusive Aryans in the north, still occupies the main central part of the southern peninsula, the Dekhan. The earliest of Indo-European tongues is the Sanskrit, especially its earlier or Vedic dialect, the dialect of the religious hymns, which, with auxiliary literature of somewhat later date, became the Bible of the Hindus, the so-called Veda. At the period of the oldest hymns, the Sanskrit-speaking peoples appear to have been not yet in possession of the great Ganges basin, but nearly or quite confined, rather, to the valleys of the Indus and its branches, in the northwestern corner, the region bordering nearest on Iran. The date is incapable of being determined with any exactness; probably it was nearly or quite 2000 B. C. The classical Sanskrit is a dialect which, at a later period, after the full possession of Hindustan and the development of Brahmanism out of the simpler and more primitive religion and polity of Vedic times, became established as the literary language of the whole country, and has ever since maintained that character, being still learned for writing and speaking in the native schools of the Brahmanic priesthood. From the fact that inscriptions in a later form of Indian language are found dating from the third century B. C., it is inferred that the Sanskrit must at least as early as that have ceased to be a vernacular tongue. The next stage of Indian language, to which the inscriptions just referred to belong, is called the Prakritic. One Prakrit dialect, the Pali, became in its turn the sacred language of southeastern Buddhism, and is still taught and learned as such in Ceylon and Farther India; the others are represented partly in the Sanskrit dramas, as the unlearned speech of the lower orders of characters, and partly by a limited literature of their own. Finally, there are the modern dialects of India, numerous and various, but rudely classifiable under the three comprehensive names of Hindî, Mahrattî, and Bengâlî, having literatures of more recent origin. The so-called Hindustânî, or Urdu, is Hindî with a great infusion of Arabic and Persian words, introduced by Mohammedan influence.

The boundaries of this great family are more distinctly drawn than those of any other. But they are not absolute or immovable. There are one or two isolated tongues in Europe which may yet be pronounced Indo-European. Thus, the Skipetar, or language of the Albanians, on that part of the west coast of European Turkey which lies close opposite the heel of Italy: it is believed to be the representative of the ancient Illyrian, and more probably Indo-European than anything else. And the Etruscan, the obscure and much-discussed tongue of that peculiar people with whose relations to the early Romans, until finally conquered and assimilated by Rome, every school-boy is familiar, after being assigned to almost every distant race on earth, has recently (1874) even been declared Indo-European and Italican by scholars of high rank and authority; their opinion, however, is generally rejected. It is evident enough that in theory such cases of doubtful classification are to be expected. There is no limit to the degree to which a language may, by special disturbing causes, become altered in its material and structure, even to the effectual disguise of its original relationships.

There are many reasons why the Indo-European family is of predominant importance among the languages of the world; why it has thus far received a very large share of the attention of linguistic scholars, and must always continue to receive, even if not the same share as hitherto, yet a larger than any other family. The least of these reasons is that it is our own family; though that is, after all, no illegitimate plea in enhancement of the interest with which it is invested for us. Of more importance is the circumstance that it belongs to the race which has long been the leading one in the history of the world, and which at the present day, as for some time past, has not even a rival. The grand and highly-developed institutions of great nations are those which most demand and best repay study. The tongues and the history of the Greeks and Romans are that part of antiquity which will continue to form, even as it constitutes at present, a leading subject in all liberal education. And the whole history of Indo-European language will have its share by reflection in this educational value, because it casts light on the study of Greek and Latin, of the Romanic languages, of the Germanic languages, of the Slavonic languages, on all that is nearest and dearest to those nations which are pursuing the study.

But there are other and more imperative reasons why the study of Indo-European language has been the training-ground of the science of language; why the two have almost grown up together, and in the minds of some have even perhaps been confused and identified with one another. The student has at best a most imperfect and fragmentary record before him. If the whole history of human speech were represented by a great sheet of paper, the part of it to be marked as known, or as accessible to direct knowledge, would be almost ludicrously small. For most human races, only the present spoken dialects lie within reach; then a few lines of light run back into the past to various distances toward the Christian era; a much smaller number beyond that point; four or five, probably, into the second thousand years before Christ; and only one, the Egyptian, to a time considerably remoter yet. And how much of language-history, as of human history in every department, may lie behind even that point, we are only recently beginning to realize. Such being the condition of the whole field, how was a fruitful beginning to be made except just as it has been made—namely, by taking up that body of historically-related facts which was widest in its range, deepest and most abundant in its penetration of the past, and most advanced in its development out of original conditions? By grasping this and reducing it to manageable order, discovering the general hidden under the particular, tracing tendencies and laws, the student might hope to acquire the ability to deal with other like bodies of facts, of narrower range and offering less abundant facilities. The character of preëminence in this line belongs to the Indo-European, beyond dispute and beyond comparison: where we have equal or greater penetration of the past, as in Egyptian, Chinese, and the Semitic tongues, there is either (as in the two former) a peculiar jejuneness of development, or at any rate (as in the last) a variety and wealth which is greatly inferior. To blame philologists, therefore, for their devotion hitherto to Indo-European study is in the highest degree unreasonable; one might as properly blame historians for their devotion to the study of European civilization and of its sources in the past. To cast reproach upon them, moreover, for their attention to the past, to the partially understood records of extinct and almost forgotten tongues, and to declare that the true and fruitful field for linguistic research is the living and spoken dialects of the present day, is not less narrow and erroneous. It overlooks the character of linguistics as a historical science; it forgets that the explanation of the present is by the past, and that the record of by-gone conditions casts on existing conditions a light that nothing else could yield. More precisely, it exaggerates and pushes forward unduly the equally true fact that the comprehension of the past is complete only by the help of the present. It would be most unfortunate to check the zeal of those who are submitting present language to the most rigorous investigation, especially on its phonetic side, or to cast the slightest reflection on the deep and far-reaching value of their work; there is hardly another more promising direction of linguistic inquiry: only they, on their side, should refrain from impliedly contemning their predecessors, and should realize that they are striking in now when the way is prepared for making their labors fruitful. So the minute study of the customs, institutions, beliefs, and myths of rude peoples now existing was, not long ago, comparatively a mere matter of curiosity; it gains its most valuable bearing from the study of civilization in its historical development. It was of little use to watch and study *nebulæ* until geology and astronomy together had learned so much about the constitution and history of our solar system as to have found out how to interpret the facts observed.

So also, in the claims here put forth as to the priority and preëminence of the Indo-European tongues as a subject of linguistic study, there is nothing which must be in the slightest degree understood as depreciating the importance of the study of other families, even its indispensability to the comprehension of Indo-European language itself. The science of language is what its name implies, a study of all human speech, of every existing and recorded dialect, without rejection of any, for obscurity, for remoteness, for lowness of development. The time has come when questions are rising in abundance in the history of Indo-European speech which cannot possibly be answered until the languages of lower organization are more thoroughly understood. And it must be distinctly laid down as a fundamental principle in linguistics, that no fact in human expression is fully estimated, until it is seen in the light of related facts all through the domain of universal expression. Only, it is not possible, in philology any more than in other branches of study, to help letting facts arrange themselves along certain leading lines, and converge their light where light is most desired.

We have reached, as was seen above, the certain conclusion that all the known Indo-European languages are descended from a single dialect, which must have been spoken at some time in the past by a single limited community, by the spread and emigration of which—not, certainly, without incorporating also bodies of other races than that to which itself belonged by origin—it has reached its present wide distribution: even as a similar process, in historical times, has brought its two leading modern branches to fill the New World, a region almost vaster than that which it occupies in the Old. Of course, it would be a matter of the highest interest to determine the place and period of this important community, were there any means of doing so; but that is not the case, at least at present. As for the time, the less said about that the better, in this transitional period of opinion as to the age of man on the earth. The question whether the first man was born only 6,000 years ago, or 12,000, or 100,000, or 1,000,000, as the new schools of anthropology are beginning to claim, is one of which the decision must exercise a controlling influence on that which we have here in view. As for the testimony of language itself, there is none, of any authority; the philologists will doubtless claim that they do not see how to compress the growth of Indo-European language into the shortest of the periods named, but they have not yet found a rule with which to measure the time they actually need. To give even a conjecture at present would be foolish.

Nor is the place perceptibly easier to determine. Man has ever been a migratory animal, and if he has had a million years, or a tenth part of the number, to wander in, it must be next to impossible to fix the starting-point of any division of the race. How little could be inferred as to the history of movement of the Celts from their present distribution! If some barbarous race had conquered and exterminated or absorbed the Germans of the continent, what erroneous conclusions might not be drawn from their presence only in Scandinavia and Iceland! And there are probabilities of just as baffling occurrences in the history of the Indo-Europeans. Men have long, and on well-known grounds, been accustomed to look upon the southwestern part of Asia as the cradle of the human race; and, mainly under the influence of this opinion, so long rooted that it sways the minds even of those who reject the authority of the testimony on which it is founded, it is by many asserted with great confidence that the Hindu-Kush mountain-region, or that Bactria, is the Indo-European cradle: the only bit of tangible evidence which they are able to allege being that that is the region where the Iranians and Indians separated, and that the Iranian and Indian dialects are the most primitive of the family. But to plead this is equivalent to maintaining that slowness or rapidity of change in language is dependent on stability or change of place in the speaking community: which is so grossly wrong that it needs no refutation. In fact, the condition of these languages is reconcilable with any possible theory as to the original site of the family. As to the interconnections of the different branches with one another, the best scholars have for some years past been settling down upon the opinion that the separation of the five European branches from one another must have been later than their common separation from the two Asiatic branches, which latter then continued to exist as one community almost down to the historical period. Upon this last point, there is unanimity of opinion; the oldest forms of Persian and Indian speech are as closely like one another as, for instance, the more dissimilar of the Germanic dialects; the two branches are ranked together under the common name of "Aryan;" and the

Indian branch is thought to have parted from the common home in northeastern Iran not very much earlier than 2000 B. C. Within the European grand division, the Germanic and Slavonic are by nearly all regarded as specially related; opinions are more nearly divided as to whether the Celtic is a wholly independent branch, or closely akin with the Italican. In all this there is evidently nothing which should point our eyes definitely toward an original home. The separation of Aryan from European *may* just as well be due to a spread and migration of the former into Asia as of the latter into Europe: and localities in Europe as well as in Asia have actually been pitched upon by eminent scholars. But it is useless to pretend to come to a definite conclusion where the data are so indefinite. Evidences of real weight bearing on the question may possibly yet be found; but certainly none such have been hitherto brought to light.

Owing to the exceptional abundance of the material for study of the history of Indo-European speech, and the amount of study which has been devoted to it, it is far better understood than is the history of any other division of human language. Partly, therefore, because of the high intrinsic interest of the subject, and partly as a standard of reference in the treatment of the structural growth of other languages, we have to follow out in a little detail, though still with all possible brevity, the ascertained history of the common foundation of the Indo-European languages.

But we have first to consider the question—if, indeed, it can be called a question—as to how the prehistorical periods of language are to be investigated. Not even the Indo-European has more than a small part of its history illustrated by contemporary documents: how are we to learn anything beyond the point where the records fail us? The answer, it is believed, is a plain and a confident one: we have to study the forces at work under our observation, and the methods of their working; and we have to carry them back into the past by careful analogical reasoning, inferring from similar effects to similar causes, just as far as the process can be made to work legitimately, never assuming new forces and modes of action except where the old ones are absolutely incapable of furnishing the explanation we are seeking—and, even then, only under the most careful restrictions. This is the familiar method of the modern inductive sciences; and its applicability to the science of language also is beyond all reasonable doubt. The parallel between linguistics and geology, the most historical of the physical sciences, is here closest and most instructive; and it has often been resorted to for illustration. The geologist infers the mode of formation of ancient sandstones and conglomerates from that of modern sandbanks and gravel and pebble-beds; and so on, through the whole series of strata, sedimentary and eruptive; he accounts for the occurrence of fossils by the engulfing or burying of extant species. And the true geologic method has been so thoroughly worked out, and is so strictly applied, that the scientific man who abandons it, and resorts to arbitrary hypotheses, even to account for facts which for the time seem unexplainable by ordinary means, is at once put down as "unscientific," and bidden to wait until the growth of knowledge shall bring around the possibility of solving his problem, if it shall finally be found soluble, in an admissible way.

Of course, the circumstances and conditions of action of the same forces may differ greatly. The admission of the unity of geologic history by no means implies that the earth has always worn the same aspect as at present; it is even a prevailing opinion among geologists that the whole solar system was once a nebulous mass of whirling vapor; but this result is reached by the inductive method. The essential unity of linguistic history, in all its phases and stages, must be made the cardinal principle of the study of language, if this is to bear a scientific character. To assume outright, as some do, either explicitly or impliedly, that ancient modes of language-making were and must have been different from modern, and that the former are not to be judged by the latter, would, if linguistic science were as matured and well-established a branch of study as geology, be enough to exclude the assumer from the ranks of scientific linguists. Here, again, the difference of conditions, of the grade of historic development, has to be fully allowed for; and the student may arrive at the recognition of a primitive condition of language to which the present is as unlike as a civilized country, teeming with the public and private works of its inhabitants, is unlike the wilderness through which the savage roams; or even as the existing cosmos is unlike the nebulous chaos; yet the present must be regarded as the consequence of a gradual accumulation of results in one unbroken line of action. We must beware, too, of claiming that we understand the present forces and their action in all points so thoroughly that we can judge the past by them completely, or even that processes which would now strike us as anomalous may not come hereafter to appear regular; but we are authorized to refuse to admit them until a clear case shall be made out in their favor; they are never to be granted as postulates.

Now we have seen above, in the chapters devoted to

detailed examination of the changes of language, that the general effort of language-making is toward the provision of expression, for the needs of communication and the uses of thought, by such means as lie most availably at hand; that a prominent part of the movement is the reduction of coarser and more physical, material, sensible designations to finer and more formal uses, both by constant shifts of meaning, by the attenuation of words once of full material meaning to the value of form-words, and by the conversion of words formerly independent into formative elements, suffixes and prefixes, signs of modified meaning or of relation attached to and forming part of other words. In the earliest traceable condition of our language, the use of formative elements was the prevailing means of denoting relations, so much so as to constitute the distinctive characteristic of the common Indo-European language; and to explain this feature is to explain Indo-European growth.

It was in the simple practice of composition that we found (p. 120 *seq.*) the germ of synthetic form-making; and we noticed a number of real forms as made by this means, with the help of only those tendencies which are universally prevalent in human speech. The adverbial endings *ly* and (French) *ment*, the tense-signs *d* and (French) *ai*, the derivative suffixes *less* and *dom*, and so on, are, in all respects, precisely as true and as good formative elements as anything in Indo-European speech; it is only the historical student, not the speaker, who knows them as different from the *s* of *loves* and the *th* of *truth*, which go back for their origin to a period greatly remote in comparison. And all form-making of which we know anything in the historical period is of this same kind, by external accretion; all the cases of an apparently different character (we exemplified them by *man* and *men*, *rēad* and *rĕad*, *sing* and *sang*) being demonstrably inorganic, accidental, results of the putting to use of a difference of secondary value, wrought out by phonetic change from forms originally made by concretion.

This being so, we are required by the principles of inductive investigation to endeavor to make this sole recognizable method of formation found active in historical times explain the growth of Indo-European language in the ancient times. If it is sufficient, we are not only not called upon, but actually forbidden, to bring in any other method to aid; or, at any rate, nothing but the most direct and cogent evidence can have the right to compel our admission of any other. And such evidence is by no means to be found in our simple inability to trace any given element or elements, or even a great many such, to the independent words out of which they grew, and to describe the series of changes of form and meaning which converted the one into the other. The linguistic record is too hopelessly fragmentary for that. As every period in the changeful life of the earth denudes or covers up or dislocates a part of the record of geological succession, so the changes of every age contribute to break the continuity of linguistic succession, in every part—in the transfers of meaning, in the formation of words, in the making of means of derivation. While there is so much in the peculiar and recent formations of even the Germanic and Romanic languages that baffles the inquirer and seems to defy explanation, it would be most unreasonable to expect that words and forms of vastly more ancient growth will be completely and in all parts amenable to analysis. If we can find any trustworthy evidences of the operation of the method of combination in the earliest synthetic forms, we have the right to assume it, in default of proof to the contrary, to have been the sole operative principle, then as well as later.

And it is claimed by the leading school of comparative philology that the principle in question is actually sufficient to account for the whole structure of Indo-European language; that the latter presents no forms which demand the admission of any other genesis than by addition of element to element; that wherever, by our analytical processes, we succeed in detaching from a word a subordinate part, indicating some modification or relation of a radical idea, there we are to recognize the trace of a formerly independent word, which has lost its independence and become an affix, by the same processes which have made *love-did* into *loved*, *true-like* into *truly*, *habere habeo* into *aurai*, *verâ mente* into *vraiment*, and so on.

But in this doctrine is involved another very important one: that, namely, of a primitive body of monosyllabic roots as the historical beginnings of Indo-European speech-development. Its necessity as a corollary from the former is clear enough: if all formative elements come by accretion and integration, then only that can have been original which is left when these have been stripped off, to the very last one: and what is left is the root; and it is, in our family of language, a monosyllable. This is the doctrine actually held by most students of language; the dissidents are few, and have nothing to say, in defense of their unbelief, except what is easily refuted as misapprehension or want of logical consistency. Though at first sight repellent to some, it involves nothing that has a right to trouble the scientific inquirer, any more than the acceptance of a primitive state of rudeness with reference to the arts of life or the condition of knowledge. And as there are races now living on the earth which have never gained command of more than the simplest tools, modes of dress and shelter, and the like, so (as we shall see more particularly in the twelfth chapter) there are those which have never developed their language out of this radical stage. If we see in later times conjugational and declensional inflections formed and brought into use, there can be no invincible obstacle in the way of our reasoning back to a time when such things did not exist; if we see parts of speech like prepositions, conjunctions, and articles coming into being, we may regard as possible a period when the first distinction of parts of speech was made. Whether such possibilities were ever realities, is a matter to be determined by sufficient scientific evidence.

It is to be noticed that this doctrine does not commit us to the recognition of any actually traceable list of roots as being the beginnings of development in our family. If it shall be shown hereafter—as it is already shown, or at least made probable, with regard to some—that any of the elements now generally regarded as roots are of composite structure, containing a formative element fused with a root (as in our *count*, *cost*, *preach*, etc., noticed above, p. 55), this will only push the name and quality of roots one step further back. The firm foundation of the theory of roots lies in its logical necessity as an inference from the doctrine of the historical growth of grammatical apparatus. It is to be noticed further that the question of roots as the historical beginnings of language is quite distinct from that of the origin of language, which we do not take up until later (fourteenth chapter): the one is exclusively linguistic, the other partly anthropological.

The Indo-European roots, then, are the elements of speech which existed prior to the whole development of the means of grammatical distinction, before the growth of inflection, before the separation of the parts of speech. They indicated each some conception in entire indefiniteness as concerns its relations, neither viewed as the concrete name of an object, nor as attribute only, nor as predicate; but as equally ready to turn to the purpose of any of the three. This is a state of things which we, with our habits of speech and thought, find it very hard to realize, but which is brought comparatively within reach of our apprehension by making acquaintance with existing tongues of a low grade of development. The roots, however, are not all of one homogeneous class; there is a little body of so-called pronominal or demonstrative roots which are distinguished from the rest as signifying position or direction with reference to the speaker, rather than any more concrete quality. They are very few, and of the simplest phonetic form: a vowel only, or a consonant with following vowel. That they are ultimately distinct from the roots of the other class, and were not rather developed out of these by attenuation of meaning, as form-words in the later stages of language-history, many students of language are very loath to believe, and not without reason; but the distinction is one which must, it seems, at any rate be admitted as antecedent to the whole growth of Indo-European forms; nor have the attempts to identify the one class with the other been as yet at all successful. The point is one of which the complete solution will probably be possible only when the languages of lower order shall have come to be more widely and deeply understood; perhaps the early devel opment of such a class of form-words was the first sign of that linguistic aptitude which has always distinguished this family, and prepared the way for its after-evolution. The other class, commonly called verbal or predicative roots, were significant in general of such acts and qualities as are apprehensible by the senses, and were much more numerous, counting by hundreds: examples are *stâ* (Greek *ἵστημι*, Lat. *stare*, our '*stand*,' etc.), *dâ*, 'give' (*δίδωμι*, *dare*), *par*, 'pass' (*περάω*, *ex-per-ior*, *fahren*, *fare*, etc.), *wid*, 'see' (*οἶδα*, *video*, *weiss*, *wot*, etc.), and so on.

An early (perhaps the first) and most important act in the history of linguistic development out of these rather scanty beginnings was that whereby a separation was made between noun (substantive and adjective) and verb. The essence of a verb is that it predicates or asserts; and the establishment of a distinct form by which predication shall be signified has by no means been reached in all languages. There are many tongues which do not formally distinguish *giving* (adjective or substantive) and *gift* from *gives*: they put the subject and predicate side by side, as 'he giver,' 'he good,' and leave the mind to supply the lacking copula. The making of a verb is nothing more than the establishment of certain combinations of elements in an exclusively predicative use, the supplying of a copula in connection with them and not with others. This was accomplished by adding certain pronominal elements to the verbal element: *dâ-mi*, *dâ-si*, *dâ-ti*; the former having already gained at least a quasi-personal significance, as designating that which is nearer or remoter. Precisely how we shall explain *dâ-mi*, for instance—whether as meaning more 'give I,' or 'giving (adj.) I,' or 'giving (subst.) mine,' or 'giving here'—seems a matter not worth contending about; since, at the period in question, noun and adjective and verb were equally present in the one element, and pronoun and adverb in the other; and there was as yet no distinction of 'I' and 'mine.' The combinations adduced above gave three verbal persons; they were made exclusively singular in number by the addition of a plural and a dual, most often explained (though very doubtfully) as formed by a composition of pronominal elements in the ending: *masi*, for example, being *ma-si* 'I [and] you,' i. e. 'we.' The forms thus made contained no implication of time, were not properly a "tense;" but a past was by-and-by made by prefixing an adverbial element, the "augment" of the Greek, pointing to a 'then' as adjunct of the action: *a-dâ-mi*, 'then give I,' i. e. 'I gave;' and the form, by reason of the accented addition at the beginning, was shortened at the end, to *ádâm* (Skt. *ádâm*, Gr. ἔδων)—whence the distinction between secondary and primary endings, conspicuous in some of the languages of the family. But yet another tense, of completed action, was made by reduplication or repetition of the root: *dâ-dâ-mi*, 'give-give I,' i. e. 'I have given' (the reduplication being then variously abbreviated); and this in Latin and Germanic has become the general preterit, the augment-tense having been lost; our *sang*, *held*, etc., are its descendants. As handed down to us, however, few of the "present" tenses of Indo-European verbs are of the simple formation above illustrated; more usually, the root appears in some way extended, either by another reduplication (Skt. *dadâmi*, Gr. δίδωμι), or by the addition of sundry formative elements (Lat. *cer-no*, *cre-sco*, Gr. δάμ-νη-μι, δείκ-νυ-μι, etc., etc.): all of them supposed to have been at first means employed for denoting the continuousness of an action, like our *am giving*, though they later lost their restriction to this sense. In some verbs, along with the new present and its continuous preterit or proper "imperfect," the preterit and moods of the simpler root were retained in use, with a more undefined past meaning, becoming the Greek (and Sanskrit) "second aorist" (as *ἔδων, ádâm*, beside imperfect *ἐδίδων, ádadâm*). For other verbs, a tense of like value was formed by help of a sibilant, *s*, of doubtful origin, making what is called in Greek the first aorist. Besides these, a future, also containing the same sibilant sign, was made before the separation of the branches, and is best retained in Greek and Sanskrit; the full form of its suffix is *sya:* Sanskrit *dâ-syâ-mi*, Greek *δώσω* (or older *δωσιω*), 'I will give.' There were some imperative persons, with no special mood-sign, but with peculiar endings. Of other moods, there were a subjunctive and an optative, marked by insertions between root and ending, of somewhat doubtful character. Then, finally, there was a reflexive or "middle" voice for all these various forms, with its characteristic in the personal endings themselves: an extension of them, prevailingly (but hardly successfully) explained as a repetition, once with subjective, once with objective.

This appears to have been the entire fabric of the Indo-European verb prior to the separation of the branches. It has been variously preserved, contracted, expanded, in the later history of the branches. The Sanskrit has preserved most faithfully the outward forms; the Greek has best retained the original uses, and has added most, so that its verb is far the richest in the family. The Latin lost much, but added a great variety of modern formations. The Germanic lost all save present and perfect, with their optative (called by us subjunctive), and with the imperative; apart from the preterit with *did*, often already referred to, its new additions have been made in the way of analytic combination. To follow out further the details of the verb-history, interesting as the task would be, would take us too long.

The genesis of the noun as a part of speech, in its two forms, substantive and adjective, was implied in that of the verb: when one set of forms became distinctly verb, the rest were left as noun. And everything in Indo-European speech from predicative roots is by origin either verb or noun, a form either of conjugation or of declension. On the other hand, the further we go back, the less are substantive and adjective distinguished from one another; they are made by the same suffixes, they share the same inflection: things, in fact, are named from their qualities; and whether the quality-denoting word shall be used attributively or appellatively is at the outset a matter of comparative indifference; though the two come finally to be distinct enough. The characteristic of the noun is the case-ending, as that of the verb is the personal ending; case and number are to the noun what person and number are to the verb, fitting it to enter into definite relations in the sentence. The Indo-European cases are seven, besides the vocative, which is not a case in the same sense with the rest, since it stands in no syntactical relation with anything else. The accusative is the *to*-case, marking that toward which the action of the verb is immediately directed, and hence becoming also the case of the direct object; the ablative is the *from*-case; the locative, the *at*- or *in*-case; the instrumental, that of adjacency or accompaniment, then of instrument or means—the *by*-case, in both senses of *by*. Then the dative is the *for*-case, and the genitive the *of*-case, that of general relation or concernment. The nominative, finally, is the case of the subject, and its ending, so far as at present appears, more formal than that of any of the others; the vocative is most often accordant with it, and has, at any rate, no inflectional sign of its own.

The subject of the genesis of the case-endings is much more obscure than the history of the verb. The genitive suffixes show most signs of kindred with the ordinary suffixes of derivation. Pronominal elements seem clearly visible among some of the rest; but every point is too doubtful to allow of summary presentment; and for more than this there would be no room here. How the distinctions of number are combined with those of case is by no means plain; the endings of singular, dual, and plural have the air of being independent of one another, nor are there demonstrable indicators of number, such as in languages of lower type are often found inserted between theme and ending. Yet the earliest language is mainly free from that diversity of modes of inflection according to which, in the middle period, words are arranged in different "declensions." First, uniformity, at least approximate, of declension in all words; then correspondence in the declension of themes having the same final; then, the characteristic finals being lost, a confusion of declensions—such has been the general history of development.

One more matter of distinction, that of gender, is so mixed up with those of case and number as not to be completely separable from them. The problem of the treatment of this element in Indo-European language is still very far from being completely solved. Its foundation appears to lie in the distinction of sex among those creatures which have conspicuous sex; but such constitute only an exceedingly small part of the creation; and the distinctions of gender involve everything that exists, and in a manner which is only in the smallest part accordant with natural sex. The world of untraceably sexual or of unsexual objects is not, as with us, relegated to the indifferent "neuter;" great classes of names are masculine or feminine partly by poetical analogy, by an imaginary estimate of their distinctive qualities as like those of the one or the other sex in the higher animals, especially man; partly by grammatical analogy, by resemblance in formation to words of gender already established. At any rate, in the common Indo-European period, all or nearly all attributive words were inflected in three somewhat varying modes, to indicate generic distinctions; and the names of things followed one or other of these modes, and were masculine or feminine or neuter. The distinction was partly in the case-ending, partly in the derivative theme or base, though there was hardly a suffix, derivative or inflectional, that was rigidly of one gender only; it was most marked as characterizing the feminine; masculine and neuter were hardly separated except in the nominative and accusative cases.

The noun-inflection was shared also by the pronouns, in all the three varieties of case, number, and gender. In those demonstrative words, however, which acquired a specific personal character, as denoting the speaker and the spoken-to, gender was undistinguished. And the words of pronominal origin exhibit certain irregularities of inflection, different from those of the general mass of nouns.

Although a case-ending of itself makes a noun, and

there are many primitive Indo-European nouns which are made by such alone, the great mass of them have other elements interposed between root and ending, which we call suffixes of derivation; and these even come, in time, to be divided into two well-marked classes: primary, or such as are appended directly to verbal roots; and secondary, or such as are added only after other derivative endings. Of these, likewise, too few among the most ancient ones are recognizable in their independent character, and traceable through their changes of application, to allow of our illustrating here the method of their growth. But though the subject is full of obscurity in its details, there is no mystery in the principles involved: the processes which have formed modern suffixes are fully capable of having produced also the ancient ones.

As the two sides of meaning and application in the predicative or verbal roots are verb and noun, so in the demonstrative (which do not make verbs) the two sides may be said to be pronoun and adverb. From the latter class come those earliest words of place and direction, readily convertible also into words of time, which are of adverbial quality. Yet even these appear to be originally and properly case-forms of pronouns: and, in fact, there is no fundamental distinction to be recognized between adverbial suffixes and case-endings. Moreover, the class of adverbs, after being established as a class, continues to receive accessions of case-forms, through its whole history, down to the latest, from which we have already drawn examples (pp. 41, 122). Prepositions, in our sense of the term, are of yet more recent origin, created a separate part of speech by the swinging away of certain adverbs from apprehended relation to the verb, and their connection in idea with the noun-cases which their addition to the verb had caused to be construed with it. We see them coming into distinct existence in the oldest languages of the family, as the Sanskrit; and their increase of number and consequence ever since is apparent. Conjunctions, though we nowhere find them absolutely wanting, are of secondary origin, being among the most characteristic products of the historical development of speech. To be able to put clauses together into periods, with due determination of their relation to one another, is a step beyond the power to put words alike determinately together into clauses.

These are the Indo-European "parts of speech:" that is to say, the main classes of words, having restricted application and definite connection, into which the holophrastic ('equivalent to a whole phrase') utterances of a primitive time have by degrees become divided; the separated parts, members, of what was once an undistinguished whole. But there is one other class, the interjections, which are not in the same and the proper sense a "*part* of speech;" which are, rather, analogous with those all-comprehending signs out of which the rest have come by evolution. A typical interjection is the mere spontaneous utterance of a feeling, capable of being paraphrased into a good set expression for what it intimates: thus, an *ah!* or an *oh!* may mean, according to its tone, 'I am hurt,' or 'am surprised,' or 'am pleased,' and so on; only there is no part of it which means one of the elements of the statement while another part means another. Yet, such creatures of conventional habit in regard to expression have we become by our long use of the wholly conventional apparatus of language, that even our exclamations have generally a conventional character, and shade off into exclamatory utterance of ordinary terms. A man's feelings must be very keenly touched in order to draw out of him a purely natural interjection, in which absolutely no trace of the acquired habits of his community shall be perceptible. And the interjectional employment of common words, or of incomplete phrases, is a very common thing in the general use of speech; emotion or eagerness causing the usual set framework of the sentence, the combination of subject and predicate, to be thrown aside, and the conspicuous or emphatic elements to be presented alone—a real abnegation of the historical development which, under the growing dominion of consciousness over instinct and of reason over passion, has wrought the sentence out of the root.

In this too brief and imperfect sketch of the history of Indo-European speech, no attempt has been made to define the order in which the parts of the inflectional development followed one another. Success is not to be hoped for in any such attempt until the history of less highly developed and of almost undeveloped languages shall be far better understood than it is at present. For, to reason these matters out on Indo-European ground alone is at any rate impossible: the period lies too far back, its evidences are too fragmentary and difficult of interpretation; we are not competent to judge them. As to the impossibility of determining the absolute time occupied by the history, enough, perhaps, has been already said: that it should have taken less than a very long time, there is no reason whatever for believing. The whole was a series of successive steps, of which one led to another and these to yet others; a growth of habits which were in themselves capacities also; and each step, the formation of each habit, was a work of time, not less in the olden time than it would have to be in the modern period: though whether a work of not less time, we can hardly venture to say, since the rate of growth may fall under the government of conditions which we cannot, as yet, fully appreciate.

There has also been, so far as synthetic structure is concerned, an evident climax, followed by an anti-climax, in this history. During the immense prehistoric period, and prior to the separation of the branches from one another, the inflectional system of the noun, and less distinctly that of the verb, reached a fullness which has since undergone a gradual reduction. Not that there has been generally a diminution of ability to express distinctions; but means of another kind have been more and more resorted to: auxiliaries, form-words, instead of suffixes, formative elements in words; and these later means we are accustomed to call analytic, as distinguished from synthetic. *He might have loved* and *he will be loved*, as contrasted with their Latin equivalents *amavisset* and *amabitur*, may be taken as typical examples of the two modes of expression. This fact has been adduced as evidence against an original radical condition of language, by some scholars, who prefer to assume a primitive period of excessive polysyllabism. But with evident injustice; the argument would be a good one only if no such thing as the making of forms were known in language, but only their wearing-out and loss. If we see how collocation and combination and integration and mutilation and corruption all work in succession on the same material in every part of language, producing forms and destroying them again, it is plainly within the competency of the changing circumstances and habits of the language-making community to give the history of development a climactic form. The constructive methods, once inaugurated, are made effective up to the provision of a sufficient apparatus for the expression of relations; and for a time, until this point is reached, their efficiency is greater than that of the destructive processes, which also have been all the time at work—then the relation is gradually reversed, and there is more wearing-out than replacement by synthetic means, though this latter also never entirely ceases; collocations remain such, instead of going on to combination and integration; there is still abundant new provision, but it is of another sort. The habit of construction has changed; though to a very different degree in the divided parts of the great community. If there is a law which governs this climactic phase of development, it has not yet been worked out and exhibited; nor is it likely ever to be so, although we can trace some of the determining influences which have contributed to bring about the effect.

It is time now for us to leave the family which has so long occupied us, and to review, in a much briefer manner, the structure of the other grand divisions of human language. But, founding upon the example of historic growth which we have just been studying, it is desirable first to turn our attention to some general features of the doctrine of linguistic structure.

CHAPTER XI.

LINGUISTIC STRUCTURE: MATERIAL AND FORM IN LANGUAGE.

The distinction of material and form; examples: number, gender, case, etc., in nouns; comparison and concord of adjectives; time, mood, and other distinctions in verbs. Form by position. Inferences. National and individual prejudices; comparative value of different languages. A language represents the capacity of its makers. Rude beginnings of all speech.

To understand, in a general way, the structure of Indo-European speech, in its character and its uses, is to us no difficult task; the subject is already more or less familiar. Though the parts of this structure which our own language still possesses are but fragmentary, they are at least akin with the rest, and lead the way to the knowledge of the whole. It is comparatively a question only of less and more; and many of us know the more, as exhibited in those tongues of the family which have retained a larger share of the original structure, or have supplied its loss more fully. We cannot, however, go on profitably to examine the character of other languages without discussing a little, by way of introduction, the principles of grammatical structure. It will be possible to do this, sufficiently for our purpose, in a wholly simple and unpretentious manner, drawing illustration from phenomena with which almost every one is familiar, and especially out of our own English.

The distinction of the more material and the more formal, relational parts of expression has been noticed and illustrated by us often already. The *s* of *brooks*, for example, is formal in relation to *brook* as material; the added letter indicates something subordinate, a modification of the conception of *brook*, the existence of it in more than one individual: it turns a singular into a plural. *Men* has the like value as regards *man*, the means of making the same formal distinction having come to be of a different kind from the other, an internal change instead of an external. *Brooks* and *men* are not mere material; they are "formed" material, signs for conceptions with one important characteristic, number, added. But then, by simple contrast with them, *brook* and *man* are also "formed;" each implies, not by a sign, but by the absence of an otherwise necessary sign to the contrary, restriction to a single article of the kind named. According to our habits of speech, no one of these words, no one of our nouns in general, can be used without a distinct recognition by the mind of the number of things signified.

But there are many other definable qualities or circumstances belonging to brooks and men besides number. They are, for example, of very different sizes. And we have a similar formal means, though only a very limited one, of signifying this: a small *brook* is to us a *brooklet;* a small *man*, a *mannikin.* It is perfectly conceivable that a language should take constant cognizance of this element of size, distinguishing always the large, the medium, and the small individuals of a kind, by diminutives and magnificatives. The Italian almost does as much as that, by a peculiarity which has grown up in it since it became a separate language. But while we call a small brook a *brooklet*, we call a large one a *creek*, or a *river*, or something of that sort; or we apply *small* and *large* to it, in all their varying degrees: and so with *giant* and *dwarf*, and all the limiting adjectives, as applied to man. All this classification which is made by independent words is as truly expression of form as is that which is made by affixes. Another equally real quality, the differences of which are apparent in every case that comes before the mind, is, in many animals, age; and we can say *man*, *lad*, *boy*, *child*, *infant*, etc., as *horse* and *colt*, *cow* and *calf*, and their like; and the Latin *senex* and German *greis* show the extension of the same system in the other direction, where we have to use the method of description by independent words.

Once more, *man* in its distinctive sense indicates a male animal, and we have a different word, *woman*, for a female of the same kind; and so all through the list of animals in which sex is a conspicuous or an important distinction: as *brother* and *sister*, *bull* and *cow*, *ram* and *ewe:* nor is there a language in the world which does not do the same. Only, as we have already seen, our own family of languages (along with two or three others) has erected this distinction of sex into a universal one, like number, making it a test to be applied in the use of every word; breaking away from the actual limits of sex, and sexualizing, as it were, all objects of thought, on grounds which no mortal has yet been wise enough to discover and point out in detail. And, though we in English have abandoned the artificial part of the system, we retain its fundamental distinction by our use of *he*, *she*, and *it;* the test of sex is to us a real and ever-present one. The modern Per sian has lost from his language even that degree of generic distinction; and to him, as to the Turk or the Finn, whose ancestors never acknowledged any grammatical gender, it seems no less strange to use one pronoun for a male being and another for a female than it would seem to us to use one for a small, or a young, or a near, or a white object, and another for a large, or an old, or a remote, or a black object. And he has really reason on his side; it is our usage that is the exceptional one, and needs justification. There is in the nature of things no necessity for our choosing among the various accidents of a conception any particular ones, to the exclusion of the rest, as subjects of grammatical distinction—although, of course, there may be reason enough why one is practically better worth distinguishing than another. There is a second, somewhat analogous yet not identical, distinction made by us, also solely by the use of pronouns—namely of *who* and *which* or *what*—between persons and non-persons; and the American Indians have one between things animate and things inanimate, with (as in the case of our gender) abundant figurative and personifying transfer: either of these is perhaps as valuable in itself, and as capable of higher uses, as is the Indo-European distinction of the three genders.

We will notice only one more item in connection with the noun, its cases. Our language has preserved to most of its nouns their old genitive case, though not without restriction of the limits of its former uses. And in the pronouns we distinguish the object from the subject or nominative case: *he him, they them*, etc. By this difference, the distinction of subject and object relation is kept so clearly before us that we transfer it in apprehension to the whole class of nouns, and reckon them also as possessing objective cases, though there is really none such in the language. We do not recognize a dative, though we have some really dative constructions—as in "I give *him* the book"—because there is not in use even one dative of different form from the accusative. Just so, the Latin and Greek reckon accusatives neuter, though these are not in a single instance different from the nominatives, because the two cases are usually unlike in other words; so the Latin reckons an ablative plural different from the dative, because there is in a part of its words an ablative singular different from the dative. This transfer of a formal distinction only partially made to the words in which it is not made at all is an important feature in the history of forms. Our two or three cases seem to compare but ill with the Sanskrit seven; yet these compare as ill, in one sense, with the Scythian fifteen or twenty: and, on the one hand, we are able, by the help of another instrumentality, to express all that is expressed by either Sanskrit or Scythian; while, on the other hand, we imply a great deal more than we or they distinctly express; if we were to use different signs for all the shades of case-relation which we can recognize by analysis in our speech, we should have to multiply our list of prepositions many times.

For a part of our adjectives of quality, we have forms (strictly, derivative rather than inflectional) denoting two "degrees" of increment: *high*, *higher*, *highest;* they seem to have been at the beginning rather intensive than strictly comparative. But, as means of comparison, they cover only a small part of the conceivable ground, and cover it only rudely. The possible degrees of a quality are indefinitely numerous, and there are descending as well as ascending grades, which have in theory an equal right to notice: many of them we clearly mark by our analytic substitutes for the old derivatives; and we frame such kindred means of expression as are exemplified by *reddish* and *bluish*, German *röthlich* and *bläulich* ('redlike,' etc.: resembling the quality, but not quite it), French *rougeâtre* and *bleuâtre*. Most of the later tongues of our family still retain that adaptedness of the qualifying adjective, in gender and number and case, to the noun qualified, which, inherited from the time when adjective and substantive were not separated, was charasteristic of their ancestors; to this we preserve nothing whatever that is correspondent; that an adjective should change its form on account of the character of the noun it belongs to is as strange to us as to many languages it is that the verb should change its form on account of the character of the subject of which it predicates something.

In fact, we have almost reduced to a nullity also the concord of the verb and its subject. How there came to be such, we have seen in the foregoing chapter: the endings were the actual subject-pronouns themselves; and the distinction of person and number in the verb was the necessary concomitant and result of that in the pronouns and nouns. Nor is it yet quite a nullity: while we say *I love*, but *thou lovest* and *he loves*, and while *they love* stands over against *he loves*, so long shall we continue, by an apprehended extension of these clearly-felt distinctions, to reckon three persons and two numbers in all our verbal inflection. But our triple distinction of persons is far from exhausting the possibilities of personal relation; many tongues have a double first person plural, one inclusive and one exclusive of the person or persons addressed: one *we* which means 'I and my party' as opposed to you; and one that means 'my party and yours,' as opposed to all third persons. Others, again, distinguish genders in verbal inflection: 'he loves' has one ending, 'she loves' has another. We have seen that some older languages of our family have a dual number; and it would be quite as proper in theory, only not so manageable in practice, to have a whole decimal system of numbers, just as of numerals.

But the attendant circumstances which present themselves for inclusion in verbal expression, and in one or another language find expression, are simply numberless; and the richest verbal scheme that was ever put together takes account of only a part of them, even when supplemented by the resources of analytic phraseology. To us, the element of time is the conspicuous and pressing one; the denoting of an action appears almost to require an implication of tense-relation. Yet many languages do not regard this element as calling for inclusion in the fundamental structure of the verb rather than others; and they leave it to be inferred from the connection, or intimated by external means, particles, auxiliaries, as we on our part treat other elements which they weave into the verbal structure. To any given act of *speaking*, for example, there cleaves some qualification of time; but so also of place, of manner, of purpose. Equally modifications of the indefinite act of speaking are speaking repeatedly or habitually, rapidly, with violence, under compulsion, for another, or causing, ceasing, appearing to speak, declaring another to speak, speaking to one's self—and so on, indefinitely: and these, or many of them, are actually incorporated in derivative verbal forms by races who treat the tense-element less elaborately than we. And our tense-making is on the smallest scale, as compared with the infinite possibilities of tense-distinction. We have not even, as some languages have, a nearer and remoter past, a nearer and remoter future. That a thing was done long ago is as true a temporal relation as that it happened in past time at all; but we intimate only the latter by an inflection, and the former by relational words; and therefore, to our way of thinking, he who wants the inflection has too little, and he who converts the other into an inflection has too much. Our triple forms for each tense—*I love, I do love, I am loving*—by their incessant use, and the necessity constantly imposed on us of choosing among them, keep before our minds certain distinctions which are comparatively unnoticed in French or German; yet they are in the French and German minds also, and if any of them rises to prominent importance, those languages have sufficient means of intimating them. It is good English or German to say "I picked up the book that lay there;" but to the Frenchman it would be a gross blunder to use the same tense for the instantaneous act of picking up and the continuous condition of lying; the difference is clearly involved in our thought as well as his; only our language does not compel our attention to it. The case is quite the same with our moods, those means of defining the contemplated relation between subject and predicate, or modifications of the copula. There are infinite shades of doubt and contingency, of hope and fear, of supplication and exaction, in our mental acts and cognitions, which all the synthetic resources of Greek moods, with added particles and adverbs, which all the analytic phraseology of English, are but rude and coarse means of signifying. And an Algonkin verb makes a host of distinctions which are so strange to us that we can hardly learn to appreciate them when defined.

There is one other mode of formal distinction which demands a moment's notice from us: namely, position. In "you love your enemies, but your enemies hate you," the distinction of subject and object is dependent solely on position, and is given by that means with all necessary clearness. In a language of which the inflections are so much worn-out as are ours, this method counts for much; and there are tongues in which it is of even superior importance. Those, on the other hand, which have a greater abundance of inflections possess a freedom of arrangement which to us is surprising, and almost puzzling.

The principal conclusions intended to be suggested by this brief exposition, and to be made of use in comparing the structure of various languages, are, it is believed, sufficiently clear. In the first place, the realm of formal relation is infinite, unexhausted by the formal resources of even the richest language, or of all languages: however much may be expressed, there is vastly more of the same kind left unexpressed, to be inferred by the intelligent mind from the perceived conditions of the particular case, or passed over as unessential to the ordinary purposes of communication—which is, at the best, only a rude and fragmentary means of putting one mind, or heart, into communion with another. There are no relations to which a language must necessarily give expression; there are only certain ones which are more naturally suggested, of which the expression is more practically valuable, than others: and what these are, we can learn only from the general study of languages; our own educated preferences are no trustworthy guide to them. In the second place, there is no absolute dividing-line between what is material and what is formal in a language; material and form are relative words only, names for degrees, for poles of a continuous series, of which the members shade into one another. And, as we saw in the fifth chapter, the grandest internal movement in a growing and improving language is that from more material to more formal uses, whereby both words and phrases take on a less gross and physical meaning, even to the extent of being attenuated into form-words, or, in combination with other elements, into formative elements —both alike indicators of relation. Hence, in the third place, the means of formal expression are of the utmost variety; they are not to be sought in one department of a language only, but in all; they are scattered through the whole vocabulary, as well as concentrated in the grammatical apparatus. Deficiency in one department may be compensated, or more than compensated, by provision of resources in another. There is no human tongue which is destitute of the expression of form; and to call certain languages, and them alone, "form-languages," is indefensible, except as the term may be meant to describe them as possessing in a higher or exceptional degree a quality which they really share with all the rest.

In judging other languages, then, we have to try to rid ourselves of the prejudices generated by our own acquired habits of expression, and to be prepared to find other peoples making a very different selection from our own of those qualifications and relations of the more material substance of expression which they shall distinctly represent in speech, and also sharing these out very differently among the different modes of formal expression. It is a common error of uncultivated, and of narrowly though highly cultivated peoples, to regard themselves alone as speakers, and all others as babblers, "barbarians," unintelligent because to them unintelligible talkers. We are in no danger of doing that; but we are in danger still of over-estimating the peculiar traits of our speech, and depreciating those of others' speech. Nothing is harder than to be perfectly impartial here; to judge the comparative merit of one's own and of another language requires a grasp of all the particulars involved, a power of analysis and comparison, and a freedom from both national and individual prejudice, of which only exceptionally endowed and exceptionally trained minds will be capable. Even great scholars are liable here to great errors. There are eminent English-speaking philologists who regard English analysis as the only reasonable or "logical" mode of expression, and look down on Greek synthesis as something characteristic of a rude and undeveloped intellectual condition; there are many more, doubtless, of various nationality, who undervalue the resources of English, and are loath to assign a high rank to a tongue which has lost or thrown away so much of its inherited structure.

On the whole, perhaps the best and most trustworthy test of the value of a language is, what its speakers have made it do. Language is but the instrument for the expression of thought. If a people has looked at the world without and within us with a penetrating and discerning eye, has observed successfully the resemblances and differences of things, has distinguished well and combined well and reasoned well, its language, of however apparently imperfect structure, in the technical sense of that term, enjoys all the advantage which comes from such use; it is the fitting instrument of an enlightened mind. There is nothing in the grammatical form of either Greek or English that may not be degraded to serve only base uses.

In another sense also a language is what its speakers make it: its structure, of whatever character, represents their collective capacity in that particular direction of effort. It is, not less than every other part of their civilization, the work of the race; every generation, every individual, has borne a part in shaping it. Whether, however, the language-making capacity can be correlated with any other, so that we may say, a highly-organized speech could not be expected from a histoi ical community whose work in this or that other respect shows a deficiency of excellence, is extremely doubtful; thus far, at any rate, nothing of value has been done in that direction. The Chinese is, as we shall see in the next chapter, a most striking example of how a community of a very high grade of general ability may exhibit an extreme inaptitude for fertile linguistic development. We may suitably compare this with the grades of aptitude shown by various races for plastic or pictorial or musical art, which by no means measure their capacity for other intellectual or spiritual products. No uncultured people ever spends consciously any time or effort upon its speech; this cannot be thought over and worked up into better shape; it must come by the way, as incident to the work of thought, as result of unreflective effort at communication. That race which possesses most of the right kind of regulative force will turn out a product that is admirable; and the contrary.

Only, also, the possibility of a radical change of history, a new turn of development, is different at different periods of growth. After a certain stage of advance in definite and established expression is reached, the conservative forces, depending on acquired habits of speech, are too strong to be overcome, and the language goes on forever on the course which the directing hands of the earlier generations have determined. This is a point upon which we have no right yet to speak with definiteness; we may hope some day to understand it better: to be able, for example, to lay down exactly what conditions the stagnation of Chinese speech. There are other departments of civilization in which a race does not always show itself able to develop unaided its own best capacities. The Celtic and Germanic tribes, which have proved themselves equal to taking leading places in the world's history, might have remained comparative barbarians to the present time, if they had not received Greek civilization, as shaped over and reorganized by Rome. But though a nation may borrow culture from its neighbors, it does not in the same way borrow linguistic development; no race ever adopted a new mode of structural growth for its native speech by imitation of another; though many a community has, under sufficient external inducement, exchanged its native speech for another; and borrowing, as we have already seen, especially accompanies transfer of culture, and is capable of going on to such an extent as vastly to enrich the borrowing speech, and fit it for higher uses.

While a people's capacities and acquirements make its language, we must not fail to notice also the contrary truth, that its language helps to determine its intellectual character and progress. The powerful reflex influence of language on mental action is a universally admitted fact in linguistics; to allow it is only to allow that rooted habits, learned by each generation from its predecessor, have a controlling influence on action—which is axiomatic. But the subject belongs to a much more advanced and elaborate discussion of language than this work makes any pretense of being; and it has never yet been worked out fruitfully.

On the analogy of Indo-European speech alone we have a right to assume, at least provisionally, that whatever of inflective structure may be possessed also by other languages, whatever of formal and formative apparatus they may contain, of any kind, has been wrought out by somewhat similar methods, from a similar initial stage of rude and gross material. If there shall be found languages in which this is demonstrably not the case, we can modify or abandon the assumption hereafter; but it will require very definite and cogent evidence to make such demonstration. For language is an instrumentality; and the law of simplicity of beginnings applies to it not less naturally and necessarily than to other instrumentalities. Some seem to imagine that to regard men as having begun to talk with formless roots, which we now arrive at "by abstraction" from the material of living languages, is like regarding them as having begun the use of physical instruments with the bare abstract motive powers—the inclined plane, the wheel, the pulley. But such a par allel is as absolutely erroneous as anything can be: the analogues of the motive powers, rather, would be the attributive and predicative relations, the assertive, interrogative, and imperative modes, and their like. The analogue of the root is the stick or the stone which was indubitably man's first instrument: a crude tool or weapon, used for a variety of purposes to which we now adapt a corresponding variety of much more intricate and shapely tools. And to hold that formed words, divisible into radical and formative elements, were first in the uses of speech, is just as defensible as to hold that men began to labor with hammers and saws and planes and nails, and to fight with iron-headed lances and bows and catapults. In each single root was present at the outset—as may be present in a single interjectional monosyllable now—a whole assertion, or inquiry, or command, to which the tone and accompanying gesture, or the mere circumstances of its utterance, furnished the sufficient interpretation: just as in the stick or stone was present—and may, on an emergency, be made present still—a variety of instruments or weapons.

Again, to maintain, for the purpose of explaining the variety of later languages, that the expressions of the earliest men must have been potentially different in the different races, as the seeds or germs which develop into different animals or plants are different; that a formative principle must have been present in the material of one language and not of another; that in the elements which came afterward to be put to formative uses there was from the beginning a form-making function inherent, and so on—all this is sheer mythology. One might as well claim that in the stick or stone, as used by some races, there was lying *perdu* a well-membered instrument or machine, which somehow developed out of it in the hands of its users, and that in the wood and metal of certain regions were inherent machine-making functions, not possessed elsewhere. Language comes to be just what its users make it; its offices correspond to their capacities; if there is a higher degree of formative structure in one language than in another, the reason lies in the difference of quality of the two races, their different capacity of education and growth; not at all in the character of the beginnings from which both alike started, nor of the materials which both alike have ever since had at command.

CHAPTER XII.

OTHER FAMILIES OF LANGUAGE: THEIR LOCALITY, AGE, AND STRUCTURE.

Classification by families. Scythian or Ural-Altaic or Turanian family; doubtful members of it. Monosyllabic family: Chinese, Farther Indian, etc. Japanese. Malay-Polynesian; other insular families: Papuan, Australian. Dravidian. Caucasian languages. Semitic family; question of its relationships. Hamitic: Egyptian, etc. South African or Bantu. Middle African languages. Basque. American Indian languages.

We have called a certain body of languages a family, the Indo-European. The name "family," we saw, was applied to it by strict analogy with the use of the same term elsewhere: the languages in question had been found, on competent examination, to show good evidence of descent from a common ancestor. We had, however, to confess that the limits, even of this best-known of families, cannot be traced with absolute precision; one or another tongue, not now thought of, or else doubtfully regarded, as Indo-European, may one day make good its title to a place with the rest. We have also seen that, by the operation of completely comprehensible causes, no language on earth exists in a state of absolute accordance through the whole community that speaks it; it is a group, even if a very limited one, of related dialects. This being the case, it is the first task of the comparative study of languages to divide all human speech into families, by recognizable signs of relationship: only thus can there be made any such examination of their character and history as shall lead the way to the other results which the science seeks to attain. And such a classification has in fact been made. It is, of course, in parts only a tentative and provisional arrangement, held liable to rectification, both by addition and by the giving up of what is now held even with a fair degree of confidence: for it not seldom happens that lines which in a half-light appear definite and fixed dissolve away when full illumination is turned upon them. The cautious philologist combines only so far as trustworthy evidences take him, leaving the rest to be settled when more knowledge is won.

As a matter of fact, moreover, linguistic scholars have hitherto been able to put together into families only those languages which have a common structure. That is to say, only tongues which have shared at least a part of their growth out of the original radical stage (provided they have left it) have yet been found to exhibit reliable evidence of relationship. No one, it is evident, has a right to declare *à priori* that there cannot remain even from the initial stage sufficient signs of common descent, in branches whose whole structural development has been separate: in fact, philologists are feeling about among the roots of certain families for such signs, and may one day succeed in bringing them to light; but thus far no definite results have been reached. We shall have occasion to note in the next chapter the difficulties which environ the inquiry, and to point out the reasons why, on a large scale, it is likely to fail of success.

The first family, then, which we take up is that of

which the leading branches occupy more or less of European soil, alongside those of our own kindred. Of these branches there are three. The first, the Finno-Hungarian, or Ugrian, is chiefly European: it includes the Finnish, with the nearly related Esthonian and Livonian, and the remoter Lappish in the Scandinavian peninsula; the Hungarian, an isolated dialect in the south, wholly environed by Indo-European tongues, but of which the intrusion into its present place, by immigration from near the southern Ural, has taken place within the historic period; the dialects from which the Hungarian separated itself, the Ostiak and Wogul, in and beyond the Ural; and the tongues of other related tribes in eastern Russia, as the Ziryanians, Wotiaks, Mordwins, etc. The Finns and Hungarians are the only cultivated peoples of the branch: there are fragments of Hungarian language from the end of the twelfth century, but the literature begins only four centuries later, and scantily, the people formerly using the Latin much more than their own speech for literary purposes; the earliest Finnish records are of the sixteenth century; the language has a mythic poem, the Kalevala, written down in this century from the mouths of popular singers, of especial originality and interest.

The second branch, quite nearly related with this one, is the Samoyed, belonging to a Hyperborean race, which stretches from the North Sea to beyond the Yenisei, and up the course of this river into the central mountains of the continent, the Altai range, probably the starting-point of its migrations. It has no culture, nor importance of any kind.

The third branch, the Turkish or Tartar (more properly Tatar), only touches and overlaps the European frontier at the south. The race to which it belongs, after having been long the restless foe of the Iranians on their northeastern frontier, finally, after the Mohammedanizing of Persia, forced its way through, worked on westward, captured Constantinople in the fifteenth century, and was arrested there only by the combined and long-continued efforts of the powers of central Europe. It is stretched out at present from European Turkey (in which it nowhere forms the mass of the population) over a great part of central Asia, and even, in its Yakut branch, to the mouth of the distant Lena. The Yakuts, Bashkirs, and Kirghiz, the Uigurs, Usbeks, and Turkomans, and the Osmanlis of Asiatic and European Turkey, are some of the principal divisions of the race. The Uigurs, getting their alphabet and culture from Nestorian missionaries, were the first to produce a scanty literature, as far back as the eighth to the tenth centuries; the southeastern peoples have records ("Jagataic") of the fourteenth to the sixteenth; the abundant and varied but little original literature of the Osmanlis dates from the time of their European conquests; it is full of Persian and Arabic materials.

Respecting the family relationship of these three branches there is no question. As to the common name by which they shall be called, usage is very diverse. "Turanian" is perhaps more frequent than any other, but there are grave objections to its genesis and application, and, till use shall pronounce more definitely in its favor, it is hardly fit to be employed in scientific description. "Ural-Altaic," "Scythian," "Tartaric" are others, employed by various authors: the first has its advantages, but is unwieldy, and implies rather more knowledge as to the movements of the family than we actually possess; we may use here "Scythian," provisionally, and disclaiming for it any marked or partisan preference.

Scythian language is the type of what is called an "agglutinative" structure, as distinguished from the "inflective" Indo-European. By this is meant that the elements of various origin which make up Scythian words and forms are more loosely aggregated, preserve more independence, than do the Indo-European; there is far less integration of the parts, with disguise and obliteration of their separate entity. All our own formations, as has been seen, begin with being agglutinations; and such words as *un-tru-th-ful-ly* preserve an agglutinative character; if all our words were like it, there would be no marked difference between the two families as to this fundamental item. For the Scythian formative elements are also only in small part traceable to the independent words out of which they have grown; they are, like the Indo-European affixes, mere signs of relation and of modification of meaning. But Scythian formations do not go on to fuse root and ending, even to the replacing of an external by an internal flection. As a rule, the root maintains itself unaltered in the whole group of derivatives and inflection, and each suffix has an unchanged form and office: whence, on the one hand, a great regularity of formation, and, on the other hand, a great intricacy. Thus, in Turkish, for example, *lar* (or *ler*) forms plurals everywhere; to it are added the same case-endings which alone make the singular cases; and pronominal elements indicating possession may be yet further interposed between the two: so *ev*, 'house,' *ev-den*, 'from a house,' *ev-üm-den*, 'from my house,' *ev-ler-üm-den*, 'from my houses.' The case-relations indicated by these endings or suffixed particles are numerous, in some dialects rising to twenty.

The verb exemplifies the same peculiarity still more strikingly: there are half a dozen modifying elements capable of insertion, singly or in variously combined groups, between root and endings, to express passive, reflexive, reciprocal, causative, negative, and impossible action; so that from the simple root *sev*, for example, we may make the intricate derivative *sev-ish-dir-il-e-me-mek*, 'not to be capable of being made to love one another,' which is then conjugated with the various forms of the simple verb; thus bringing the possible inflective forms from one root up to a number which is immense as compared with any Indo-European verb.

But the distinction of verb and noun in these languages is much less original, fundamental, and sharply drawn than with us. The verbally used forms are, rather, but one step removed from nouns used predicatively, with subjective or possessive pronominal elements appended. The types of verbal forms are, for example, (Turkish) *dogur-um*, 'striking I,' i. e. 'I strike,' and *dogd-um*, 'act of striking mine,' i. e. 'I have struck;' and the third person is without ending: *dogdi*, 'he has struck,' *dogdi-ler*, 'they have struck,' literally 'striking,' 'strikings.' To say this is not to say that these languages have no real verb; since to make a verb it needs only that certain forms be set apart and strictly devoted by usage to the expression of the predicative relation; but it does imply a decided inferiority in the grade of clearness of this most fruitful of formal distinctions, and may shade off into a total absence of it. Of tenses and moods such as those instanced above, and others made with auxiliaries, these languages have a plenty; and their variety of resource in derivatives is very great; so that all the formal apparatus is provided which is needed for shaping by the right usage into a sufficient instrument of thought; and the most cultivated of the dialects do indeed come so near to "inflection" that their falling short of it is hardly more than nominal.

The Scythian adjective is as bare of inflection as the English; and there is an utter absence of gender as one of the categories of noun-inflection or of pronominal distinction, just as in Persian. Relatives and conjunctions are also nearly unknown, the combinations of dependent clauses being, as is natural in languages where the verb is a less definite part of speech, rather by case-forms of verbal nouns. These constructions make upon us the impression of great intricacy, and invert that order of the members of the sentence to which we are accustomed.

In the phonetic structure of these languages, the most striking trait is the so-called "harmonic sequence of vowels." There are, namely, two classes of vowels, light and heavy, or palatal (*e*, *i*, *ü*, *ö*) and other (*a*, *o*, *u*); and it is the general law that the vowels of the various endings shall be of the class of that in the root, or in its last syllable—thus marking the appurtenance and dependency of the endings in their relation to the root in a manner which, though undoubtedly at first euphonic only (like the Germanic *umlaut*), has lent itself usefully to the purposes of formal distinction. Every suffix, then, has two forms, a light and a heavy: we have *al-mak*, but *sev-mek*; *ev-ler*, but *agha-lar*, and so on. In some dialects this assimilative process is of a wonderful degree of intricacy.

There is field and scope in these languages for a comparative grammar of the highest interest and importance; but no one has yet taken up the work seriously and comprehensively; the science of language has advanced far enough to demand its execution, which, it is to be hoped, will not be long deferred. One obstacle in its way, the lack of really ancient records, from a time comparable to that of the early Indo-European documents, is likely to be removed, if recent claims shall prove well-founded. There is, namely, in the Mesopotamian and Persian records, a third language, the so-called Accadian, of greatly disputed character and connections, but which has been for some time past persistently declared by one party of its students to be Ugrian, an ancient dialect of the Finno-Hungarian stock, and a grammar of it has lately been written (by M. Lenormant) on that understanding. This is a point of very high importance, but we have no right yet to consider it fairly settled; it is doubtful whether so exact and comprehensive knowledge and so sound method have yet been applied as to yield a trustworthy result. What adds greatly to the interest of the matter is that this language and its community are demonstrably the original owners of the cuneiform mode of writing, which has been borrowed and adapted by both Semitic and Indo-European peoples: it would follow, then, that the original basis of culture in that great and important centre of the world's civilization was Scythian. We have no right to deny the possibility of this; at the same time, it is so inconsistent with what we know of the activity of the race elsewhere that we have a right to regard it with provisional incredulity, and to demand a full demonstration before yielding it our belie'

Along with the three branches we have bee considering are generally ranked, as belonging to the same family, two others, the Mongolian and the Tungusic: but the evidence for their inclusion with the rest is confessedly less positive, and we are justified in holding a doubtful position as regards them. Their languages are of a much lower grade of development, verging even upon monosyllabic poverty, having nothing which can be called a verb, possessing even no distinction of number and person in their predicative words. This may well enough be the result of arrested growth, but whether it demonstrably is so is another question, to which we demand a more competent and satisfactory reply than has yet been given. An opposing consideration of no slight weight is the different physical type ("Mongolian") of these races, which connects them rather with the extreme eastern Asiatics than with the Europeans. Another is their possession of a "classificatory" system of estimation and designation of relationship (Mr. L. H. Morgan), as opposed to the analytic or "descriptive" one of the other branches. It is not, then, undue skepticism that leads us to limit the Scythian family for the present to its three demonstrated branches. Just in this direction there has been such an excess of unscientific and wholesale grouping, the classification of ignorance, that a little even of overstrained conservatism ought to have a wholesome effect.

The Mongol territory occupies a great space on the inhospitable plateau of central Asia; and, as a consequence of the great movement by which, in the twelfth and thirteenth centuries, the race became the conquerors and devastators of almost the whole world, fragments of it are scattered far westward, one even occupying a considerable tract astride the Volga, near its mouth. The Mongols reach eastward along a great part of the northern frontier of China, and are there succeeded by the Tungusic tribes, who range still farther east and north, almost to the coasts. Of these tribes, the only one of note is the Manchu, whose great deed and title to historic fame is its conquest and administration of China during the past two centuries. Both Mongols and Manchus have alphabets, their usual ones derived through the Uigur Turkish from the Syriac; their literatures are quite modern only, and reflections of Chinese originals.

If in Mongol and Manchu we are close upon the absence of all inflective structure, in the Chinese we actually reach that condition. The Chinese is a tongue composed of about five hundred separate words, as we should reckon them, each a monosyllable. But in this language tone is pressed into the service of ordinary intellectual distinction, and the words are multiplied to over fifteen hundred by the significant variety of intonation. Nor are these words, like English monosyllables, worn-out relics of a formerly inflected condition of speech; there is no good reason to doubt their being the actual undeveloped roots of the language, analogous with the Indo-European roots except in the results of use by an enlightened community for communication and thought during thousands of years. They have been crowded with meanings of every kind, and of various degrees of formality; they have been combined into standing phrases, with balance of parts and unity of emphasis, as in our *I shall have gone*, *by the way*, and so on; many of them have become auxiliaries, signs of relation, indicators of special uses analogous with those of our parts of speech; but yet they have never been made into actual parts of speech, nor united into inflectional systems. If they had gone through any such process as this, the present speech would show plainly the results of it: there would be a much greater number and variety of words; they would fall into related groups; and they would be more sharply defined and discriminated in their uses. The Chinese word admits of employment indifferently as one and another part of speech, and plainly by an inherent non-distinction of their various offices.

The Chinese language is therefore, in one most important and fundamental respect, of the very lowest grade of structure and poverty of resource. But it is also the most remarkable example in the world of a weak instrumentality which is made the means of accomplishing great things; it illustrates, in a manner which the student of language cannot too carefully heed, the truth that language is only an instrumentality, and the mind the force that uses it; that the mind, which in all its employment of speech implies a great deal more than it expresses, is able to do a high quality of work with only the scantiest hints of expression, catching from the connection and from position the shades of meaning and the modes of relation which it needs. It is but a difference of degree between Chinese inexpressiveness and the frequent overloading of distinctions which in our view characterizes some of the agglutinative idioms: for example, the American Indian; and, with a right view of language, one is as explainable as the other. A few scratches on a board with a bit of charcoal by a skilled artist may be more full of meaning, may speak more strongly to the imagination and feeling, than a picture elaborated by an inferior hand with all the resources of a modern art-school.

The abundant and varied literature of China goes back in its beginnings to about 2000 B. C., an antiquity exceeded in only two or three other countries of the world. Though a tongue of so bald structure is comparatively little liable to disguising alteration, the Chi nese of to-day is quite unlike what it was so long ago—to what extent and how, learned men are now making effort to determine. A still more obvious measure of the progress of alteration is given by the dialectic varieties of the existing language, which are so great that almost every hundred miles along the southern coast brings one to a new speech, nearly or quite unintelligible to dwellers in other districts. The literary dialect is one in its written character, but somewhat discordant in its spoken form, through the whole empire. Some hold that here and there, in the dialects, the line which separates utter uninflectedness from a rude agglutination has been overstepped.

The various languages of Farther India—as the Annamese or Cochin-Chinese, the Siamese, and the Burmese, with the tongues of numerous other wilder and less important tribes or races—are sufficiently unlike to Chinese and to each other in material to pass for wholly unrelated. But they are all alike in the capital point that they are uninflected; and this cannot but be regarded as a strong indication of ultimate relationship between them. We can point out, indeed, no reason why one race more than another should exhibit an incapacity for linguistic development; and if we met with monosyllabic tongues in different parts of the earth, we should have no right to infer their connection; but that the dialects of one corner of Asia should share a peculiarity so exceptional can hardly be other than the result of a common fixation of the monosyllabic type. At any rate provisionally, therefore, we class all these together as the southeastern Asiatic, or monosyllabic family. The Farther Indian tongues are inferior to the Chinese in just that manner and degree which was to be expected in dialects of inferior races and lower culture. They abound in such means of definition as auxiliaries and indicative particles.

How far the limits of the family thus constructed extend, is a question which only further research can determine. Running up the southern border of the Asiatic plateau, from northern Farther India westward, is a region occupied by a great and far from homogeneous mass of dialects, generally called Himalayan, of a low type of structure, which are at any rate not sufficiently known to be classified as distinct from the family we have been considering. With them goes the Tibetan, though this has an alphabet, of Indian origin, and a Buddhist literature, from the seventh century down.

Among all these peoples, the position of the Chinese is a striking and exceptional one, as that of the only race possessing a wholly independent and highly-developed civilization, with attendant literature. It is somewhat like the position of the Accadians—if they be proved Scythian—among the other Scythian peoples. China has been as grand a centre of light to all its neighbors as Mesopotamia; but with this marked difference: by a persistency which is one of the most striking facts in the history of the world, it has maintained its own institutions, political and religious and linguistic, substantially unchanged from the very dawn of the historic period.

The nation which has profited most by Chinese teaching, which has alone shown the capacity to assimilate and continue the Chinese culture, with adaptations to its own peculiar character, is the Japanese. It is of the same pronounced physical type which we are accustomed to call Mongolian. Attempts have been made to connect its language with those of the Mongols and

Manchus, but they have not met with approved success, and the Japanese still stands alone. It is by no means monosyllabic, but rather an agglutinative dialect of extremely simple structure, with hardly an established distinction between noun and verb, and with no determinate flexion; the relations of case, and number and person are indicated by analytic means, by separate particles or auxiliary words; number in part by duplication. Variations of the radical verbal idea akin with those exemplified above from the Turkish are also made, by various compounded elements. Combination of separate root-words, often with considerable contraction or mutilation, is very common; but it does not tend as with us, to the production of formative elements and of forms, except coarsely and restrictedly. Relatives and subordinating conjunctions are wanting. The language is burdened with the over-elaborate recognition of degrees of dignity in the speaker and the persons addressed or spoken of, almost to the disuse of simple pronouns. The Chinese vocabulary is imported *en masse* into the more learned styles, especially of writing. The phonetic structure of the language is very simple and euphonious. The oldest literary remains are from the seventh and eighth centuries.

The shores and peninsulas and islands of the north-eastern corner of Asia are occupied by a variety of races and languages, which are too little known, and of too little interest, to demand attention from us in this hasty review.

On the islands, however, which lie off the south-eastern part of the continent, and through most of the groups and isolated islets that dot the Pacific, north to Formosa, east to Easter island, south to New Zealand, and west even to Madagascar, on the very border of

Africa, are found the scattered members of a vast and perfectly well-developed family, the Malay-Polynesian. From what central point the migrations of the tribes and their dialects took place, it is not possible to tell: the family is strictly an insular one, the hold which a part of the Malays have on the mainland in Malacca being only recently gained (since the twelfth century). The Malays proper have adopted Mohammedanism, and taken for use the Arabic alphabet; and they have a tolerably abundant literature, reaching up into the fourteenth century. Some of the other less conspicuous tribes—as the Battaks, Mancassars, and Bugis, and the Tagalas of the Philippines—have alphabets, which are believed to come ultimately from India, but nothing that can fairly be called a literature. But in Java and its dependencies, especially Bali, the introduction of culture and writing from India dates back even to the first century of our era, with a considerable literature, founded on the Sanskrit. Elsewhere in the family, record begins only with the labors of Christian missionaries in the most recent period.

The family is divided (Friedrich Müller) into three great branches: 1. The Malayan, filling on the one hand the great islands nearest to Asia, and on the other hand the Philippine and Ladrone groups; 2. The Polynesian, in most of the smaller groups, with New Zealand and Madagascar; 3. The Melanesian, of the Fijian and other archipelagos off the northeastern corner of Australia. The various Polynesian dialects are clearly and closely related; the Melanesian show the extreme of dialectic division, with other peculiarities—which, along with the darker hue and other physical differences of their speakers, have been plausibly explained as due to an imposition of Polynesian speech upon a population chiefly Papuan. The Malayan dialects are farthest developed, making most approach toward something like a rude flexion. For, in general, the languages of the family are almost as bare of derivative and inflectional combinations as is the Chinese itself; their grammatical relations are indicated by pronouns and particles, which only in the Malayan group, and in derivation rather than inflection, take on the aspect of affixes: gender, case, number, mood, tense, person, are wanting; nor is there any distinction of noun from verb; the verb is a substantive or adjective used predicatively without copula. The roots, if we may call them so, the most ultimate elements accessible to our analysis, are prevailingly dissyllabic; and their reduplication, either complete or by abbreviation, is a means of variation of which great use is made, and for very various purposes. Only the pronouns have distinct numeral forms, and the first person has the double plural, inclusive or exclusive of the person addressed, referred to above (pp. 218, 219). The determinative particles are more often prefixed than suffixed.

The Malay-Polynesian languages are more simple in regard to their phonetic structure than any others in the world. Hardly any of them have more than ten consonants; many only seven. And they do not allow a syllable to begin with more than one consonant, or to close with a consonant.

Not the whole population of the Pacific islands belongs to this family. The mass of the great islands Borneo and New Guinea, with the more inaccessible parts of the Philippines and others, are inhabited by a black and woolly-haired race, the Papuans or Negritos, resembling the Africans though not related with them, and quite distinct from the Malay-Polynesians, by whose incursions they have been exterminated or crowded back from parts of their ancient possessions. Their languages are almost utterly unknown.

Australia, again, and the neighboring Tasmania, were inhabited, when discovered, by a third island-race, of dark color but straight-haired, and of nearly or quite the lowest known grade of endowment. Their greatly varying dialects are polysyllabic and agglutinative, of simple phonetic character, and especially different from the Polynesian in using exclusively suffixed instead of prefixed particles.

In reviewing the Indian branch of the Indo-European family, we saw that the tribes of our kindred had worked their way in through the passes of the northwest, driving out or subjecting a more aboriginal population. This primitive race still holds in possession most of the great southern peninsula, beyond the chain of mountains and wild highlands which cuts it off from the wide valleys of Hindustan proper. The so-called "Dravidians" number thirty to forty millions: their principal languages are the Tamil, Telugu, Canarese, and Malayâlam or Malabar; there are several others, of inferior importance; and the Brahuî, of Beluchistan, has been claimed to show signs of affinity with the group. The Dravidian tongues have some peculiar phonetic elements, are richly polysyllabic, of general agglutinative structure, with prefixes only, and very soft and harmonious in their utterance; they are of a very high type of agglutination, like the Finnish and Hungarian; and the author has been informed by an American who was born in southern India and grew up to speak its language vernacularly along with his English, a man of high education and unusual gifts as a preacher and writer, that he esteemed the Tamil a finer language to think and speak in than any European tongue known to him.

Excepting that they show no trace of the harmonic sequence of vowels, these languages are not in their structure so different from the Scythian that they might not belong to one family with them, if only sufficient correspondences of material were found between the two groups. And some have been ready, though on grounds not to be accepted as sufficient, to declare them related. The comparative grammar of the Scythian languages has not yet been so reduced to form that it should be possible to define the boundaries of the family, either on the east or in the south.

Among the less familiar languages of Asia we have occasion to notice further only that intricate and problematical group known as the Caucasian. As the name denotes, its locality is the region between the Caspian and Black Seas, filled by the Caucasus range and its dependent hills and valleys. The chief dialects on the south of the main crest are the Georgian, Suanian, Mingrelian, and Lazian, all plainly related to one another, and the first having an alphabet, derived along with its religion from Armenia, and a literature of some antiquity. The principal groups on the north are the Circassian, Mitsjeghian, and Lesghian, the first bordering the Black Sea, the last the Caspian. The variety of sub-dialects, especially of the Lesghian, is very great. There is no demonstrated affinity between the southern and northern divisions, nor between the members of the northern; how many independent groups there may be is yet undetermined; and also, whether there is any tie of analogical structure to bind them together into a family, or whether they are the relics of ultimately separate families, left stranded, as it were, on the mountains, and defended by them and by the great seas in front and behind from the movements of migration which have swept the families elsewhere out of existence.

Last among the Asiatic languages, we come to the Semitic, so called because in the genealogies of the Genesis the communities which speak them are mostly described as descendants of Shem. They fill the immense, but barren and thinly-populated peninsula of Arabia, with its northern border-lands, of Mesopotamia and Syria and Palestine, and with a district in Abyssinia, lying opposite its southwest corner. The northern division is composed of the Assyrian and Babylonian, the Canaanitic dialects (chief among them the Hebrew and Phœnician), and the Syrian, or Aramaic; the southern division contains the Arabic and Abyssinian dialects. This is their ancient territory: the Phœnician was carried to its colonies, and, as Carthaginian, might perhaps have become the tongue of Mediterranean civilization, but that the long struggle for supremacy ended with the complete overthrow of Carthage by Rome; the Hebrew, replaced in vernacular use, even in its own home, four centuries before Christ, by the Syrian (Chaldee, Aramaic), has led ever since the artificial life of a learned language, scattered among the civilized nations; the Arabic, as the sacred dialect of a conquering people and religion, has been carried, since the seventh century, over a part of the world comparable with that which the Latin came finally to occupy: it is the speech of the whole northern border of Africa; it has crowded out the other Semitic branches, and has filled with its words the Persian, Turkish, and Hindustani, and to a less extent the Malay and Spanish vocabularies. It has given birth, however, to no such group of independent derived languages as the Latin can show.

The ancient Hebrew literature is familiar to us far beyond the rest, being our "Bible;" its earliest parts go back into the second thousand years before Christ. The Phœnician has left no literature, and the inscribed coffin of a king of Sidon (probably 500 B. C.) is its chief monument; a very recently discovered Moabite tablet (of 900 B. C.) gives us a specimen of another ancient Canaanitic dialect, almost identical with Hebrew. The Aramaic has an abundant Greco-Christian literature, beginning from the second century, besides its share in the Talmudic writings. The Assyrian has a fragmentary literature in the inscriptions and tablets of Nineveh and Babylon, from a period beyond that of the earliest Hebrew. The Arabic begins its record mainly with the rise of Islam; since that time it is one of the richest literatures in the world. In southwest Arabia prevailed a very different body of dialects, usually styled Himyaritic, now preserved only in the jealously-guarded remains of an earlier civilization. With the Himyaritic is most nearly akin the Abyssinian group, which, in two principal literary dialects, the earlier Geëz or Ethiopic and the later Amharic, has a considerable literature, beginning in the fourth century.

The Semitic family of languages and races is, after the Indo-European, by far the most prominent in the history of the world. None but the Semites have, since the dawn of the historic period, seriously disputed with our family the headship of the human race; and, of the three great conquering religions, two, Christianity and Mohammedanism, are of Semitic birth—although the former won its world-wide dominion in connection with its transfer to the hands of Indo-Europeans, the Greeks and Romans. That we have put off, then, our examination of Semitic language to this point is mainly owing to its exceptional and anomalous character. Semitic speech stands more alone in the world than any other, than even the nakedly isolating Chinese or the indefinitely synthetic American. For, as regards all other tongues, the basis of radical elements and the principle of their combination being given, it is easy enough in theory to explain their various structures, as products of one general method of development. But no such thing is at present practicable for the Semitic; this contains two characteristics—the triliterality of the roots and their inflection by internal change, by variation of vowel—which belong to it alone.

What we call the Semitic root, namely, is (except in the pronouns and a wholly insignificant number of other cases) a conglomerate of three consonants, no more and no less: thus, for example, *q-t-l* represents the conception of 'killing,' *k-t-b* that of 'writing.' By this is not meant, of course, that such conglomerates were, like the Indo-European roots, the historical germs of a body of derivative forms; but, as we arrive at the root in Indo-European by taking off the variously accreted formative elements, we arrive at such a Semitic root by removing its formative elements. The latter includes no vowel that has an identity to preserve; the addition of any vowel makes a form. Thus, in Arabic (the best preserved and most transparent in structure of the various dialects), *qatala* is a verbal third singular, 'he killed;' as it were, the base of a system of personal forms, made, like ours, by pronominal endings: thus, *qataltu*, 'I killed,' *qatalat*, 'she killed,' *qataltumâ*, 'ye two killed,' *qatalnâ*, 'we killed.' A change of vowels, to *qutila*, makes of it a passive, 'he was killed;'

and from this we have by a like process *qutiltu*, *qutilat*, *qutiltumâ*, *qutilnâ*, etc. Another change, to *aqtala*, signifies 'he caused to kill,' with its passive *uqtila ;* and so on. Then (*u*)*qtul* is imperative, 'kill!' and something like this is base of another set of persons, formed partly by prefixes, partly by suffixes: as *yaqtulu*, 'he kills,' *taqtulu*, 'she kills,' *yaqtulûna*, 'they (men) kill,' *naqtulu*, 'we kill,' etc. Then, *qâtil* is present participle, 'killing,' and *qatl* infinitive, 'act of killing;' while *iqtâl* is 'causing to kill' as noun, and *muqtil* the same as adjective. And *qitl*, 'enemy,' and *qutl*, 'murderous,' are specimens of derivative noun and adjective. These forms at once suggest our *sing*, *sang*, etc., already often used as illustrations; yet there is an immense difference between the two cases: the Semitic phenomena are infinitely more intricate and various; and then they are the very life and soul of the inflection of the language, not in a single item reducible to anything more original, out of which they should be seen to grow, by an "inorganic" process. If we could conceive that, at some peculiarly plastic period in the history of a Germanic dialect, by an abnormal extension of the analogy of *sing*, *sang*, etc., the popular taste taking a sudden bent toward such formations, all the rest of the language should come to be patterned after that model, with consequent complete oblivion of the state of things out of which *sing*, *sang*, etc. proceeded—that would be something analogous with the present condition of Semitic.

The other peculiarities of the language are trifling as compared with these, not different in kind or degree from such as are variously found in other tongues. The structure of the verb is quite unlike ours. The element of time does not enter distinctly into it; the (only) two so-called tenses are explained as indicating primarily complete and incomplete action, and each fills various offices of tense. In Assyrian, the tense of complete action has gone almost entirely out of use. Of forms analogous with our moods, too, there is great poverty. But, as we have found the case in more than one other family, there is a disposition to the formation of numerous conjugations from one root, representing the radical idea in a causative, a reflexive, an intensive, a conative form, and so on. In Arabic, where these changes are fullest, there are some fifteen such conjugations; and about a dozen of them, each with its passive, are in tolerably frequent use. The tense of incomplete action (*yaqtulu*, etc.) has the aspect of being younger than the other, and of standing at only one remove from a noun; since its endings of number are mainly coincident with those of ordinary noun inflection, and it denotes person by prefixes, while the other (*qatala*, etc.) indicates person and number together by added endings, evidently of pronominal origin. Both tenses distinguish masculine from feminine subject, except in the first person. We find the distinction of gender (masculine and feminine only) here again for the first time since we left the Indo-European family. The nouns have the same three numbers as the verb, but of case distinction there is almost nothing. Derived nouns are formed by the help both of internal flexion and of external additions, both prefixes and suffixes; but only directly from the root: those successive derivations, by ending added to ending, in which the Indo-European abounds (as *true*, *tru-th*, *truth-ful*, *un-truthful-ly*) are quite unknown. Nor are compounds formed, save in exceptional cases. Finally, connecting particles, as means of the intertwining and subordination of clauses.

their conversion into a period, are almost wanting: Semitic style is bald and simple, proceeding from assertion to assertion. Another marked peculiarity is the persistency of radical meaning in derivative and figurative expression: the metaphorical or other transfer by which a new term is won, instead of soon passing out of memory, as in Indo-European, lets the old meaning continue to show through. Picturesqueness, pictorial vividness, therefore, are leading characteristics of Semitic language.

The scale of dialectic differences is much less in Semitic than in Indo-European; all the great branches, even, are as it were the closely related members of a single branch. This is not necessarily because their separation has been more recent than that of the branches of our family; for Semitic speech has shown itself much more rigid and changeless than Indo-European—or, it is believed, than any other variety of human speech. The ground of this difference doubtless lies partly in the character of the speakers; but it is also in part to be plainly read in the character of the language itself, with its rigid framework of three consonants appearing in the whole body of derivatives of each root, with its significant and therefore more carefully maintained variations of vowel, and with its incapacity of new formations by composition. Its primitive development, if development it was, was into so individual and sharply defined a type that it has since been comparatively exempt from variation.

There are two ways of looking at the peculiarities of Semitic structure. One, by far the simpler and more comfortable, is to pronounce them original and inexplicable, an indefeasible part of the appanage of the Semitic mind, to be taken as presented, and no questions asked. This, however, is virtually to declare them outside the pale of science, to abnegate with regard to them the right of the linguistic student to ask after the *why* of what he finds anywhere in language. The other way is to put this question and pursue it, not daunted by the acknowledged difficulties of the case. If all other languages have had a history of development into their present shape, then doubtless the Semitic also; if all the rest have started from pronounceable roots, composed of a combination of consonant and vowel, and have grown by external accretion of other similar elements to these, then it is not lightly to be believed that the Semitic has not done the same. That is to say, there must probably lie behind the consonantal triple roots and the internal flexion of the Semitic something more analogous with what is seen to lie at the basis of all other human speech; and there must have been a history of change from the one of these conditions to the other—whether we shall or shall not prove able to retrace the history and restore the primitive condition. Most linguistic scholars, as might be expected, take the latter view; and the attempt has been repeatedly made to reduce the roots to a more primitive form; but no definite and solid results have been yet attained. The most plausible conjectural account of the matter, probably, yet suggested has been that the universality of the three root-consonants is due (as in our hypothetical case above) to the inorganic extension of an analogy which had in some way become a dominant one; and that a stage of dissyllabic or trisyllabic derivative nouns lies between the primitive roots and their present shape. But to offer a plausible conjecture is one thing, and to demonstrate its value as a true explanation is another; and until something like a demonstration is reached (which possibly may never be), there will doubtless continue to be those who will look upon Semitic triliterality and internal flexion as original, as not only inaccessible to explanation but calling for none.

It must, however, be admitted that with the retracing of Semitic root-history is indissolubly bound up the historical connection of Semitic language with any other form of human speech. So long as Semitic flexion remains what it is, it cannot be identified with that of any other language; so long as Semitic roots remain what they are, no resemblances which may be traced between them and those of any other language can have real value. It has been a favorite subject of effort with scholars, ever since the beginning of linguistic study, to connect the germs of Semitic and Indo-European speech, and to prove the two families and the races that speak them branches of an ultimately common stock. There are many things which tempt to this: the two peoples are, at the beginning of their cultural history, near neighbors and mutual helpers; they are the two great conquering and civilizing white races, exchanging influence and institutions with one another through the ages: how natural to connect them more closely with one another than with mankind in general! This consideration goes all the way back to the representation of Shem and Japhet as sons of one father. But here, again, plausible theory is one thing, and scientific dem onstration another. If the items of apparent agreement which great scholars have hunted up between Semitic and Indo-European had been pointed out as existing between Indo-European and Zulu or Papuan, no one would think them of any account; and they are really worth no more where they are, as scientific evidence. It cannot be too strongly insisted on that, until the anomalies of Semitic language are at least measurably explained, it is too soon to say anything about a relationship between it and any other tongue.

The same rule is to be applied to the current assertions of Semitic relationship in the opposite direction, with the tongues which are grouped together to form the "Hamitic" family. In this family, the Egyptian occupies the same commanding position as the Chinese among the monosyllabic tongues of southeastern Asia. Egypt is the home of by far the oldest civilization of which we have any records. The question as to the chronology of its earliest monuments is not, to be sure, settled beyond dispute; but the present tendency of scientific inquiry seems decidedly toward recognizing as well founded even the extreme claims put forth respecting them, and fixing the reign of the first historical king at nearly 4000 B. C.; and even at that time the race must have been a powerful one, with a highly developed civilization. The knowledge of Egyptian language has been recovered in our own century, after being utterly lost for near two thousand years, and remarkable discoveries of new material in the country itself, and advances in Egyptian learning in Europe, are at this very time going on; so that many of the historical and chronological questions about which we are disputing will be fully settled for the generation that succeeds us.

The key to the decipherment of the ancient Egyptian was furnished in its descendant, the modern Coptic. The Coptic records are Christian only, written in an alphabet derived from the Greek, and dating back to the early centuries of our era. But the language was extinguished in vernacular use by the Arabic, three or four centuries ago. Several slightly different dialects are to be recognized in its literary remains.

The Egyptian language, old and new, was of the utmost simplicity of structure. It hardly knew a distinction between root and word; its fundamental elements (not always monosyllabic) were brought directly into the combinations of the sentence, without formal means of distinction of one part of speech from another. Nor even in inflection is such distinction clearly made; noun and verb are separated in part by the connection only: *ran-i*, for example, is literally 'naming-mine,' and means either 'my name' or 'I name or call.' The personal inflection of the verb is by means of affixed pronouns, loosely agglutinated to it, that of the third person being omissible when a subject noun is expressed. Mood and tense are marked, within narrow limits, by prefixed auxiliary words. The noun has no declension: relations of case are denoted by connectives; its use as noun is generally marked by a prefixed "article." And in this article, as in the pronominal elements generally, is made in the singular a distinction of masculine and feminine gender—a marked peculiarity of the language, putting it so far into one class with the Semitic and Indo-European. This particular, however, is one of which the reach and importance are wont to be greatly exaggerated; in its general character, the language can sustain no comparison at all with the other two mentioned; it is little richer or more developed than the lowest tongues of the eastern Asiatic races.

It must be clearly apparent from this description how venturesome is the assertion of a relationship between the Egyptian and Semitic. There are, to be sure, certain remarkable resemblances between the pronouns of the two languages; but to rely on these as sufficient proof of connection is not an acceptable proceeding. In many languages, signs of relationship, abundantly traceable through their whole material, are especially conspicuous in the pronouns; of connection proved by pronominal evidence solely, or chiefly, there are no examples. And the question is, whether pronominal words could possibly retain an almost undisguised identity while the rest of the language was undergoing such a tremendous revolution as should alone be able to convert Egyptian poverty of inflection and fixity of root and freedom of radical form into the strictly regulated wealth and internal flexion of the Semitic. And the provisional answer must be in the negative. We do not need to deny the possibility of ultimately proving the Semitic related with the Hamitic, any more than with the Indo-European; we have only to see that no sufficient evidence of it has yet been brought forward, nor is likely to be so until the riddle of Semitic structure is solved.

Two other groups of languages in northern and northeastern Africa are held to be ultimately related with the Egyptian, forming along with it the Hamitic family. They are the Libyan or Berber group (Kabyle and Tamashek, and, more doubtfully, Hausa), and, southward from Egypt, the Ethiopian, or Cushitic group (Beja, Galla, Dankâli, Somâli, etc.).

Nearly the whole of the narrower southern peninsula of Africa is occupied by the branches of a single very distinct family, best called the South-African (known also as Bantu, Chuana, Zingian). It has no culture and no literature, except what it has produced by the aid of Christian missionaries in the most recent time. It is strikingly characterized by its extensive use of prefixes: a word without a formative prefix being here nearly as unknown as, in the synthetic period of Indo-European, a word without a formative suffix. Different prefixes distinguish various classes of nouns, and numbers in those classes: thus, in Zulu, *um-fana* is 'boy,' and *aba-fana* 'boys;' *in-komo* is 'cow,' and *izin-komo* 'cows;' *ili-zwe* is 'country,' and *ama-zwe* 'countries,' and so on. Then, in the clauses into which any one of these words enters as dominant member, other members relating to them—as adjectives, possessives, verbs—take into their structure representative parts of the same prefix: e. g. *aba-fana b-ami aba-kulu, ba tanda*, 'my large boys, they love;' but *izin-komo z-ami izin-kulu, zi tanda*, 'my large cows, they love.' This is like Latin or Greek inverted; an alliterative instead of a rhyming congruence. Verbal mood and tense are signified in part by suffixes, as are also conjugational distinctions analogous with those made in Scythian and Semitic language: thus, from *bona*, 'see,' come *bonisa*, 'show,' *bonana*, 'see each other,' *bonisana*, 'show each other,' and so on. Case-relations are signified by prefixed prepositions. The South-African languages are thus by no means unprovided with the formal means of sufficiently various distinction. Those of them which border on the Hottentot dialects have in their alphabets peculiar sounds called "clicks," made by sharp separation of the tongue from the roof of the mouth, with suction.

The clicks are a marked feature of the Hottentot, and look as if they had been introduced into the South-African from thence, perhaps along with mixture of blood. There is no relationship whatever between the two families; nor, probably, between the Hottentot and the Bushman. Of the last mentioned, the scientific investigation is now just beginning (Bleek); the other, chiefly on the ground of its partial distinction of genders, has been by some accounted a branch of the Hamitic family, strayed away into the far south and greatly degraded in type; but the connection is confidently denied by others.

Between the South-African and Hamitic domains, in a broad band extending across the widest part of the African continent, is found an intricate and heterogeneous mass of dialects, of which the classification is a matter of much difference of opinion among even the latest investigators, and which are of too little importance to be dwelt on by us. The region is that of the typical negro; yet there are also in it races of a lighter tint: the variety of physical characteristics in Africa, among races which we in our ignorance lump together as one, is not inconsiderable.

Before leaving the eastern continent, we must return to Europe for a word or two upon one language which has as yet found no place for notice—the Basque, now spoken, in four principal dialects and a number of minor varieties, in a very limited mountain-district at the angle of the Bay of Biscay, astride the frontier, but chiefly on the Spanish side. It is believed to be the modern representative of the ancient Iberian, and to have belonged to the older population of the peninsula, before the irruption of the Indo-European Celts. Traces of local nomenclature show it to have occupied also at least the southern part of France. The Basque may then be the sole surviving relic and witness of an aboriginal western European population, dispossessed by the intrusive Indo-European tribes. It stands entirely alone, no kindred having yet been found for it in any part of the world. It is of an exaggeratedly agglutinative type, incorporating into its verb a variety of relations which are almost everywhere else expressed by independent words.

The Basque forms a suitable stepping-stone from which to enter the peculiar linguistic domain of the New World, since there is no other dialect of the Old World which so much resembles in structure the American languages. Not that the latter are all of accordant form. Although it is usual among philologists to account them as making together but a single great family, this is in no small part a classification of ignorance, and should be held only provisionally, ready to be changed, if necessary, when additional knowledge is won. As regards the material of expression, it is fully confessed that there is irreconcilable diversity among them. There are a very considerable number of groups, between whose significant signs exist no more apparent correspondences than between those of English, Hungarian, and Malay: none, namely, which may not be merely fortuitous. So, for example, between the neighboring tongues of the Algonkin, Iroquois, and Dakota groups, the speakers of which we have every reason to regard as ultimately related, on the ground of common physical characteristics, gifts, and institutions. Indeed, there is even linguistic evidence to the same effect. The case seems to be clearly one where the style of structure of a language is more permanent than the material, constituting of itself a satisfactory proof of relationship. That is to say, while the material elements of these tongues have been highly variable since their separation from one another, till identities in this department are no longer traceable—a feature in their history which we shall understand and judge more truly when the special laws of their growth and change shall be much better comprehended—there still remains, un altered in its main features, their common mode of managing and combining the linguistic material, of apprehending the relations which are to be expressed in language, and the way in which they shall be expressed.

And this common mode of structure, which, in its various aspects and degrees, is at least generally characteristic of American language, is called the polysynthetic or incorporating. Its marked tendency is toward the absorbing of the other parts of the sentence into the verb. Not the subject alone, as in Indo-European, enters into combination with the root for predicative expression, but the objects also, of every kind of relation, and the signs of time and place and manner and degree, and a host of modifiers of the verbal action, for purposes unknown to any grammatical system with which we are ordinarily familiar. It has been deliberately calculated, by one long versed in the chief Algonkin dialects (Rev. T. Hurlbut), that 17,000,000 verbal forms may be made from an Algonkin root; and even if our credence were to extend to only the thousandth part of this, enough would be left to be very characteristic of a structural style. Everything tends to verbal expression: nouns, and adjectives, and even adverbs and prepositions, are regularly conjugated; nouns are to a great extent verbal forms: e. g. 'home' is 'they live there,' or 'where they live.' Or, to express it more accurately, our grammatical terminology does not at all suit these languages; we are involved in contradictions and absurdities as soon as we attempt to apply it to them. Of course, the tendency is toward the formation of words of immense length, and of an intricate structure that gives expression to a host of things left by us to be understood. The longest word in Eliot's

Massachusetts Bible, however, is of eleven syllables: *wut-appesituqussun-nooweht-unk-quoh*, which renders "kneeling down to him" in our version; but it really means 'he came to a state of rest upon the bended knees, doing reverence unto him' (J. H. Trumbull). All the parts of such combinations must be recognized in their separateness; the word must be in all its members significant and self-explaining. And the separate elements are not, as is often represented, a reduction to manageable fragments of long words for which they stand; they are rather the desired significant element among those which compose the other word. Of course, there are infinite possibilities of expressiveness in such a structure; and it would only need that some native-American Greek race should arise, to fill it full of thought and fancy, and put it to the uses of a noble literature, and it would be rightly admired as rich and flexible, perhaps, beyond anything else that the world knew. As it is, it makes upon us the impression of as much exceeding the due medium of formal expressiveness as the Chinese comes short of it; it is cumbrous and time-wasting in its immense polysyllabism. Partly as a result of its multiplicity of accessory details, it seems to us deficient in simple abstract terms: as having, for instance, separate roots for washing all kinds of objects, in all kinds of ways, but none for 'washing' pure and simple. There is something of our prejudice in this, however; so a Chinaman or Englishman might criticise a Latin adjective unfavorably, saying: "The Latin is deficient in the power of abstraction, of considering a quality apart from its accidental accessories: so *magnus*, for example, does not signify simply *ta*, 'great,' but a quality of great of a first degree, and as belonging to only one object, and to one that is (for some unassignable reason) regarded as masculine and can be only the subject of a verb; *magnas* indicates in like manner an objective and feminine and plural greatness; but for the bare idea of *ta*, 'great,' the Latin has no expression."

There are other characteristics of American speech, of universal or general prevalence, like the distinction of animate and inanimate gender (which would seem to be quite as significant, and as capable of being applied to higher formative uses, as is our own sexual gender), the possession of the inclusive and exclusive first persons plural, the classificatory system of designation of relationships, and so on; but they are of only minor importance, as compared with the general style of structure.

The polysynthetic structure does not belong in the same degree to all the American languages; on the contrary, it seems to be altogether effaced or originally wanting in some. So, for example, a monosyllabic or uninflective character has been claimed for the Otomi in Mexico, and for one or two dialects in South America; and all sign of polysynthetism has been denied (C. F. Hartt) to the great Tupi-Guarani stock, on the eastern side of the South American continent. It remains yet to be determined how far such exceptions are real, and how far apparent only. But the common character is recognizable in so large a part of American tongues, from the Eskimo of the extreme north to the Antarctic Ocean, that the linguist regards them, with considerable confidence, as members of a family, descendants of one original speech, of unknown age, locality, and derivation. Attempts have been made to connect them with some dialect or family of the Old World, but with obviously unavoidable ill-success. If, for example, there is not left in Algonkin, Iroquois, and Dakota enough of the material once common to the ancestors of all to furnish ground for trustworthy identifications, much less are they to be identified with tongues from which they have been so much longer separated that even their structure is of a different character. It is not proper, perhaps, to limit the possibilities of the future; but there appears to be no tolerable prospect that, even supposing the American languages derived from the Old World, they can ever be proved so, or traced to their parentage.

An exhaustive classification of the American languages is at present impossible; and to give what can already be given would demand much more space than can be afforded here. There are many great groups, and a host of lesser knots of idioms, or of dialects isolated or unclassified. The Eskimos line the whole northern coast, and the northeastern down to Newfoundland. The Athabaskan or Tinné occupies a great region in the far northwest (the Apache and Navajo in the south also belong to it), and is flanked on the west by the Selish and other smaller groups. The Algonkin had in possession the northeastern and middle United States, and stretched westward to the Rocky Mountains; within its territory was included that of the Iroquois. The Dakota (Sioux) is the largest of the families occupying the great prairies and plains of the far West, to the Rocky Mountains. Beyond them is found the extensive Shoshone family, and, north of it, the Sahaptin and Selish families. Still further, on the Pacific coast, occurs a perplexing variety of dialects. The Muskokee and Cherokee group filled the States of the southeast. In Colorado and Utah commence the towns of the settled and comparatively civilized "*pueblo*

Indians," rising to the more advanced culture of the Mexican peoples, attaining its height in the Mayas of Central America, and continued in the empire of the Incas of Peru. The Quichua of the latter, with the related Aymara, are still the native dialects of a considerable part of South America; with the Tupi-Guarani, already referred to, on the east, in the valleys of the Amazons and its tributaries.

The condition of American languages is thus an epitome of that of the language of the world in general. Great and wide-spread families, limited groups, isolated and perishing dialects, touch and jostle one another. Such, in the vicissitudes of human affairs, must be the history of races and of their dialects. What families, once covering great tracts of the earth's surface, have been wiped out without a trace, what others have been reduced to mere fragments, what have started from a narrow beginning, and, by prosperous growth and by working in parts of other races, have risen to prominence—on such points as these we must remain forever only imperfectly informed. We need to guard against supposing that, when we have succeeded in classifying all existing languages and determining their relations, we shall have gained a complete outline of the history of human language: the darkness of the past may hide a great deal of which we do not even catch a glimpse.

Some of the questions bearing on this point will engage our attention in the next chapter.

CHAPTER XIII.

LANGUAGE AND ETHNOLOGY.

Limitations to the scope of linguistic science: materials of speech not analyzable to the end; annihilation, transmutation, new creation, possible in it; cumulative character of evidences of relationship. Impossibility that language can prove either unity or variety of the human race. Relation of language to race, as transmitted institution only; exchange of language accompanying mixture of blood. Insolubility of the ethnological problem. Contributions to it of archæology and linguistics; merits of the latter; importance of the testimony of language to race. Reconciliation of the various lines of ethnological evidence. Inferior value of other classifications of language as compared with the genetic.

The classification of languages given in the preceding chapter has confessedly represented only the present state of knowledge, and is liable to amendment hereafter, as further investigation shall bring more light. But its main features will probably stand unaltered. The leading independent families will continue separate to the end. One and another of those now recognized, it is true, may hereafter assume a dependent place, as branches of a wider and more comprehensive family, but there is no reasonable ground for anticipating that such will ever be the case with them all. To maintain this is not so much to limit the future of linguistic science, as, rather, to recognize the limits which in the nature of things are set to its progress; as a brief and simple exposition will show.

We must not fail to appreciate the essential difference between the material of the physical sciences and that of our subject; that we have to deal with the usages of men, in all of which intervenes that indefinite element, the human will as determined by circumstance, by habit, by individual character; and that these do not admit an analysis penetrating to the ultimate elements. There is no natural substance which the chemist may not aspire to analyze; into whatever new forms and combinations an element may enter, he has tests which will detect its presence; neither new creation nor annihilation is possible; all change is but recombination of material always existing; there is no transmutation of one element into another. But it is altogether different with speech. A word, a whole family of words, perishes by simple disuse, and is as if it had never been, unless civilization is there to make a record of its departed worth. A whole language, or family of languages, is annihilated by the destruction of the community that spoke it, or by the adoption of another language by that community. When the Gauls learned Latin, there was nothing saved which, without the aid of external evidences, should show what their primitive speech had been; when the Etruscans were Latinized, but for the scattering words which they had written down, their speech passed out of all reach of knowledge: and many a dialect has doubtless gone out in a like way, leaving no such telltale records. The actual creation of the new in speech is, as we have seen, very rare; yet there is nothing whatever to prevent it save men's preferences. And it amounts, for all purposes of analysis, to a new creation, when a derivative word gets so far from its primitive, in form and meaning, that the tie between them is traceable only by external, historical evidence: and of such cases all language is full. A formative element is annihilated when it is worn off from every form which it once made; such a one is created when it is fully established in its derived and subordinate use: no process of analysis that we have or of which we can conceive would ever find the lost *masi* of our first persons plural, or detect the presence of *did* in *loved:* there is wanted the historical support, for lack of which a host of other like cases cannot be accounted for.

The changes of linguistic usage are all the time separating in appearance what really belongs together: *bishop* and *évêque* are historically one word; so are *eye* and *auge;* so are *I* and *je* and *ik* and *ἐγών* and *aham;* though not one of them has an audible element which is found in any other. And then, the same changes are bringing together what really belongs apart: the Latin *locus* and the Sanskrit *lokas,* 'place, room,' have really nothing to do with one another, though so nearly identical and in closely-related languages; likewise Greek ὅλος (*holos*) and English *whole;* and so on. We may take the English language (as too many do), and compare it with every unrelated dialect in existence, and find a liberal list of apparent correspondences; which then a little study of the English words will prove unreal and fallacious. This is, above all others, the decisive fact which stands in the way of a comparison that shall penetrate to the bottom of the matter. If there were no resemblances in either the material or the structure of language save such as have a historical basis, we might let them be swept away as much as they would; what was left, if anything were left, would suffice to prove relationship. As it is, the process of proof is not direct and absolute, but cumulative; the result comes from a sufficient number of particulars of which each, taken by itself, would prove nothing. We have had expressly to allow that two dialects may diverge from a common original so far that all sign of their kinship shall be lost; there may be a plenty of the altered products of common material in them both; but if it have gotten into the condition of *bishop* and *évêque*, it is of no use to the linguist. Accidental correspondences are capable of rising to a certain percentage; if all that appear stand at or near this figure, the case is one hopeless of settlement.

This cumulative character of the signs of relationship, the uncertain value of any single item, and the need of historical evidence to support their interpretation, set limits to the reach and competence of linguistic investigation. Thus far, the recognized families are such as have had a common development. There are even some of which the sole uniting tie is a common style of structure. If we cannot prove the American languages related except by the characteristic of polysynthetism, nor the southeastern Asiatic except by that of monosyllabism, it is obviously impossible to prove American and Chinese related by the material correspondences of their roots. In the present stage of linguistic science, root-comparisons are surrounded with too many uncertainties and dangers to have any value. All that have been made thus far are worthless; whether the future will show anything better, we may leave for the future to determine. There is no harm in any one's rating even too highly the possibilities of a progressive science like linguistics, provided he do not let his sanguineness warp his judgment as to what shall have been at any given time already accomplished, and lead him to take plausible fancies for tried and approved facts. He who realizes the immense difficulty of arriving at the ultimate roots even of a family like the Indo-European, despite the exceptional antiquity and conservation of its oldest dialects, will be likely to be saved from hanging his expectations on root-comparisons.

It is, then, impossible that linguistic science should ever be able to prove, by the evidence of community of the first germs of expression, that the human race in the beginning formed one society together. Even if the number of families be lessened by future research, it will never be reduced to one.

But it is even far more demonstrable that linguistic science can never prove the variety of human races and origins. As we have repeatedly seen, there are no limits to the diversity which may arise by discordant growth between languages originally one. Given any angle of divergence, and the law of increasing divergence (p. 165), and the distance of the ends of two lines may be made, by their production far enough, to exceed any assignable quantity; and in linguistics, as has been just pointed out, there comes, far short of infinite prolongation, a distance across which the historical scholar, with his limited vision, cannot see: and that is, for all practical purposes, infinity. The understanding now won of the methods of growth and change in speech has taken away all possibility of a dogmatic assertion on the part of the linguistic scholar that language has a various origin. If every tongue had from the beginning its own structure and material complete, then language-history would run back only in parallel lines, with no indication of convergence. But the difference of English and German and Danish comes by divergent growth from a common centre; that of English and Russian and Armenian and Persian is by similar divergence from a more distant centre: and we cannot say that English and Turkish and Circassian and Japanese may not owe their difference to the same cause. The lines of development of all families of language do point back to one original common condition of formless roots; and precisely what these roots were, in shape and meaning, we cannot in most families even begin to trace out; we cannot, then, deny that they may have been the same for all. We may talk of probabilities as much as we please; but of impossibility there is actually nothing in the assumption of identity of origins.

This, again, implies that linguistic science cannot assume to prove the diversity of human races. But it deserves to be pointed out that there is an additional difficulty in the way of the same proof. If we must regard it as at least possible (whether we admit it as an established conclusion or not) that men made the beginnings of their own speech, as well as created all its after-development, then we shall be obliged also to allow that a period of some length may have elapsed before any so settled store of expression had been won that it should show itself in the later forms of language; and during this period the race, though one, might have spread and separated, so that the abiding germs of the speech of each part should be independent. As a general conclusion, the incompetence of linguistic science to pass any decisive judgment as to the unity or diversity of the human race, or even as to that of human speech, appears to be completely and irrevocably demonstrated.

Another highly important anthropological question,

connected with and suggested by our classification of languages, concerns its relation to the ethnologist's classification of races. And here we have to make at the outset the unreserved confession that the two do not by any means correspond and agree: wholly discordant languages are spoken by communities whom the ethnologist would not separate in race from one another; and related languages are spoken by men of apparently different race. And the view we have taken of language is entirely consistent with this. We have seen that there is no necessary tie between race and language; that every man speaks the language he has learned, being born into the possession of no one rather than another; and that, as any individual may learn a language different from that of his parents or of his remoter ancestors, so a community (which is only an aggregate of individuals) may do the same thing, not retaining the slightest trace of its ancestral speech. The world, past and present, is full of examples of this, of every class and kind, and sundry of them have been already noticed by us in passing—as the combination of heterogeneous elements, now using only English as their native tongue, found in the American community; the Celts of Gaul, the Normans of France, the Celts of Ireland and Cornwall, the Etruscans of Italy, and all the other communities whose idioms have been crowded out and replaced by the Latin, the English, the Arabic. There are conquering languages which are always encroaching upon the territory of their neighbors, as there are others which are always losing ground.

The testimony of language to race is thus not that of a physical characteristic, nor of anything founded on and representing such; but only that of a transmitted institution, which, under sufficient inducement, is capable of being abandoned by its proper inheritors, or assumed by men of strange blood. And the inducement lies in external circumstances, not in the nature of the language abandoned or assumed. Political control, social superiority, superiority of culture—these are the leading causes which bring about change of speech. Or rather, these are the added circumstances which, in the case of a mixture of communities, decide which element of population shall give, chiefly or wholly, its tongue to the resulting community. If there were no such thing as mixture of blood, then there would at least be next to nothing of the shifting of speech. Borrowing there would still be, but not substitution.

It is mixture of communities which creates the great intricacy of the ethnological problem, on its linguistic side as on its physical; which renders it, in fact, insoluble except approximately; and which, so far as the history of races is concerned, makes the linguist as glad of the help of the physicist as *vice versâ*. The ethnologist has to confess the same possibility which was admitted on the part of the linguists at the end of the preceding chapter. During the long past, there have been indefinite encroachments, superpositions, mixtures, displacements, destructions, among human races (or derived branches of a unitary race), as among human languages (or derived branches of the unitary human language). In neither department is it likely that the history will ever be unraveled with anything approaching to completeness: especially, since the great extension which the generally-admitted period of man's existence on the earth has lately received. Opinions are by no means as yet agreed upon this point; but even those who still refuse to accept the new doctrine are preparing themselves to believe by-and-by, if the evidence to that effect shall turn out irresistible, that the life of man has lasted for scores, if not for hundreds, of thousands of years. This is a doctrine of the highest interest to the ethnologist; but it balks his hopes of being able to trace more than a little way into the thick darkness of early time the lines of race-history; it gives the precedence to anthropology as the science of man's development as a whole race, or a congeries of undistinguishable races, as yet not sufficiently differentiated in their capacities and products to be held apart from one another; and to zoölogy as alone capable of answering the question as to his origin.

The records of the earliest and rudest period of man's activity are of two kinds: the products of their art and industry, wrought by their hands; and the primitive materials and forms of their speech, wrought for the uses of their minds; the latter the instrument of sociality, as the former of individual subsistence and defense; both turning, each in its own way and measure, to the education and equipment of the higher capacities of the race, and its advance toward self-control, the control of Nature, and civilization. Both kinds of record are eagerly sought and carefully scanned by historical students, as evidences of a remoter past than the pen of history or the voice of legend reports. But, of the two, the linguistic remains are infinitely the more important and instructive; and it is almost they alone which can serve the purpose of the ethnologist, since the others are indicative rather of a grade of development than of the special endowments or habits of a race. The linguistic evidence has over even the physical the advantage that it is far more abundant and varied, and therefore manageable. The differences in the kingdom of language are not like those which pre vail within the limits of a single species of animals; they are equal, rather, in range to those which belong to the whole animal kingdom. It is, to the other, like a microscopic image thrown up by optical means upon a wall, where its parts may be examined and measured and described and compared by even the unskilled student. Breadth of knowledge and competent judgment are to be won in physical ethnology only by rare opportunities, peculiar gifts, and prolonged training. Though languages are traditional institutions, they are of a special kind, capable of application to ethnological purposes far beyond any other, as being so various and so distinct as they are, capable of being looked at objectively, and handled and compared with accuracy. They are persistent, also, at least to a degree far beyond other institutions.

To admit that a language can be exchanged, therefore, is by no means to deny its value as a record of human history, even of race-history; it is only to put that value upon its proper basis, and confess those limitations which can in no manner be avoided, and of which a due consideration is needful to the proper use of linguistic evidence. It still remains true that, upon the whole, language is determined by race, since each human being usually learns to speak from his parents and others of the same blood. And the marked exceptions to this rule take place in the full light of historical record. Civilization facilitates mixture, as it does communication. It is not the wild and obscure races which are, or have ever been, mixing blood and mixing or shifting speech upon a grand scale; it is the cultivated ones. If one barbarous tribe overcomes another, unless the conquerors absorb the conquered into their own community, there is not usually a change of speech: but nations like the Romans and Arabs, who come with the force of an organized polity and a literature, extend their speech widely over strange peoples. Where the information derivable from language, therefore, is most needed, there it comes with the greatest presumption of accuracy.

Hence, when the ethnological relations of a community or of a group of communities are to be settled, the first question is as to the affinities of its speech. This does not necessarily decide the case; the linguistic evidence may be overborne by some other; but nothing can be determined without it; it lays the basis for further discussion. We need only to quote an example or two in illustration of this. The Basques are a white, "Caucasian" race; there is nothing in their other ethnological characteristics which should forbid our connecting them with any great division of the white race; but their speech at once cuts them off from every other, and we accept its decision as authoritative. Out of what mixtures the original Iberians may have grown, we cannot tell; nor can we ever absolutely know that the Basques did not borrow their Euskarian dialect, as the French their Romanic dialect; there are indefinite possibilities lying behind; but the language tells us a great deal, and probably all that will ever be within our reach. Again, of the Etruscans there are records and descriptions and pictures, and products, art and industrial; but to settle the relationship of the race the ethnologists with one consent appeal to the infinitesimal remnants of Etruscan speech: a single page of connected Etruscan text, with but a hint of its meaning, would in the briefest time settle the question whether the race is to be connected with any other on earth, or whether, like the Basque, it is an isolated fragment. There lies before us a vast and complicated problem in the American races; and here, again, it is their language that must do by far the greatest part of the work in solving it. American ethnology depends primarily and in bulk on the classifications and connections of dialects; till that foundation is laid, all is uncertain; although there are points involved which may not yield even to the combination of all attainable evidence, from every quarter.

We are to look for no real reconciliation between the results won by the two great branches of ethnological study until their methods are more fully established than at present; nor is it worth while to hurry the process—least of all, to attempt prematurely an artificial and superficial scheme of combination. All that will come in good time, if we only have patience. Within its own domain, each is supreme. The classifications and relations of speech are what they are, without any reference to underlying questions of race; and yet, those questions cannot be kept down and ignored by the linguist: his study is too thoroughly a historical one, it involves too much of the element of race in the later periods, to allow of our leaving that element out of account for the earlier. As one of the leading branches of historical investigation, as claiming to make its contribution to the elucidation of the past, it must offer its results to be criticised by every other concurrent branch. And to exaggerate its claims, or to put them upon a false basis, is both needless and harmful. If any one is not content with the degree of dignity and authority that belongs to the science of language when kept within the very strictest limits which a sound and impartial criticism is impelled to draw, there are other departments in which his aid will be welcomed, and he had better turn to them.

There is one more point calling for brief notice in

connection with our classification of the dialects of the world. That classification aimed at being a strictly genetical one, each family embracing those tongues which, by the sum of all available evidences, were deemed traceable to a common ancestor. To the historical philologist, still deep in the labor of determining relations and tracing out the course of structural development, this is by far the most important of all; indeed, the value of any other at present is so small as to be hardly worthy of notice. The wider distinction of languages as isolating, agglutinative, and inflective, which has a degree of currency and familiarity, offers a convenient, but far from exact or absolute, test by which the character of linguistic structure may be tried; the three degrees lie in a certain line of progress, but, as in all such cases, pass into one another. To lay any stress upon this as a basis of classification is like making the character of the hair or the color of the skin a basis of classification in physical ethnology, or the number of stamens or the combination of leaves in botany: it ignores and overrides other distinctions of an equal or of greater importance. If the naturalist had the actual certainty which the linguist has of the common descent of related species, he would care little for any other classification, but would spend his strength upon the elaboration and perfection of this one. The linguist has enough of this still left to do; and till it is all accomplished, at any rate, any other is of small account to him.

CHAPTER XIV.

NATURE AND ORIGIN OF LANGUAGE.

Language an acquisition, a part of culture. Its universality among men; limitation to man; difference between human and other means of expression. Communication the direct motive to the production of speech; this the conscious and determining element in all language-history. Natural cries as basis of the development; question as to their nature and range; postulation of instinctive articulate utterances uncalled for. Use of the voice as principal means of expression. Imitative element in the beginnings of speech; range and limits of onomatopœic expression. The doctrine of roots. Sufficiency of this view of the origin of language; the opposing miraculous theory. Capacity involved in language-making; difference in this respect between men and lower animals. Relation of language to development of man; rate and manner of its growth.

Our examination of the history of language, of its mode of transmission, preservation, and alteration, has shown us clearly enough what we are to hold respecting its nature. It is not a faculty, a capacity; it is not an immediate exertion of the thinking power; it is a mediate product and an instrumentality. To many, superficial or prejudiced, inquirers this seems an unsatisfactory, even a low, view; but it is because they confound together two very different senses of the word *language*. Man possesses, as one of his most marked and distinctive characteristics, a faculty or capacity of speech—or, more accurately, various faculties and capacities which lead inevitably to the production of speech: but the faculties are one thing, and their elaborated products are another and very different one. So man has a capacity for art, for the invention of instruments, for finding out and applying the resources of mathematics, for many other great and noble things; but no man is born an artist, an engineer, or a calculist, any more than he is born a speaker. In regard to these various exercises of our activities our condition is the same. In all alike, the race has been undergoing almost from the beginning a training of its capacities, step by step, each step being embodied in a product. The growth of art implies a period of rude shapings, and a rise to higher and higher production by improving on former models and processes. Mechanics still more clearly has the same history; it was by the use of ruder instruments, by the dexterity acquired in that use and the consequent suggestion of improvements, that men came finally to locomotives and power-looms. Mathematics began with the apprehension that one and one are two, and its development has been like that of the others. And every new individual of the race has to go through the same series of steps, from the same humble beginnings. Only, he takes them at lightning-speed, as compared with their first elaboration; because he is led onward by others over a beaten and smoothed track. The half-grown boy now is often a more advanced mathematician or mechanician than the wisest of the Greeks: not because his gifts are superior to theirs, but because he has only to receive and assimilate what they and their successors have wrought out for him. Though possessing the endowments of a Homer or a Demosthenes, no man can speak any language until he has learned it, as truly learned it as he learns the multiplication-table, or the demonstrations of Euclid.

Now these collected products of the exercise of man's developing powers, which are passed on from one generation to another, increasing and changing as they go, we call institutions, constituents of our culture. Something of them is possessed by every section of humanity. There is no member of any community, however barbarous, who is not raised vastly above what he would otherwise be by learning what his fellows have to teach him, acquiring their fragments of knowledge, however scanty, and their arts—including the art of speech. Doubtless the most degraded community has more to teach the most gifted individual than he would have learned, to the end of his life, by the use of his own faculties unaided; certainly this is so as regards speech. Every one acquires that which the accident of birth places within his reach, exercising his faculties upon that foundation, expanded and at the same time constrained by it, making to it his individual contribution, if he have one to make: just as truly in the case of language as of any other part. Language is in no way to be separated from the rest: it is in some respects very unlike them; but so are they unlike one another; if it be the one most fundamentally important, most highly characteristic, most obviously the product and expression of reason, that is only a difference of degree.

We regard every language, then, as an institution, one of those which, in each community, make up its culture. Like all the constituent elements of culture, it is various in every community, even in the different individuals composing each. There are communities in which it has come down within the strict limits of race;

in others it has been, partly or wholly, taken from strange races; for, like the rest, it is capable of being transferred or shifted. Race-characteristics can only go down by blood; but race-acquisitions—language not less than religion, or science—can be borrowed and lent.

The universality of language, we may remark in passing, is thus due to nothing more profound or mysterious than that every division of the human race has been long enough in existence for its language-capacities to work themselves out to some manner of result. Precisely so, there is a universal possession by men of some body of instruments, to help the hands in providing for human needs. This universality does not at all prove that, if we could see coming into being a new race, by whatever means brought the existing race into being, we should find it within any definite assignable period possessed of instruments—or of speech.

But, as things are, every community of men has a common language, while none of the lower animals are possessed of such; their means of communication being of so different a character that it has no right to be called by the same name. No special obligation rests upon the linguist to explain this difference, any more than upon the historian of art or of mechanics to explain why the lower animals are neither artists nor machine-makers. It is enough for him to point out that, the gifts of man being such as they are, he invariably comes to the possession of this as well as of the other elements of culture, while not one of the lower races has shown itself capable of originating a civilization, in any element, linguistic or other; their utmost capacity being that of being trained by the higher race to the exercise of activities which in their own keeping had remained undeveloped, of being taught various arts and acts, performed partly mechanically, partly with a certain hardly determinable degree of intelligence. But the subject is one upon which erroneous views are so prevalent that we can hardly help giving it a brief consideration.

The essential difference, which separates man's means of communication in kind as well as degree from that of the other animals, is that, while the latter is instinctive, the former is, in all its parts, arbitrary and conventional. That this is so, the whole course of our exposition has sufficiently shown. It is fully proved by the single circumstance that for each object, or act, or quality, there are as many names as there are languages in the world, each answering as good a purpose as any other, and capable of being substituted for another in the usage of any individual. There is not in a known language a single item which can be truly claimed to exist *φύσει*, 'by nature;' each stands in its accepted use *θέσει*, 'by an act of attribution,' in which men's circumstances, habits, preferences, will, are the determining force. Even where the onomatopœic or imitative element is most conspicuous—as in *cuckoo* and *pewee*, in *crack* and *whiz*—there is no tie of necessity, but only of convenience: if there were a necessity, it would extend equally to other animals and other noises; and also to all tongues; while in fact these conceptions have elsewhere wholly other names. No man can become possessed of any existing language without learning it; no animal (that we know of) has any expression which he learns, which is not the direct gift of nature to him. We are not less generously treated in this latter respect than the animals; we have also our "natural" expression, in grimace, gesture, and tone; and we make use of it: on the one hand, for communication where the usual conventional means is made of no avail—as between men of different tongue, or those who by deafness are cut off from the use of speech—and, on the other hand, for embellishing and explaining and enforcing our ordinary language: where it is of a power and value that no student of language can afford to overlook. In the domain of feeling and persuasion, in all that is intended to impress the personality of the communicator upon the recipient, it possesses the highest consequence. We say with literal truth that a look, a tone, a gesture, is often more eloquent than elaborate speech. Language is harmed for some uses by its conventionality. Words of sympathy or affection can be repeated parrot-like by one whose heartless tone takes all value from them; there is no persuasion in a discourse which is given as if from a mere animated speaking-machine. And herein comes clearly to light the true sphere of natural expression; it indicates feeling, and feeling only. From the cry and groan and laugh and smile up to the lightest variations of tone and feature which the skilled elocutionist uses, it is emotional, subjective. Not a tittle of evidence has ever been brought forward to show that there is such a thing as the natural expression of an intellectual conception, of a judgment, of a cognition. It is where expression quits its emotional natural basis, and turns to intellectual uses, that the history of language begins.

Nor is it less plain what inaugurates the conversion, and becomes the main determining element in the whole history of production of speech; it is the desire of communication. This turns the instinctive into the intentional. As itself becomes more distinct and conscious, it lifts expression of all kinds above its natural basis, and makes of it an instrumentality; capable, as such, of indefinite extension and improvement. He who (as many do) leaves this force out of account, cannot but make utter shipwreck of his whole linguistic philosophy. Where the impulse to communication is wanting, no speech comes into being. Here, again, the parallelism between language and the other departments of culture is close and instructive. The man growing up in solitude would initiate no culture. He would never come to a knowledge of any of the higher things of which he was capable. It needs not only the inward power, but also the outward occasion, to make man what he is capable of becoming. This is characteristic of his whole historical attitude. Races and generations of men have passed away in barbarism and ignorance who were as capable of civilization as the mass of the present civilized communities: indeed, there are such actually passing away around us. It is in no wise to deny the grand endowments of human nature that we ascribe the acquisition of speech to an external inducement. We may illustrate the case by a comparison. A stone has lain motionless for ages on the verge of a precipice, and may lie there for ages longer; all the cosmic forces of gravity will not stir it. But a chance thrust from some passing animal jostles it from its equilibrium, and it goes crashing down. Which, shall we say, caused the fall? gravity, or the thrust? Each, in its way; the great force would not have wrought this particular effect but for the aid of the petty one; and there is nothing derogatory to the dignity of gravitation in admitting the fact. Just so in language: the great and wonderful powers of the human soul would never move in this particular direction but for the added push given by the desire of communication; when this leads the way, all the rest follows.

Our recognition of the determining force of this element is far from implying that communication is the sole end, or the highest end, of speech. We have sufficiently noticed, in the second chapter, the infinite value of expression to the operations of each individual mind and soul, and its fundamental value as an element in the progress of the race. But it is here as elsewhere; men strive after that which is nearest and most obvious to them, and attain thereby a vast deal more than they foresaw. In the devising and constructing of instruments, of all kinds, men have had directly in view only what may be called the lower uses of them, their immediate contributions to comfort and safety and sensuous enjoyment; but the result has been a calling-out of many of the higher powers which could find appropriate exercise in no other way, a reduction of Nature to service in a manner that allows a part of the race to engage in the more elevated and elevating occupations; and a discovery of truths in bewildering abundance. A yet closer parallel is afforded by the closely kindred art of writing, which adds to and enhances all the advantages belonging to the art of speech, and is as indispensable to the highest culture as is speech to the lower; but, like speech, it came into being by a process in which the only conscious motive was communication; all its superior uses followed in the train of that, and were unthought of until experience disclosed them; indeed, they are even yet unthought of by the greater part of those who derive advantage from them. And this last is true, to a degree which we must not fail to observe, of spoken language also: its higher uses are not conscious ones. Not one in a hundred, or a thousand, of those who speak realizes that he "uses language;" but there is no one who does not know well enough that he can talk. That is to say, language, to the general apprehension of its users, is simply a means of receiving from others and giving to them: what it is to the individual soul, what it is to the race, few have reach of vision to see. And least of all is such penetration to be credited to primitive man: he, especially, needs some motive right before his eyes, and of which he can feel every moment the impelling force; and the desire to communicate with his fellows is that motive, the sole and the wholly sufficient one. He has no thoughts swelling in his soul and demanding utterance; he has no foreboding of high capacities which only need education to make him a little lower than the angels; he feels nothing but the nearest and most urgent needs. If language broke out from within, driven by the wants of the soul, it ought to come forth fastest and most fully in the solitary; since he, cut off from other means of improvement, is thrown back upon this as his only resource: but the solitary man is as speechless as the lower animals.

There might be ground for questioning this conclusion as to the decisive value of the impulse to communication in the initiation of language-history, if the after-course of that history showed entire independence of it. That is no acceptable scientific explanation which calls in a special force at the beginning, like a *deus ex machina*, to accomplish what we cannot see to be otherwise feasible, and then to retire and act no more. But communication is the leading determinative force throughout. This it is for which and by which we make our first acquisitions; this leads us, when circumstances change, to lay our old acquisitions aside and make new; this determines the unity of a language, and puts a restraint upon its dialectic variation; this is, both consciously and unconsciously, recognized by every individual as the regulator: we speak so as to be intelligible to others; we hear and learn that we may understand them; we do not speak simply as we ourselves choose, letting others understand us if they can and will.

If this be so, then we have virtually solved, so far as it admits of solution, the problem of the origin of language; we have ascertained what was the original basis, and what the character of its development. The basis was the natural cries of human beings, expressive of their feelings, and capable of being understood as such by their fellows. That is to say, the basis so far as audible speech is concerned; for it is not to be maintained that this was the only, or even the principal, means of primitive expression. Gesture and grimace are every whit as natural and as immediately intelligible; and in the undeveloped condition of expression every available means will unquestionably have been resorted to, perhaps with a long predominance of the visible over the audible. But it cannot be that the use of the voice for expression should not have been suggested and initiated by Nature's own endowments in this direction.

Here, however, comes in a question respecting which even the most recent opinions, and among those who in general accept the view of language here taken, are divided. How wide was this basis, and of what and how definite character? Did it consist of articulate sounds instinctively attached to certain conceptions? Was there a limited natural vocabulary of actual words or roots, of the same kind with later language, and needing only to be extended into the latter? There are those who would answer these questions in the affimative, and who hold, therefore, that the fruitful way to investigate concretely the problem of the origin of language is to study the means of expression of the lower animals, especially of those which stand nearest to man, in order to find there something analogous with the roots of our speech. But this view has its basis in the clinging impression, which many of those who reason and write about language cannot possibly get rid of, that there is somehow a real internal connection between at least a part of our words and the ideas which these represent—if one could only find out what it is. If we recognize the truths that all existing human speech is in every part and particle conventional, that all of which there is record in the past was of the same character, and that there is an utter absence of evidence going to show that any uttered sound, any combination of articulations, comes or ever came into existence as the natural sign of an intellectual conception—we shall be led to look with extreme disfavor upon any suggestion of this kind. Beyond all question, it is wholly uncalled for by necessity: the tones significant of feeling, of which no one can deny the existence because they are still an important part of our expression, are fully capable of becoming the effective initiators of language. Spoken language began, we may say, when a cry of pain, formerly wrung out by real suffering, and seen to be understood and sympathized with, was repeated in imitation, no longer as a mere instinctive utterance, but for the purpose of intimating to another, "I am (was, shall be) suffering;" when an angry growl, formerly the direct expression of passion, was reproduced to signify disapprobation and threatening; and the like. This was enough to serve as foundation for all that should be built upon it.

It is further to be considered, in judging this point, that, as we approach man, the general capacities increase, but the specific instincts, the already formed and as it were educated capacities, decrease. It is among the insects that we find those wonderful arts which seem like the perfected results of training of a limited intellect; it is among birds that we find specific modes of nest-building and a highly art-like, almost artistic, song. Man is capable of acquiring everything, but he begins in the actual possession of next to nothing. Except suckling, he can hardly be said to be born with an instinct. His long helpless infancy, while the chicken and the calf run about and help themselves from the very day of their birth, is characteristic of Nature's whole mode of treatment of him. There is no plausibility in the suggestion that he should have begun social life with a naturally implanted capital of the means of social communication—and any more in the form of words than in that of gestures. It is a blunder of our educated habit to regard the voice as the specific instrument of expression; it is only one of several instruments. We might just as hopefully look among the higher animals for the particular and definite beginnings out of which our clothes, our buildings, our instruments, are a development. In these departments of human production, we see clearly enough what the natural beginning should have been. No animal save man is known to make any attempt at dressing; but if any did, it would amount to nothing; for there are tribes of men that go utterly, or almost utterly, naked; and no one, probably, would think of suggesting that the rudiments of dress are not a turning to account, for perceived purposes of comfort or decency, just such materials as Nature placed in man's way. The earliest shelters were of the same sort: it would be of high interest to find the animals nearest to man showing that kind of capacity which he possesses, of putting to use freely, simply as directed by circumstances, the varied resources of Nature; but probably the idea has never come into any one's head that man, as an animal uneducated, would be found building a particular style of shelter (as the beaver its dam, the oriole its hanging nest, the wasp its cells), out of which have grown, by a process showing nowhere a *saltus* or *lacuna*, the huts and palaces and temples of the more educated races. And the same thing is true of instruments: clubs and stones we allow to have been the first, only because Nature offers such most conveniently within reach of the beings who were gifted with mind enough to see how they could be made available for perceived needs.

Now it is only an unclear or a false view of the nature of speech that prevents any from seeing that its case is entirely analogous with these others, and that to postulate, and then seek for traces of, a primitive basis for language in the form of specific articulate signs for ideas is an uncalled-for, even a necessarily vain and futile, proceeding. It is, indeed, a matter of high interest, and promising of valuable instruction, to investigate as closely as possible the means of communication of the lower animals, so as to determine its character and scope; but the point calling for special attention is, how far the natural tones and utterances and postures and movements are used secondarily and mediately, for the purpose of signifying something, in rudimentary correspondence with what we have seen to be the infer able beginnings of human language-making. We need not be surprised to find, in more than one quarter, such methods of communication in use, only limited, and, for lack of the right kind and degree of capacity in their users, incapable of development; and these would be the real analogues of speech, and would bridge the *saltus* of which some are so afraid. If the Darwinian theory is true, and man a development out of some lower animal, it is at any rate conceded that the last and nearest transition-forms have perished, perhaps exterminated by him in the struggle for existence, as his special rivals, during his prehistoric ages of wildness; if they could be restored, we should find the transition-forms toward our speech to be, not at all a minor provision of natural articulate signs, but an inferior system of conventional signs, in tone, gesture, and grimace.

As between the three natural means of expression just mentioned, and constantly had in view by us in this discussion, it is simply by a kind of process of natural selection and survival of the fittest that the voice has gained the upper hand, and come to be so much the most prominent that we give the name of *language* ('tonguiness') to all expression. There is no mysterious connection between the thinking apparatus and the articulating apparatus, whereby the action that forms a thought sets the tongue swinging to utter it. Apart from the emotional (and non-articulate) natural cries and tones, the muscles of the larynx and mouth are no nearer to the soul than those of voluntary motion, by which, among other things, gestures are produced. Besides the lack of all evidence in language, rightly understood, to indicate such connection, it is sufficiently disproved, in a positive way, by the absence of vocal expression in the deaf, whose thinking and articulating apparatus is all in normal order, but who, by the numbing of the single nerve of audition, are removed from the disturbing infection of conventional speech; it ought to be many times more instructive to watch the "natural utterances" of a person thus affected than to study the jabberings of monkeys. The analogy between gesture and speech here is in the highest degree instructive. The hands and arms are muscular instruments under control of the same mind which produces conceptions and judgments. Among their manifold capacities, they are able to make gestures, of infinite variety, all of which are reported by the vibrations of the luminiferous ether to a certain apprehending organ, the eye, both of the maker and of others. There is a natural basis of instinctive gesture, which to the human intellect is capable of suggesting a method of intimation of intended meaning, developable into a complete system of expression; and it is so developed for the use of those who by lack of power to hear are cut off from the superior advantages of the other means of expression. In the same manner, the larynx and the parts which lie between it and the outer world are muscular organs, movable by the same will which moves the arms and hands. The parts have other offices to perform besides that of shaping tone; and the tone which it is the sole office of the vocal chords to generate is for other purposes as well as that of utterance: yet, along with other things, they can produce an indefinite variety of modified vibrations, reported through the sympathetic vibrations of the air to another apprehending organ, the ear, both of the producer and of others; and the sounds so reported are capable of combination into groups practically infinite in number. There is a natural basis of tonic expression; and on this and by its suggestion human intelligence has worked out a great number of diverse systems of expression, used, one or other of them, by all ordinarily endowed men.

There is nothing here to require the admission of a peculiar connection between thought and articulate utterance. In a certain sense, it is true, the voice may fairly be said to have been given us for the purpose of speech; but it is only as the hands have been given us to write with; our speaking organs do also our tasting, breathing, eating. So iron has been given us to make rails with for fast traveling: that is to say, among the various substances provided in the world for man's various uses, iron is the one best suited to this use; its qualities had only to be discovered by men, in the course of their experience of Nature, and, when the time for the use came, the perception of its adaptedness, and the application, necessarily followed. In the course of man's experience, it has come to light that the voice is, on the whole, the most available means of communication, for reasons which are not hard to understand: it acts with least expenditure of effort; it leaves the hands, much more variously efficient and hard-worked members, at leisure for other work at the same time; and it most easily compels attention from any direction. Only the smallest part of its capacities are laid under contribution for the uses of speech; of the indefinite number of distinguishable sounds which it can produce, only a fraction, of twelve to fifty, are put to use in any one language; and there is nothing in the selection to characterize a race, or to be used (except in the same historical way as language in general) for ethnological distinction: from among the many possibles, these have chanced to be taken; mainly the sounds easiest to make, and broadly distinguished from one another.

Under these determining considerations, vocal utterance has become everywhere the leading means of expression, and has so multiplied its resources that tone, and still more gesture, has assumed the subordinate office of aiding the effectiveness of what is uttered. And the lower the intellectual condition of the speaker and the spoken-to, the more indispensable is the addition of tone and gesture. It belongs to the highest development of speech that the word written and read should have something like the same power as the word spoken and heard; that the personality of the writer, even his frame of mind, should be felt, and should move the sympathetic feeling of the reader. And yet, it should also be noted here that, as we saw in the twelfth chapter, there are languages (e. g. Chinese) in which tone and inflection come to be used, in a secondary and conventional way, to eke out the too scanty resources of intellectual designation.

If we thus accept the impulse to communicate as the governing principle of speech-development, and the voice as the agent whose action we have especially to trace, it will not be difficult to establish other points in the earliest history. Whatever offered itself as the most feasible means of arriving at mutual understanding would be soonest turned to account. We have regarded the reproduction, with intent to signify something, of the natural tones and cries, as the positively earliest speech; but this would so immediately and certainly come to be combined with imitative or onomatopoetic utterances, that the distinction in time between the two is rather theoretical than actual. Indeed, the reproduction itself is in a certain way onomatopoetic t imitates, so to speak, the cries of the human animal, in order to intimate secondarily what those cries in their primary use signified directly. Just as soon, at any rate, as an inkling of the value of communication was gained, and the process began to be performed a little more consciously, the range of imitation would be extended. This is a direct corollary to the principles laid down above. Mutual intelligence being aimed at, and audible utterance the means employed, audible sounds will be the matter most readily represented and conveyed; just as something else would come easiest to one who used a different means. To repeat once more the old and well-worn, but telling, illustration: if we had the conception of a dog to signify, and the instrumentality were pictorial, we should draw the outline figure of a dog; if the means were gesture, we should imitate some characteristic visible act of the animal—for example, its bite, or the wagging of its tail; if it were voice, we should say "bow-wow." This is the simple explanation of the importance which is and must be attributed to the onomatopoetic principle in the early stages of language-making. We have no need of appealing to any special tendency toward imitation. Man is, to be sure, an imitative animal, as we may fairly say; but not in an instinctive or mechanical way; he is imitative because he has the capacity to notice and appreciate what he sees, in other animals or in nature, and to reproduce it in imitative show, if anything is to be gained thereby—whether amusement, or artistic pleasure, or communication. He is an imitator just as he is an artist; the latter is only the higher development of the former.

The scope of the imitative principle is by no means restricted to the sounds which occur in nature, although these are the most obvious and easiest subjects of significative reproduction. What it is, may be seen in part from the range of onomatopoetic words in known languages. There is a figurative use of imitation, whereby rapid, slow, abrupt, repetitive motions are capable of being signified by combinations of sounds which make something such an impression on the mind through the ear as the motions in question do through the eye. And we can well conceive that, while this was the chief efficient suggestion of expression, men's minds may have been sharpened to catch and incorporate analogies which now escape our notice, because, having a plentiful provision of expression from other sources, we no longer have our attention keenly directed to them. Our judgments on such points as this can only be partially trusted, and must be tested with extreme caution, because we are all of us now the creatures of educated habit, and cannot look at things as men uneducated and with no formed habits would do. We can safely investigate and combine and speculate in this direction, if we keep fully in mind the governing principle that mutual intelligence is the end, and that whatever conduces to mutual intelligence, and that alone, is the acceptable means. We shall thus be saved from running off into, or toward, that most absurd doctrine, the absolute natural significance of articulate sounds, and the successful intimation of complex ideas by a process of piecing these elements together.

There are one or two further points connected with this theory of the imitative origin of language which call for a few words of explanation. In the first place, it does not rest on a discovery of the signs of onomatopœia as predominant in the early traceable stages of language. Those stages are still too far from the beginning to furnish any such discovery. The intent was to find means of mutual intelligence; and when this was won, the way it came was a matter of small consequence, and might be left to be covered up. This has been, as we abundantly saw above, a governing tendency in the growth of speech down to the present time. Speakers know not and care not whence their words came; they know simply what they mean; even the wisest of us can trace the history of only a small part of his vocabulary, and only a little way. The very earliest dialects are as exclusively conventional as the latest; the savage has no keener sense of etymological connection than the man of higher civilization. Nothing has done so much to discredit the imitative theory with sound and sober linguistic scholars as the way in which some pass beyond the bounds of true science in their attempts to trace our living vocabularies to mimetic originals. The theory does, indeed, rest in part on the undeniable presence of a considerable onomatopœic element in later speech, and on the fact that new material is actually won in this way through the whole history of language; onomatopœia is thus raised to the rank of a *vera causa*, attested by familiar fact; and nothing that is not so attested—for example, the assumed immediate intellectual significance of articulate combinations—has the right to stand as a *causa* at all; but it rests also in part, and in the main part, on the necessities of the case, as inferred from the whole traceable history of speech and its relation to thought, its use and its value. Here is just the other support which it needs: no account of the origin of language is scientific which does not join directly on to the later history of language without a break, being of one piece with that history.

But, in the second place, it may at first sight seem

to some that there is a break in the history: for why do we not still go on to make words abundantly by onomatopœia? A moment's thought will show the baselessness of this objection. The office of onomatopœia was the provision, by the easiest attainable method, of the means of mutual intelligence; in proportion, then, as it became easier to make the same provision by another method, the differentiation and new application of signs already existing, the primitive method went into comparative disuse—as it has ever since continued, though never absolutely unused.

Once more, our theory furnishes the satisfactory solution of a difficulty which has had influence with some minds. Why should the germs of speech be what we have called roots, elements indicative of such abstract things as acts and qualities? surely concrete objects are soonest and most easily apprehended by the mind. Without stopping to dispute on more philosophical grounds this last assertion, claiming instead that we apprehend only the concreted qualities and acts of objects, it will be more to the point with those who feel the difficulty to note that the process of speech is one of signifying, and that only the separate qualities of objects, at any rate, are capable of being signified. To revert to our former example: there may be a state of mind in which there should exist a confused concrete impression of a dog, just sufficient to make it possible to recognize another as agreeing with one already seen, but without any distinct sense of its various attributes. But so long as that is the case, no production of a sign is possible: it is only when one has so clear a conception of its form that he can signify it by a rude outline picture, or of its characteristic acts that he can reproduce the bite, or wag, or bark, in imitation of them, that he is ready for an act of language-making of which the dog shall be the subject. And so with every other case; the first acts of comparing and abstracting must precede, and the first signs must follow; even as we have before seen that it is through the whole history of speech: the conception first, then the nomenclative act. And *bow-wow* is a type, a normal example, of the whole genus "root." It is a sign, a hint, that calls before the properly prepared mind a certain conception, or set of related conceptions: the animal itself, the act, the time and other circumstances of hearing it, and what followed. It does not mean any one of these things exclusively; it comprehends them all. It is not a verb, for that adds the idea of predication; nor is it a name: it may be put to use in either of these two senses. What it comes nearest in itself to meaning is 'the action of barking'—just that form of abstraction into which we now most naturally and properly cast the sense of a "root." And so with both the other suggested signs. Only, the outline figure has a decidedly more concrete character than either of the others, and is in a certain way their antithesis. It is a curious fact, and one tellingly illustrative of how the character of the sign depends on the instrumentality by which it is made, that hieroglyphic systems of representation of thought (which are in their origin independent systems, parallel with speech, though they are wont finally to come into servitude to speech) begin with the signs for concrete objects, and arrive from these, and secondarily, at the designation of acts and qualities. In Chinese, a combination of the hieroglyphs of sun and moon makes the character for 'light' and 'shine;' in speech, on the contrary, both luminaries are apt to be named from their shining (see above, p. 83). In Egyptian, a picture of a pair of legs in motion means 'walk;' while, with us, the *foot* is so named as being the 'walker.'

That by the methods thus described it was possible to make a provision of signs capable of development, by processes not different from those traceable in the historic period of language, into such vocabularies as we find actually existing, it does not seem as if any one could reasonably deny. If this is true, and if the methods are not only not inconsistent, but even in complete harmony, with the whole traceable course of human action on language, then we have found an acceptable solution of that part of the problem we are seeking to solve which is at present within our reach. A scientific solution requires that we take man as he is, with no other gifts than those we see him to possess, but also with all those that constitute his endowment as man, and examine whether and how he would possess himself of the beginnings of speech, analogous with those which our historical analysis shows to have been the germs of the after-development, but beyond which historical research will not carry us. As he would, if need were, make the acquisition now, so may he, or must he, have made it of old. This is not a part of the historical science of language, but a corollary to it, a subject for the anthropologist who is also a linguistic scholar, who knows what language is to man, and how. He is not prepared to deal with it who is merely master of the facts of many languages.

Of course, a language thus produced would be a rude and rudimentary means of expression. But that constitutes, in the mind of the modern anthropologist, no bar to the acceptance of the theory. If we deny to primitive man the possession of the other elements of civilization, and hold him to have gradually developed them out of scanty beginnings made by himself, then there is no reason why we should not hold the same view in respect to language, which is only such an element. Even in existing languages the differences of degree are great, as in existing states of culture in general. An infinity of things can be said in English which cannot be said in Fijian or Hottentot; a vast deal, doubtless, can be said in Fijian or Hottentot which could not be said in the first human languages. For what can be done in the way of distinct, even cultivated and elaborate, expression, by only a few hundred formless roots, we have a brilliant, almost a startling, example in the Chinese. Of how sentences can be made of roots alone, with the relations left to be supplied by the intelligently apprehending mind, the same tongue is a sufficient illustration. The Greek, or German, or English, can elaborate a thought in a period half a page long, determining by proper connectives the relation of each of its clauses to the central idea, and also, in widely varying degree and method, that of the members of each clause to one another. This is a capacity which belongs only to languages of high cultivation, working on a richly inflective basis. Many another tongue can form only simple clauses, possessing no more intricate apparatus of connection than 'ands' and 'buts,' though having form enough in its words to construct a clause of defined parts. Yet others lack this definition of parts; they strike only at the leading ideas, presenting them in such order that the hearer supplies the missing relations out of his general comprehension of what must be the intended meaning. And it is but another step backward to the primitive root-condition of speech, where an utterance or two had to do the duty of a whole clause. Men thus began, not with parts of speech which they afterward learned to piece together into sentences, but with comprehensive utterances in which the parts of speech lay as yet undeveloped, sentences in the germ; a single word signifying a whole statement, as even yet sometimes with us: only then from poverty, as now from economy. To demand that "sentences," in the present sense of that term, with subject and predicate, with adjuncts and modifiers, should have been the first speech, is precisely analogous with demanding that the first human abodes should have contained at least two stories and a cellar; or that the earliest garments should not have lacked buttons and braces; or that the first instruments should have had handles, and been put together with screws. These conditions, in the last three cases, are at once recognized as possible only to a miraculous endowment of humanity, a gifting of man, at his birth, not with capacities alone, but also with their elaborated results, with the fruits of education; and the assumption in regard to language is really precisely the same, a proper part of a miraculous theory of the origin of speech, but of no other.

The word "miraculous," rather than "divine," is here used to characterize the theory in question, because it is the only truly descriptive one. One may hold the views advocated in this chapter without any detriment to his belief in the divine origin of language; since he may be persuaded that the capacities and tendencies which lead man universally and inevitably to the acquisition of speech were implanted in him by the Creator for that end, and only work themselves out to a foreseen and intended result. If language itself were a gift, a faculty, a capacity, it might admit of being regarded as the subject of direct bestowal; being only a result, a historical result, to assert that it sprang into developed being along with man is to assert a miracle; the doctrine has no right to make its appearance except in company with a general miraculous account of the beginnings of human existence. That view of the nature of language which linguistic science establishes takes entirely away the foundation on which the doctrine of divine origin, in its form as once held, reposed.

The human capacity to which the production of language is most directly due is, as has been seen, the power of intelligently, and not by blind instinct alone, adapting means to ends. This is by no means a unitary capacity; on the contrary, it is a highly composite and intricate one. But it does not belong to the linguistic student to unravel and explain, any more than to the student of the history of civilization in its other departments; it falls, rather, to the student of the human mind and its powers, to the psychologist. So also with all the mental capacities involved in language, the psychic forces which underlie that practical faculty, and which, being by it brought to conscious action, are drawn out and trained and developed. The psychologist has a work of highest interest and importance to do, in analyzing and exhibiting this ultimate groundwork, on which have grown up the great institutions that make man what he is: language, society, the arts of life, machinery, art, and so on; and in tracing the history of education of the human powers in connection with them; and his aid and criticism must be everywhere of great value to their student. And this is most of all the case with regard to language; for language is in an especial manner the incorporation and revelation of the acts of the soul. Out of this relation has grown the error of those who look upon linguistic science as a branch of psychology, would force it into a psychologic mould and conduct it by psychologic methods: an error which is so refuted by the whole view we have taken of language and its history, that we do not need to spend any more words upon it here. Language is merely that product and instrumentality of the inner powers which exhibits them most directly and most fully in their various modes of action; by which, so far as the case admits, our inner consciousness is externized, turned up to the light for ourselves and others to see and study.

Out of the same close relation grows another and a far grosser error, that of actually identifying speech with thought and reason. This, too, we may take as sufficiently refuted by our whole argument; nothing but the most imperfect comprehension of language can account for a blunder so radical. The word *reason*, to be sure, is used so loosely, in such a variety of senses, that an unclear thinker and illogical arguer can comparatively easily become confused by it; but no one who attempts to enlighten his fellow-men on this class of subjects is excusable for such inability to grasp their most fundamental principles. Language is, upon the whole, the most conspicuous of the manifestations of man's higher endowments, and the one of widest and deepest influence on every other; and the superiority of man's endowments is vaguely known as reason—and that is the whole ground of the assertion of identity. There are many faculties which go to the production of speech; and they have other modes of manifestation besides speech. And we have only to take the most normally endowed human being and cut off artificially the avenue of a single class of sensuous impressions, those of hearing, and he will never have any speech.

If speech, then, is reason, reason will have to be defined as a function of the auditory nerve.

Whether, among the powers that contribute to the production of language, there is one, or more than one not belonging in any degree to a single animal below man, is a point which must be left to the psychologist to decide. It may fairly be claimed, however, that none such has yet been demonstrated; and also, that none such is necessary: a simple difference of degree in the capacities common to both is amply sufficient to account for the possession and the lack, on the one side and the other. A heightened power of comparison, of the general perception of resemblances and differences; an accompanying higher power of abstraction, or of viewing the resemblances and differences as attributes, characteristic of the objects compared; and, above all else, a heightened command of consciousness, a power of looking upon one's self also as acting and feeling, of studying one's own mental movements—these, it is believed, are the directions in which the decisive superiority is to be looked for. It is the height of injustice to maintain that there is not an approach, and a very marked approach, made by some of the lower animals to the capacity of language. In the ratio of what we call their "intelligence," they are able distinctly and fruitfully to associate conceptions with signs—signs, namely, which we make for them, and by which we guide and govern them. But, as an actual fact, their capacity, though rising thus far, stops short of the native production of such a sign, even of its acquisition from the higher race and its independent use among themselves. There is a long interval, incapable of being crossed by the lower animals, between their endowments and ours; and he is a coward who, out of fear for the preservation of man's supremacy, attempts to stretch it out, or to set up barriers upon it.

There is yet another important corollary from our established view of language as a constituent element of human civilization. Its production had nothing to do, as a cause, with the development of man out of any other and lower race. Its province was to raise man from a savage state to the plane which he was capable of reaching. The only development in which it was concerned is the historical development of man's faculties. Except, of course, that minor and limited change which falls within the sphere of ordinary heredity. The descendant of a cultivated race is more cultivable than the descendant of a wild one. The capacity of a yet higher cultivation grows with the slow increase of cultivation; and if a people is suddenly brought in contact with a civilization too far in advance of it, it is rather deteriorated and wasted than elevated. The power of brain, the capacity of thought, is enhanced by speech; but no such differences are produced as separate one animal species from another. All men speak, each race in accordance with its gift and culture; but all together are only one species. To the zoölogist, man was what he is now when the first beginnings of speech were made; it is to the historian that he was infinitely different. "Man could not become man except by language; but in order to possess language, he needed already to be man," is one of those Orphic sayings which, if taken for what they are meant to be, poetic expressions whose apparently paradoxical character shall compel attention and suggest thought and inquiry, are admirable enough. To make them the foundation or test of scientific views is simply ridiculous; it is as if one were to say: "A pig is not a pig without being fattened; but in order to be fattened he must first be a pig." The trick of the aphorism in question lies in its play upon the double sense of the word *man;* properly interpreted, it becomes an acceptable expression of our own view: 'Man could not rise from what he was by nature to what he was able and intended to become, and ought to become, except by the aid of speech; but he could never have produced speech had he not been at the outset gifted with just those powers of which we still see him in possession, and which make him man.'

We have already noted the linguist's inability at present to form even any valuable conjectures as to the precise point in the history of man at which the germs of speech should have appeared, and the time which they should have occupied in the successive steps of their development. Men's views are greatly at variance as to this, and with no prospect of reconciliation at present, because there is no criterion by which they can be tested. That the process was a slow one, all our knowledge of the history of later speech gives us reason to believe. As to the precise degree of slowness, that is an unessential point, which we may well enough leave for future knowledge to settle—if it can. What we have to guard especially against is the tendency to look upon language-making as a task in which men engage, to which they direct their attention, which absorbs a part of their nervous energy, so that they are thereby prevented from working as effectively in other directions of effort. Language-making is a mere incident of social life and of cultural growth; its every act is suggested or called forth by an occasion which is by comparison the engrossing thing, to which the nomenclative act is wholly subordinate. It is as great an error to hold that at some period men are engaged in making and laying up expressions for their own future use and that of their descendants, as that, at another period, men are packing away conceptions and judgments for which their successors shall find expression. Each period provides just what it has occasion for; nothing more. A generation or period may, indeed, by a successful incorporation in speech of an exceptionally fertile distinction, start a train of development which shall lead to immense consequences in the future, and lay a foundation on which a great deal shall admit of being built: such, for example (as we thought to see above), was the early Indo-European establishment of a special predicative form, a verb. This is truly analogous with those fortunate inventions or discoveries (like that of treating iron, of domesticating useful animals) which appear now and then to have given a happy turn to the history of a race, initiating an upward career of growth which would have seemed *à priori* equally within the reach of any other race. Such occurrences we are in the habit of calling accidental; and properly enough, if we are careful to understand by this only that they are the product of forces and circumstances so numerous and so indeterminable that we cannot estimate them, and could not have predicted their result. But, slower or more rapid, the production of language is a continuous process; it varies in rate and kind with the circumstances and habits of the speaking community; but it never ceases; there was never a time when it was more truly going on than at present.

What term we shall apply to the process and its result is a matter of very inferior consequence. Invention, fabrication, devisal, production, generation—all these are terms which have their favorers and also their violent opposers. Provided we understand what the thing in reality is, we need care little about the phraseology used in characterizing it. Each word may be not unfitly compared to an invention; it has its own place, mode, and circumstances of devisal, its preparation in the previous habits of speech, its influence in determining the after-progress of speech-development; but every language in the gross is an institution, on which scores or hundreds of generations and unnumbered thousands of individual workers have labored.

CHAPTER XV.

THE SCIENCE OF LANGUAGE: CONCLUSION.

Character of the study of language; its analogies with the physical sciences. Its historical methods; etymology; rules of its successful pursuit. Comparative philology and linguistic science. History of the scientific study of language.

WHAT we have to observe here in conclusion with regard to the study of language must be very brief, and mainly in the way of more or less obvious corollary to what has been already said. With any one who accepts the views of language set forth above, the rest will follow as a matter of course; with one who does not, it is too late here to argue.

Whether, in the first place, men be willing to allow to the study the name of a science or not, is a matter of the smallest moment. It has its own character, its own sphere, its own importance of bearing on other departments of knowledge. If there are those whose definition of a science excludes it, let it be so; the point is one on which no student of language need insist.

What he does need to insist upon is that the character of his department of study be not misrepresented, in order to arrogate to it a kind and degree of consequence to which it is not entitled—by declaring it, for example, a physical or natural science, in these days when the physical sciences are filling men's minds with wonder at their achievements, and almost presuming to claim the title of science as belonging to themselves alone. It is curiously indicative of the present as an early and formative period in the history of this study, that there should exist a difference of opinion among its conspicuous followers as to whether it be a branch of physical or of historical science. The difference may be now regarded as pretty conclusively settled: certainly, it is high time that any one who takes the wrong view be read out of the ranks, as one who has the alphabet of the science still to learn. No study into which the acts and circumstances and habits of men enter, not only as an important, but even as the predominant and determining element, can possibly be otherwise than a historical or moral science. Not one item of any existing tongue is ever uttered except by the will of the utterer; not one is produced, not one that has been produced or acquired is changed, except by causes residing in the human will, consisting in human needs and preferences and economies. There is no way of claiming a physical character for the study of such phenomena except by a thorough misapprehension of their nature, a perversion of their analogies with the facts of physical science.

These analogies are real and striking, and are often fitly used as instructive illustrations. There is no branch of historical study which is so like a physical science as is linguistics, none which deals with such an infinite multiplicity of separate facts, capable of being observed, recorded, turned over, estimated in their various relations. A combination of articulate sounds forming a word is almost as objective an entity as a polyp or a fossil; it can be laid away on a sheet of paper, like a plant in a *herbarium*, for future leisurely examination.

Though a product of voluntary action, it is not an artificiality; what the producer consciously willed it to be is but the smallest part of what we seek to discover in it: we seek to read the circumstances which, unconsciously to himself, guided his will, and made the act what it was; we regard it as a part of a system, as a link in a historical series, as an indicator of capacity, of culture, of ethnological connection. So a flint-chip, a scratched outline of an animal, an ornament, is a product of intention; but it is also, as a historical record, pure of all intention; a fact as objectively trustworthy as is a fossil bone or footmark. The material of archæology is even more physical than that of linguistics; but no one has ever thought of calling archæology a physical science.

As linguistics is a historical science, so its evidences are historical, and its methods of proof of the same character. There is no absolute demonstration about it; there is only probability, in the same varying degree as elsewhere in historical inquiry. There are no rules the strict application of which will lead to infallible results. Nothing will make dispensable the wide gathering-in of evidence, the careful sifting of it, so as to determine what bears upon the case in hand and how directly, the judicial balancing of apparently conflicting testimony, the refraining from pushing conclusions beyond what the evidences warrant, the willingness to rest, when necessary, in a merely negative conclusion, which should characterize the historical investigator in all departments.

The whole process of linguistic research begins in and depends upon etymology, the tracing out of the histories of individual words and elements. From words the investigation rises higher, to classes, to parts of speech, to whole languages. On accuracy in etymological processes, then, depends the success of the whole; and the perfecting of the methods of etymologizing is what especially distinguishes the new linguistic science from the old. The old worked upon the same basis on which the new now works: namely, on the tracing of resemblances or analogies between words, in regard to form and meaning. But the former was hopelessly superficial. It was guided by surface likenesses, without regard to the essential diversity which might underlie them—as if the naturalist were to compare and class together green leaves, green paper, green wings of insects, and green laminæ of minerals; it was heedless of the sources whence its material came; it did not, in short, command its subject sufficiently to have a method. A wider knowledge of facts, and a consequent better comprehension of their relations, changed all this. Especially, the separation of languages into families, with their divisions and subdivisions, the recognition of non-relationships and relationships and degrees of relationship, effected the great revolution, by changing the principles on which the probable value of particular evidences is estimated. It was seen that, whereas a close verbal resemblance between two nearly related tongues has the balance of probabilities in its favor, one between only distantly related tongues, or those regarded as unrelated, has the probabilities against it; and hence, that, in order to be successful, comparative investigation must be carried on with strict regard to demonstrated affinities. While affinities are unsettled, of course, all comparisons are tentative only, and may be made in any direction, with due caution as to overestimate of the results reached. But when a family like the Indo-European is constituted, with its branches and sub-branches and dialects, all founded on the collection and thorough examination of a vast body of evidence, and by its side another like the Semitic and yet another like the Scythian, then even cross-comparisons between the branches are to be held in strict subordination to the general comparison of branch with branch, and cross-comparisons between families not less so: indeed, they are not to be admitted at all, except as possible evidences bearing on the question whether the families are not, after all, ultimately akin—a question which is ever theoretically an open one, but of which the extreme difficulty has been sufficiently pointed out in previous chapters. It is, at any rate, only when the structure and material of the families shall have become understood with equal thoroughness, by the bringing to bear of all the evidences lying within the boundaries of each, that apparent resemblances between them can be deemed genuine, or used as signs of original connection. It is not enough that such preparatory work be done in one family; all the subjects of comparison must be reduced to the same value before they can be treated as commensurable.

There are, in short, two fundamental rules, under the government of which all comparative processes must be carried on: 1. comparisons must have in view the established lines of genetic connection; and 2. the comparer must be thoroughly and equally versed in the materials of both sides of the comparison. For want of regard to them, men are even yet filling volumes with linguistic rubbish, drawing wide and worthless conclusions from unsound and insufficient premises. On the other hand, if they be duly heeded, there is no limit to the scale on which the comparative process may be carried on, and made fruitful of valuable results. We have already noticed that no fact in any language is completely understood until there has been brought to bear upon it the evidence of every other analogous fact, related or unrelated; and doubtless, to the end, so long as any corner of the earth remains unransacked, some of the views which we hold with confidence will be liable to modification or overthrow.

The comparative method is really no more characteristic of the study of language than of the other branches of modern inquiry. But it was sufficiently conspicuous in connection with the new start taken by the study early in this century to make the name of "comparative philology," like the earlier "comparative anatomy" and the later "comparative mythology," familiar and favored, for a time, beyond any other. And the title is still accurate enough, as applied to that aspect of the study in which it is engaged in collecting and sifting its material, in order to determine correspondences and relationships and penetrate the secrets of structure and historic growth; but it is insufficient as applied to the whole study—the science of language, or linguistic science, or glottology. Comparative philology and linguistic science, we may say, are two sides of the same study: the former deals primarily with the individual facts of a certain body of languages, classifying them, tracing out their relations, and arriving at the conclusions they suggest; the latter makes the laws and general principles of speech its main subject, and uses particular facts rather as illustrations. The one is the working phase, the other the regulative and critical and teaching phase of the science. The one is more important as a part of special training, the other as an element of general culture—if, indeed, it be proper to raise any question as to their relative importance, even to the special student of language; for the lack of either will equally unfit him for doing the soundest and best service.

Yet the two are certainly different enough to make it possible that a scholar should excel in the one and not in the other. The science of language runs out, on its comparative side, into an infinity of details, like chemistry or zoölogy; and one may be extremely well versed in the manipulation of its special processes while wholly wrong as regards its grander generalizations: just as one may be a skillful analyst while knowing little or nothing of the philosophy of chemistry, or eminent in the comparative anatomy of animals with no sound knowledge or judgment as to the principles of biology. To illustrate this, it would be easy to cite remarkable examples of men of the present generation, enjoying high distinction as comparative philologists, who, as soon as they attempt to reason on the wider truths of linguistic science, fall into incongruities and absurdities; or, in matters of minor consequence, they show in manifold ways the lack of a sound and defensible basis of general theoretical views. Comparative work of the broadest scope and greatest value has long been done and is still doing; but the science of language is only in the most recent period taking shape; and its principles are still subjects of great diversity of opinion and of lively controversy. It is high time that this state of things, tolerable only in the growing and shaping period of a study, should come to an end, and that, as in other sciences of observation and deduction—for example, in chemistry, zoölogy, geology—there should be acknowledged to exist a body, not of facts only, but of truths, so well established that he who rejects them shall have no claim to be considered a man of science.

To review the history of the study is a task for which we have no room remaining, and which may well enough be left here unattempted; it is a subject by itself, and has been treated in independent works.[1] The beginnings of the science lie as far back in the past as the time when men first began to inquire and to speculate concerning the facts which they observed in themselves and in the world about them. The germs of all the most important modern doctrines are to be found in the reasonings of the Greek philosophers, for example; but unclearly apprehended, and mixed with much that is erroneous. Their basis of knowledge was almost entirely limited to the facts of their own language, and hence insufficient for sound generalization. In the great progress which has taken place during the last century, resulting in the elaboration of a whole sisterhood of new sciences, it was in the nature of things impossible that linguistics should not come into being with the rest; and it came. The movement toward it was well initiated in the last century, by the suggestive and inciting deductions and speculations of men like Leibnitz and Herder, by the wide assemblage of facts and first classifications of language by the Russians under Catherine and by Adelung and Vater and their like, and by the introduction of the Sanskrit to the knowledge of Europe, and the intimation of its connections and importance, by Jones and Colebrooke. No

[1] Important authorities are: L. Lersch, *Sprachphilosophie der Alten* (1840); H. Steinthal, *Geschichte der Sprachwissenschaft bei den Griechen und Römern* (1862–3); T. Benfey, *Geschichte der Sprachwissenschaft und orientalischen Philologie in Deutschland* (1869). Dr. J. Jolly has added a sketch of the subject, in a couple of chapters, to his German version of the author's "Language and the Study of Language" (Munich, 1874); and many interesting details are given in M. Müller's "Lectures on the Science of Language," first series.

one thing was so decisive of the rapid success of the movement as this last; the long-gathering facts at once fell into their proper places, with clearly exhibited relations, and on the basis of Indo-European philology was built up the science of comparative philology. Frederick Schlegel was a forerunner of the study; more than any other man, Francis Bopp was its leader. Parallel with Bopp's great Comparative Grammar of Indo-European tongues came forth Jacob Grimm's Comparative Grammar of the Germanic branch of the family, each in its own way a masterpiece, and both together raising the historical study of language at once to the rank of a science.

Almost all these names, it will be observed, are German; and, in truth, to Germany belongs nearly the whole credit of the development of comparative philology; the contributions made to it from other countries are of only subordinate value. In Germany, the names of George Curtius, Pott, Benfey, Schleicher, Kuhn, Leo Meyer, are perhaps the most conspicuous, in the generation still mainly upon the stage; but they have so many fellows of nearly equal eminence that it is almost invidious to begin specification and to stop anywhere, without going on to include as many more. Outside of Germany, Rask in Denmark, Burnouf in France, and Ascoli in Italy, have most right to be mentioned on the same page with the great German masters.

But while Germany is the home of comparative philology, the scholars of that country have, as was hinted above, distinguished themselves much less in that which we have called the science of language. There is among them (not less than elsewhere) such discordance on points of fundamental importance, such uncertainty of view, such carelessness of consistency, that a German science of language cannot be said yet to have an existence. And, accustomed as the world is to look to Germany for guidance in all matters pertaining to this subject, until they shall come to something like agreement it will hardly be possible to claim that there exists a world's science of language. In the present condition, however, of linguistic study on the one side and of anthropology on the other, it cannot be that the period of chaos will endure much longer; if men will begin with learning to understand those facts in the life and growth of language which lie nearest to them, they will surely be guided to consistent and sensible views as to the past history, the origin, and the nature of this most ancient and valuable of man's social institutions.

INDEX.

THE END.

THE GEOGRAPHICAL AND GEOLOGICAL DISTRIBUTION OF ANIMALS. By ANGELO HEILPRIN, Professor of Invertebrate Paleontology at the Academy of Natural Sciences, Philadelphia, etc. 12mo. $2.00.

"An important contribution to physical science is Angelo Heilprin's 'Geographical and Geological Distribution of Animals.' The author has aimed to present to his readers such of the more significant facts connected with the past and present distribution of animal life as might lead to a proper conception of the relations of existing fauna, and also to furnish the student with a work of general reference, wherein the more salient features of the geography and geology of animal forms could be readily ascertained. While this book is addressed chiefly to the naturalist, it contains much information, particularly on the subject of the geographical distribution of animals, the rapidly increasing growth of some species and the gradual extinction of others, which will interest and instruct the general reader. Mr. Heilprin is no believer in the doctrine of independent creation, but holds that animate nature must be looked upon as a concrete whole."—*New York Sun.*

MICROBES, FERMENTS, AND MOULDS. By E. L. TROUESSART. With 107 Illustrations. 12mo. Cloth, $1.50.

"Microbes are everywhere; every species of plant has its special parasites, the vine having more than one hundred foes of this kind. Fungi of a microscopic size, they have their uses in nature, since they clear the surface of the earth from dead bodies and fecal matter, from all dead and useless substances which are the refuse of life, and return to the soil the soluble mineral substances from which plants are derived. All fermented liquors, wine, beer, vinegar, etc., are artificially produced by the species of microbes called ferments; they also cause bread to rise. Others are injurious to us, for in the shape of spores and seeds they enter our bodies with air and water and cause a large number of the diseases to which the flesh is heir. Many physicians do not accept the microbian theory, considering that when microbes are found in the blood they are neither the cause of the disease, nor the contagious element, nor the vehicle of contagion. In France the opponents of the microbian theory are Robin, Bechamp, and Jousset de Bellesme; in England, Lewis and Lionel Beale. The writer comes to the conclusion that Pasteur's microbian theory is the only one that explains all facts."—*New York Times.*

EARTHQUAKES AND OTHER EARTH MOVEMENTS. By JOHN MILNE, Professor of Mining and Geology in the Imperial College of Engineering, Tokio, Japan. With 38 Illustrations. 12mo. Cloth, $1.75.

"In this little book Professor Milne has endeavored to bring together all that is known concerning the nature and causes of earthquake movements. His task was one of much difficulty. Professor Milne's excellent work in the science of seismology has been done in Japan, in a region of incessant shocks of sufficient energy to make observation possible, yet, with rare exceptions, of no disastrous effects. He has had the good fortune to be aided by Mr. Thomas Gray, a gentleman of great constructive skill, as well as by Professors J. A. Ewing, W. S. Chaplin, and his other colleagues in the scientific colony which has gathered about the Imperial University of Japan. To these gentlemen we owe the best of our science of seismology, for before their achievements we had nothing of value concerning the physical conditions of earthquakes except the great works of Robert Mallet; and Mallet, with all his genius and devotion to the subject, had but few chances to observe the actual shocks, and so failed to understand many of their important features."—*The Nation.*

APPLETONS' PHYSICAL GEOGRAPHY. Illustrated with engravings, diagrams and maps in color, and including a separate chapter on the geological history and the physical features of the United States. By JOHN D. QUACKENBOS, A. M., M. D., Adjunct Professor of the English Language and Literature, Columbia College, New York, *Literary Editor;* JOHN S. NEWBERRY, M. D., LL. D., Professor of Geology and Paleontology, Columbia College; CHARLES H. HITCHCOCK, Ph. D., Professor of Geology and Mineralogy, Dartmouth College; W. LE CONTE STEVENS, Ph. D., Professor of Physics, Packer Collegiate Institute; HENRY GANNETT, E. M., Chief Geographer of the United States Geological Survey; WILLIAM H. DALL, of the United States National Museum; C. HART MERRIAM, M. D., Ornithologist of the Department of Agriculture; NATHANIEL L. BRITTON, E. M., Ph. D., Lecturer in Botany, Columbia College; GEORGE F. KUNZ, Gem Expert and Mineralogist with Messrs. Tiffany & Co., New York; Lieutenant GEORGE M. STONEY, Naval Department, Washington. Large 4to. Cloth, $1.90.

APPLETONS' ATLAS OF THE UNITED STATES. Consisting of General Maps of the United States and Territories, and a County Map of each of the States, all printed in Colors, together with Railway Maps and Descriptive Text Outlining the History, Geography, and Political and Educational Organization of the States, with latest Statistics of their Resources and Industries. Imperial 8vo, cloth. $1.50.

THE EARTH AND ITS INHABITANTS. By ELISÉE RECLUS. Translated and edited by E. G. Ravenstein. With numerous Illustrations, Maps, and Charts.

M. Reclus the distinguished French Geographer has given in this work the most thorough and comprehensive treatise on the countries of the world yet produced. Maps, plans, and illustrations are lavish. It is subdivided as follows:

EUROPE, in 5 volumes. Imperial 8vo.

ASIA, in 4 volumes. Imperial 8vo.

AFRICA, in 3 volumes. Imperial 8vo.

AMERICA. (*In preparation.*)

Price, $6.00 per volume in library binding. Sold only by subscription.

A NEW PHYSICAL GEOGRAPHY. By ELISÉE RECLUS. In two volumes. Vol. I. The Earth. Vol. II. The Ocean, Atmosphere, and Life. With Maps and Illustrations. Price, $6.00 per volume, library binding. Sold only by subscription.

New York: D. APPLETON & CO., 1, 3, & 5 Bond Street.

ANTS, BEES, AND WASPS. A Record of Observations on the Habits of the Social Hymenoptera. By Sir JOHN LUBBOCK, Bart., M. P., F. R. S., etc., author of "Origin of Civilization, and the Primitive Condition of Man," etc., etc. With Colored Plates. 12mo. Cloth, $2.00.

"This volume contains the record of various experiments made with ants, bees, and wasps during the last ten years, with a view to test their mental condition and powers of sense. The principal point in which Sir John's mode of experiment differs from those of Huber, Forel, McCook, and others, is that he has carefully watched and marked particular insects, and has had their nests under observation for long periods—one of his ants' nests having been under constant inspection ever since 1874. His observations are made principally upon ants, because they show more power and flexibility of mind; and the value of his studies is that they belong to the department of original research."

"We have no hesitation in saying that the author has presented us with the most valuable series of observations on a special subject that has ever been produced, charmingly written, full of logical deductions, and, when we consider his multitudinous engagements, a remarkable illustration of economy of time. As a contribution to insect psychology, it will be long before this book finds a parallel."—*London Athenæum.*

DISEASES OF MEMORY. An Essay in the Positive Psychology. By TH. RIBOT, author of "Heredity," etc. Translated from the French by William Huntington Smith. 12mo. Cloth, $1.50.

"M. Ribot reduces diseases of memory to law, and his treatise is of extraordinary interest."—*Philadelphia Press.*

"Not merely to scientific, but to all thinking men, this volume will prove intensely interesting."—*New York Observer.*

"M. Ribot has bestowed the most painstaking attention upon his theme, and numerous examples of the conditions considered greatly increase the value and interest of the volume."—*Philadelphia North American.*

"To the general reader the work is made entertaining by many illustrations connected with such names as Linnæus, Newton, Sir Walter Scott, Horace Vernet, Gustave Doré, and many others."—*Harrisburg Telegraph.*

"The whole subject is presented with a Frenchman's vivacity of style."—*Providence Journal.*

"It is not too much to say that in no single work have so many curious cases been brought together and interpreted in a scientific manner."—*Boston Evening Traveller.*

MYTH AND SCIENCE. By TITO VIGNOLI. 12mo. Cloth, $1.50.

"His book is ingenious; . . . his theory of how science gradually differentiated from and conquered myth is extremely well wrought out, and is probably in essentials correct."—*Saturday Review.*

"The book is a strong one, and far more interesting to the general reader than its title would indicate. The learning, the acuteness, the strong reasoning power, and the scientific spirit of the author, command admiration."—*New York Christian Advocate.*

"An attempt made, with much ability and no small measure of success, to trace the origin and development of the myth. The author has pursued his inquiry with much patience and ingenuity, and has produced a very readable and luminous treatise."—*Philadelphia North American.*

"It is a curious if not startling contribution both to psychology and to the early history of man's development."—*New York World.*

New York: D. APPLETON & CO., 1, 3, & 5 Bond Street.

MAN BEFORE METALS. By N. JOLY, Professor at the Science Faculty of Toulouse; Correspondent of the Institute. With 148 Illustrations. 12mo. Cloth, $1.75.

"The discussion of man's origin and early history, by Professor De Quatrefages, formed one of the most useful volumes in the 'International Scientific Series,' and the same collection is now further enriched by a popular treatise on paleontology, by M. N. Joly, Professor in the University of Toulouse. The title of the book, 'Man before Metals,' indicates the limitations of the writer's theme. His object is to bring together the numerous proofs, collected by modern research, of the great age of the human race, and to show us what man was, in respect of customs, industries, and moral or religious ideas, before the use of metals was known to him."—*New York Sun.*

"An interesting, not to say fascinating volume."—*New York Churchman.*

ANIMAL INTELLIGENCE. By GEORGE J. ROMANES, F. R. S., Zoölogical Secretary of the Linnæan Society, etc. 12mo. Cloth, $1.75.

"My object in the work as a whole is twofold: First, I have thought it desirable that there should be something resembling a text-book of the facts of Comparative Psychology, to which men of science, and also metaphysicians, may turn whenever they have occasion to acquaint themselves with the particular level of intelligence to which this or that species of animal attains. My second and much more important object is that of considering the facts of animal intelligence in their relation to the theory of descent."—*From the Preface.*

"Unless we are greatly mistaken, Mr. Romanes's work will take its place as one of the most attractive volumes of the 'International Scientific Series.' Some persons may, indeed, be disposed to say that it is too attractive, that it feeds the popular taste for the curious and marvelous without supplying any commensurate discipline in exact scientific reflection; but the author has, we think, fully justified himself in his modest preface. The result is the appearance of a collection of facts which will be a real boon to the student of Comparative Psychology, for this is the first attempt to present systematically well-assured observations on the mental life of animals."—*Saturday Review.*

"The author believes himself, not without ample cause, to have completely bridged the supposed gap between instinct and reason by the authentic proofs here marshaled of remarkable intelligence in some of the higher animals. It is the seemingly conclusive evidence of reasoning powers furnished by the adaptation of means to ends in cases which can not be explained on the theory of inherited aptitude or habit."—*New York Sun.*

THE SCIENCE OF POLITICS. By SHELDON AMOS, M. A., author of "The Science of Law," etc. 12mo. Cloth, $1.75

"To the political student and the practical statesman it ought to be of great value."—*New York Herald.*

"The author traces the subject from Plato and Aristotle in Greece, and Cicero in Rome, to the modern schools in the English field, not slighting the teachings of the American Revolution or the lessons of the French Revolution of 1793. Forms of government, political terms, the relation of law, written and unwritten, to the subject, a codification from Justinian to Napoleon in France and Field in America, are treated as parts of the subject in hand. Necessarily the subjects of executive and legislative authority, police, liquor, and land laws are considered, and the question ever growing in importance in all countries, the relations of corporations to the state."—*New York Observer.*

A NATURALIST'S RAMBLES ABOUT HOME. By Dr. CHARLES C. ABBOTT. 12mo, cloth, $1.50.

"The home about which the doctor rambles is clearly the haunt of fowl and fish, of animal and insect life; and it is of the habits and nature of these that he discourses pleasantly in this book. Summer and winter, morning and evening, he has been in the open air all the time on the alert for some new revelation of instinct, or feeling, or character on the part of his neighbor creatures. Most that he sees and hears he reports agreeably to us, as it was no doubt delightful to himself. Books like this, which are free from all the technicalities of science, but yet lack little that has scientific value, are well suited to the reading of the young. Their atmosphere is a healthy one for boys in particular to breathe. It awakens a noble sympathy for what is below us. It helps to overcome a natural timidity, often increased by ignorance, which detracts much from the enjoyment many would have in out-of-door recreation. Ever since the days of Izaak Walton, books like his and 'The Natural History of Selborne' have been popular; but there was never before a time when they found so many intelligent readers as they do at present."—*Boston Transcript.*

HAND-BOOK OF TREE-PLANTING; OR, Why to Plant, Where to Plant, What to Plant, How to Plant. By NATHANIEL H. EGLESTON, Chief of Forestry Division, Department of Agriculture, Washington. 16mo, cloth, 75 cents.

"Mr. Egleston's little book ought to be read by every one—by legislators considering the subject as a matter for statute law; by the farmer, by the manufacturer, by the frontiersman, and by the ordinary citizen—for the interest of all is affected by the interest of each."—*Hartford Evening Post.*

"The work especially aims to meet the wants of land-owners in those portions of country largely destitute of forests, by furnishing the very best information regarding the planting and culture of trees. The author does not discuss the merits of the various ornamental trees, but treats particularly of those classes which have a recognized value that commends them to the attention of any who may wish to plant for use and profit. But since the laws of growth and the conditions of success in planting are the same, whether one plants for use or for ornament, this manual will be found a useful guide and helper to amateurs, and to every one who is interested in tree-culture.'—*Western Christian Advocate (Cincinnati).*

FLOWERS AND THEIR PEDIGREES. By GRANT ALLEN, author of "Vignettes of Nature," etc. Illustrated. 12mo, cloth, $1.50.

No writer treats scientific subjects with so much ease and charm of style as Mr. Grant Allen. His sketches in the magazines have well been called fascinating, and the present volume, being a collection of various papers, will fully sustain his reputation as an eminently entertaining and suggestive writer.

"'Flowers and their Pedigrees,' by Grant Allen, with many illustrations, is not merely a description of British wild flowers, but a discussion of why they are, what they are, and how they come to be so; in other words, a scientific study of the migration and transformation of plants, illustrated by the daisy, the strawberry, the cleavers, wheat, the mountain tulip, the cuckoo-pint, and a few others. The study is a delightful one, and the book is fascinating to any one who has either love for flowers or curiosity about them."—*Hartford Courant.*

"'Flowers and their Pedigrees' is a series of charming essays, by Grant Allen, a well-known English writer, on the daisy, the strawberry, the mountain tulip, the origin of wheat, etc. Though specially adapted to the latitude of England, they will not be less interesting in this country."—*New York Observer.*

New York: D. APPLETON & CO., 1, 3, & 5 Bond Street.